ABEL BODIED

MURDER AT THE MALDEN BANK

Michael Cloherty

MINPIN PUBLISHING

ISBN 978-1-7371386-1-7 (hardcover)
ISBN 978-1-7371386-0-0 (paperback)
ISBN 978-1-7371386-2-4 (e-book)

To my wife, Jen, for her love and support
and our miniature pinscher, Guinness,
who lay sweetly beside me over the many years
of research, writing and revision.

The Ballad of Edward Green

On a snowy day,
In the Malden Bank,
Edward Green
Killed his friend Frank.

A wife with child,
His debt was high,
There was no choice:
The boy must die.

The barber watched
Him limp away,
But out of fear,
He could not say.

He had fled north
Before the war
And sensed the risk
Was what he saw.

On a snowy day,
In the Malden bank,
Edward Green
Killed his friend Frank.

December 15, 1863,
The first bank murder robbery.
Before Jesse James and Sundance Kid,
Edward Green gained infamy.

On a snowy day,
In the Malden bank,
Edward Green
Killed his friend Frank.

Chapter One

WILLIAM SHILOH PEERED through his barbershop window and watched the postmaster first allow a horse and buggy to pass him and then continue his confident hobble across Pleasant Street, heading straight toward the shop. William hurried away from the window and busied himself with a broom so as to look nonchalant and unconcerned when the bell rang on his door and Edward Green entered. The two men spent most of their waking hours working across the street from one another in their respective businesses yet maintained just a mere acquaintance.

Edward had visited William's shop many times before, but this was the first time the postmaster had done so since the daylight robbery of the First National Bank and the murder of the young clerk, Frank Converse, shocked the village.

Edward immediately ambled toward William, who found himself paralyzed and unsure of the intention of the man's advance.

The postmaster interlocked his fingers deep within William's hair and rubbed the barber's scalp with a fury, laughing as he did so. Edward began singing, "Jingle bells, jingle bells, jingle all the way . . ."

Edward, pausing the motion of his fingers, said, "Shiloh, have you ever heard this song?"

"I have not, sir."

"It was written by my friend Jimmy Pierpont, from Medford. I heard it first in '57 at a minstrel show in Boston. Think he lives in Georgia. Even if he is a Reb now, he was a good one. Had my share of ales with him at the Simpson Tavern."

Edward began to rub William's hair between his fingers once more. "Oh, what fun it is to ride in a one-horse open sleigh." He paused his singing. "Shiloh, have you ever been to a minstrel show?"

"No, sir."

"Of course not. I suppose you can just look at your reflection for that." Edward howled with laughter. At this, William pondered their reflected images in his mirror as Edward continued his song and the friction of his hands through William's hair. Edward's reflection was joyous and William strained to have no expression at all.

Though the sensation burned, the barber stood silent and motionless. William convinced himself that the assault would cease in a minute or two, when the postmaster would grow bored, and so he let his mind linger on the safety and happiness of his wife and children instead of focusing on his current pain and humiliation. The novelty of William's hair had eventually worn off for many of the barber's customers but never for the postmaster. Occasionally, new customers, especially the children of the rich men William served, would, with excitement and curiosity, rush toward him with arms outstretched to touch his hair, finding the texture quite exotic, so unlike their own.

William would smile and laugh, although he always considered the act of being petted like an animal purely belittling and loathsome. Yet he took some solace from the fact that the children always were gentler than the postmaster ever was.

The barber would never think to touch any of them unsolicited. Through his profession, he was well acquainted with how different their hair was from his own. He cut it, shaved it, and swept it from his floor day after day.

It was omnipresent, spreading its web mercilessly within his shop and onto his very person, seemingly dominating every inch of both. William couldn't truly rid himself of it; there was always more. It was like an extra layer of skin restraining him. He was constantly picking strands and even tufts off of his work shirt and his trousers; they adhered to his clothing as unwanted passengers, like barnacles on a whale, feeding on him, consuming him from the outside and slowly and more menacingly from the inside. He was a free man, but the ubiquitous hair of these men in his life symbolized to William that he was still very much confined within their society.

Yet, tending to these men's follicles was the very means of his livelihood. Regrettably, William couldn't cut the hair of his own people. This was just one of a myriad of implied rules for which he and his kind had to abide. Another example was he could never purchase or carry a pistol. William thought he would feel a bit more at ease if he possessed a gun, especially with the postmaster standing before him, currently assaulting him.

William was quite unsure of the postmaster's intentions and of his own safety but then considered the additional peril he would face if he were armed himself. *I might as well just shoot myself in the head, for if any of the townsfolk found a firearm on my person, the end result would surely be the same for me,* he thought.

The postmaster finally removed his hands from the barber's head, sighed, and said, "Shiloh, a shave of my face leaving my side-whiskers as they are and a bit of a trim on this mop of hair. See to it now."

"Certainly, Mr. Green!" William motioned toward the chair with a theatrical flail of his arms, feigning not to be nervous, which he was. "Have a seat, sir, and welcome back to my humble establishment. And congratulations on the birth of your daughter! May the Heavenly Father bless her!" The barber bent for a few moments and then stood, worrying that he may have curtsied a tad too long.

Edward hesitated as he leaned back, jaw clenched, nostrils flared, then his whole face and body twisted as all four limbs tried to gain a hold of the chair as if he were wrestling it into submission. The barber's eyes dilated, and his breathing intensified. His scalp still hurt. Had he said or done something wrong? Taken a liberty he shouldn't have dared? In a matter of moments, as if nothing had occurred whatsoever, Edward's grimace was replaced by a small smile as he relaxed into the chair. Relieved, William realized the postmaster's pained expression was merely caused by his boyhood injury as he adjusted one leg, and then the other, in the chair, his arms steadying his weight while his lower extremities fought to gain any fraction of comfort they could acquire.

William grasped, as he always did, that one of Edward's limbs was clearly shorter than its companion. Then, standing behind him and looking in the mirror, he scrutinized Edward's lesser leg from the opposite view. William comprehended in this moment, truly more than he ever had before, that the postmaster was not, in any way whatsoever, an able-bodied man.

"Yes, my daughter, Alice, was born just a week ago. A true blessing from above," said Edward.

William smiled and nodded. The murder of young Converse and the search for his killer was discussed on every street corner, and all William's customers would speak of almost nothing else from the very moment they entered his shop. This was especially true of William's newest and most frequent customer, the Count Joannes, who held many theories on the crime and discussed them endlessly with the barber and anyone else who would listen.

Edward was regarded as one of the most talkative men in town, so if the postmaster had spoken about the murder at all, William believed he would have caught wind of it from the other gentlemen who frequented his establishment. Edward's silence on this matter, along with other factors, led William to suspect that what he had seen on that terrible morning must be true.

Is the postmaster here to determine whether I was a witness to his crimes? No way to be certain. I must be careful with my words and actions toward him, even more so than normal, thought William. *Yet Green is now a father. Perhaps it would be wiser, better for me, to think about one that has just joined the earth's choir instead of another who has left it to sing forever with the angels. Was Frank's demise caused by the postmaster's hand? I suspect that it was.*

William sought to convince himself he hadn't seen what he knew he had indeed witnessed. *Safer just to put all these negative thoughts out of my mind. Perchance it was not the postmaster but someone else I saw on the street instead?*

The words echoed pleadingly in his head over and over. The barber knew Edward and Frank had been close friends. William's shop was on the same side of the street as the bank. The two businesses, in one-story buildings with gable roofs, were separated by a single storefront, and William often observed Edward walking across from the post office to visit the boy. William was certain Edward had done so twice on the morning of the murder and, more likely than not, a third time as well, but he forced that thought out of his mind when he realized Edward was staring directly at him.

"I'm going to Boston today to visit a man named Chute to forever capture this handsome mug of mine, Shiloh, so Alice can see what her daddy looked like when she was born."

William was surprised. "Mr. Swain is right next door, and he is a fine fellow and his photographs and portraits are well regarded, sir."

Edward turned a slight crimson. "Swain, Swain. I'm sure he's adequate for the local townsfolk, but I'm a father now and, of course, as the town's postmaster, it's only right for me to have a proper Bostonian capture me and my countenance."

William nodded and began attending to his oils and creams. He would soon apply them to Edward's neck to soften the skin before shaving him. Was Edward still looking at him? William convinced himself that if the postmaster was, it surely meant nothing. William ignored the inclination growing inside his mind to confirm if Edward's attention was on him by simply turning his head. Instead, William prepared his straight razor by wiping it with a soft cloth and then decided to apply the one tactic that appeased each and every one of his customers in any circumstance: pure flattery. After building up his confidence, he looked at the postmaster.

"Of course, sir. You're a very important man. A proper Boston photographer is what you need. Of course, of course. So your daughter can always remember the man you were when she entered the world. Mr. Green, I'm well aware and growing more and more certain of the absolute character of the man I see before me in this very moment."

William picked up his razor and drummed his fingers along its sleek handle and then continued, saying, "Your daughter is a lucky child to have such a prominent man, the postmaster of Malden, for a daddy!"

Edward offered a proud smile and then leaned his head back. With his customer gazing safely at the ceiling and apparently deep in his own thoughts, William glanced down at Edward's incongruent figure: one leg rested on the footrest while the other hung an inch or perhaps two above it, this limb twisted a bit as if it did not want to be there, but seemed delighted for the reprieve of not having to walk or stand.

This lesser limb appeared as if it were surrendering and it would take a grand force of will to return it to its journey. But it would have little choice, William thought; it would be dragged along, one way or another.

Was the postmaster suspicious of the knowledge William held of him? The barber contemplated his options. If Edward tried to attack him, he thought he could flee and surely outrun him. Yet if Edward was carrying a gun on his person, perhaps the one recently wielded for the heinous violence at the bank, William feared there could be no escape.

The postmaster had exhibited many times before that he had no qualms about belittling William or laying his hands upon him in superiority, but would Edward be exponentially more violent toward him if he perceived what William currently suspected—that the postmaster was the murderer of Frank Converse?

He had no option to fight, and he realized fleeing was also a dismal choice. William had run very far once before to attain this new life. He was weary of running. There must be another solution. William hoped and prayed to conjure a way out of this uncertain situation with the postmaster. His finger stroked along the scar on his cheek absentmindedly, repeatedly, as William often did in such times of deep deliberation, and the barber pondered what he could do.

Chapter Two

WILLIAM SHILOH HAD left his hometown of Wilmington, Delaware, in 1859 to move to Malden, Massachusetts. He had become proprietor of his own barbershop soon after arriving in town—with the assistance of a kind benefactor, Deacon Elisha Converse, the father of the young murder victim. The deacon, who owned many properties in town, lent his influence in helping William to set up his trade after the two first met outside the Baptist church. He even rented the shop to him at a discounted rate. William believed himself fortunate that Malden was a growing town with numerous men of means who required a competent barber for a shave and a hair trim. He was skilled at both and quickly built up a large clientele through word of mouth.

With the uncertainty of the war raging for over two years, mainly in the South, the barber was joyful to be in the North. William was aware that Delaware contained a larger number of free colored men than any other state, between 80 and 90 percent.

The Quakers, who held great influence in the state, particularly in its northern sections, including Wilmington, were morally against slavery from Delaware's creation. Back in 1787, they had helped enact a law forbidding ships from bringing any more slaves ashore. In the southern counties, though, there remained a number of slaves whose ancestors preceded that law, so generation after generation, their children continued to be born into bondage.

William had been apprehensive from a young age that he could easily join their ranks and never leave enslavement once the shackles were clasped.

Plus, all his life he heard the grumbling of white men who were incensed by the cost of hiring free men for labor while some of their peers lacked that expenditure.

Several years before William traveled north, a law was passed in his home state stating that if a free black man was seen as indigent, not seeking employment, idle, or poor he could be sold into servitude for a year. So William thought it was in his interest to develop a skill that would allow him to provide for himself and, more importantly, ensure his freedom. He had a sliver of safety in the North now, yet every day William prayed that the Union Army would prevail, fearful that a Confederate victory would lead to all blacks being sent south again to work on the plantations.

As he shaved the postmaster, William remembered two distinct times Elisha Converse had visited his shop, the first being soon after William arrived in Malden and when he had begun to fully trust the deacon as his spiritual advisor and his friend.

"William, you are an excellent barber. How did you choose this trade? I can assume why you have come to Malden, but could you please tell me directly? I am most interested."

"The reason I left, sir, is that the threat of the white men at home wasn't just implied, it was very real. It was their laws to make and carry out as they deemed fit."

"This is so wrong, my friend—a man cannot own his fellow man. I'm truly grateful to the Lord above that you no longer live with such fear."

But I live with so many other fears still, thought William, but he said instead, "And so my choice of calling, by forced necessity, was to become a barber, and it's been a blessing from God! For now I can live with even more freedom, as much as a colored man can manage, I'm aware, and much more than quite a bit of my brethren can, regardless of which side of the Mason–Dixon line they stand on."

William paused and adjusted the direction of his scissors as he continued trimming the man's hair.

"It is unjust," said the deacon.

William stopped cutting the deacon's hair and dropped his arms to his sides.

He contemplated whether he should continue and chose to be courageous. "Sir, my shop doesn't cater to other Negroes, and so they resent me. This causes me sadness, but it's white men such as you—I don't mean you directly, sir"—William looked at the floor and then back at the deacon—"that provide for my livelihood. Not my life, not completely. But by necessity, I must heed your rules and regulations."

"William, it is not my rules. I think you should be able to serve any customer of any skin tone." Elisha turned his head and looked him in the eye. "But many ignorant others disagree, and unfortunately, they are the majority. I pray as time goes by, I may attain more influence in this town so that I can change the hearts and minds of such men. Surely, you have heard me preach often about such things from the pulpit on Sundays."

"I have, sir, and I am grateful for that, but it is still difficult for me. Trusting you to allow me to speak my mind was—honestly, is—still hard for me. I have faith in God always, and I have gained faith in you as well, for you have shown great kindness to me. However, my mind always warns me that it is easier, often safer, to remain silent on such matters of race to white men when I am seen as an inferior, viewed as a threat."

"In my mind, William, we are all equal in God's eyes, though, sadly, many of my kind don't see it this way. I assure you, I do. Please speak your mind, William, always. Never be afraid or hold anything back that you wish to express to me."

William breathed deep; he steadfastly wanted to believe this man. It was taxing to trust any white man, yet he took a leap of faith and walked from his spot behind the deacon so he could stand directly before him.

"I've often heard said, 'No Negroes allowed,' yet I, through my trade and skill, am allowed, somewhat. It pains me, but I can't fret or carry the weight of all the others of my kind. All I can do is provide for my family and myself and then retain a bit of hope for the rest of my people. I ain't no Nat Turner; that's not my ambition. I'm a black barber. This is much better for me than being an idle free man in Delaware turned slave, which I could've been."

Elisha asked that they pray together that all men could be judged on their merits and not on the pigment of their skin, and the two clasped hands.

"Lord, I know you love us all equally, but there are many sinners amongst us who profess themselves ardent Christians. They are fraudulent if they hold such hate in their breasts," said the deacon.

The main reason why William had traveled north was so his children wouldn't be exposed to the threat of servitude, though he feared they were still vulnerable to many other prejudices. Despite this, he believed their lives were a little bit better; in fact, he often tried to convince himself that they were one hell of a lot better than they would have been if the family had not fled north.

The second conversation with the deacon that played in William's mind was far more recent, from the day before Elisha's son's funeral. William, not expecting him, quickly brushed off the barber's chair as the deacon sat down without saying a word.

After their first meeting years ago, the barber had politely asked that the deacon call him "William." In turn, the deacon said he could simply be addressed as "Elisha," if that was the case. But William Shiloh would have no part of that. "Mr. Converse" it was, but occasionally he would say, "Mr. Elisha Converse" as a compromise, with a wink and smile. Elisha would smile back.

Although he always attempted to put on a respectful and friendly tone for each gentleman who walked into his shop for a haircut or a shave, William's manner was at its most genuine around this man.

William began trimming Elisha's follicles just as he had done so many times before. But this was such a somber moment. He did not want to be the first to speak, aware the whole time he was cutting the man's hair that the deacon was staring at the mirror. William imagined he was trying to look beyond the large Bailey building and focus on an image of the bank, just out of his view, the place of his son's murder.

Elisha's eyes were moist, but no tears fell. His gaze never diverted from the reflecting glass. William considered that perhaps Elisha was only able to gaze at the bank indirectly, in the abyss of his mind, perceiving that the image and what it represented were but an illusion, that none of this was real, that his son could still be alive if he merely banished the idea of his brutal death from his thoughts.

"Frank." Elisha pronounced the single syllable as if he had just learned to speak. The dry sound from his throat echoed out, lingered in the shop, and fell upon the barber unexpectedly. William sensed the word envelop him, cover him, cajole him, beg him to release the knowledge he concealed, his bearing witness to Edward being the last person to exit the bank before Frank's bloody body was discovered. He had to say something, to respond. William attempted to convince himself the spoken name of a slaughtered boy was just the grief of a father, not an accusation directed toward him for his reluctance at uttering the name of the killer.

For this reason, sound also had to be forced from William's lungs, and his lips struggled to enunciate six syllables of his own.

"He was a fine young man."

Elisha pivoted his head toward William, no longer mesmerized by the reflection of the place which held his son's last moments. The tension lessened in his countenance as he beheld the sympathetic look of his friend.

"He was. Thank you. You are a good man as well, William. It has been difficult to dwell in the gloom of my home, so imbued with the sadness of Mary and the family. I've always felt a certain calmness as you cut my hair. Sitting here brings me respite. You are a dependable barber, and I can trust in you and your care always."

This statement provoked a shudder in William, and he almost came close to speaking what his conscience implored him to say; but his mind willed the words back down his throat, stymieing their ascent. He convinced himself to be cautious, to wait, to ponder and to pray as to how he should proceed.

William retreated back to the silence, sheltered himself there as he finished cutting, then brushed the stray hairs off the deacon. Staring at them, he shuddered again; the hairs had grown from Elisha but had been cut down and discarded. William reluctantly brushed them away. Frank had also grown from the deacon and had been cut down as well—by the postmaster. Was William also brushing away Edward's crime like the hair from Elisha's shoulders by not speaking of what he knew? His profession may be that of a barber, but he wondered that if his very calling from the Lord above was to be a witness to this crime. Was he failing God, the Converses, and himself with his silence?

William began to weep; the tears he had spotted ebbing on Elisha's eyes now exploded from his very own. They were a torrent. He felt grief, he felt remorse, he felt completely overwhelmed.

"William, my dear William." Elisha arose from his chair, placing a hand on the barber's shoulder. William thought the pressure would push him down, but instead the deacon's touch alleviated the barber's anguish. "We will find the grace and solace of the Almighty."

At this, the benevolent actions and words of a grieving father, William's cries softened. The deacon placed his left hand on the barber's other shoulder, and they both spoke to God silently, one man asking for solace and the other guidance to ease the grief of his friend while not putting himself and his family in possible jeopardy.

Thinking back on this emotional moment with the honorable, grieving deacon, William now stared down at the man responsible for Elisha's grief and his own growing anxiety.

Mr. Converse tells me that we are equal, that God sees us all as just men. But my mind is trained that this is simply not so. I have never been in physical bondage but despised the masters that wished to enslave me before I learned my trade and fled Delaware. I have prayed with the deacon for the loss of his son. The tragedy that occurred more than a fortnight ago has been in all our hearts and minds ever since.

But the perpetrator who currently sits in my chair may also consider himself master of my destiny if he believes even a little bit that I'm aware of his sins. So, what is my choice? I'm a free man, and right is right. The choice may seem black and white, but the answer is always white. No matter what I have seen to be true in my eyes, my skin will hide the truth from them, I think. Being black makes me even doubt myself and what I have certainly seen. A black man can't accuse a white man even if heaven judges it's just for him to do so.

In this case, the good deacon's son has been slain by this Judas's thirst for coin. He spends some of it today on a fancy Boston photographer when Swain offers a fair price. What else has Green done with the stained five thousand dollars?

Lord, I can speak of what I saw and be heard, or I can suffer with the knowledge. The postmaster is the killer. Am I the only one to see it? I saw him go plainly to the bank twice that morning while I was observing the street. I spied him a third time, in my mirror, exiting the bank as I was preparing to go out on an appointment. Ten minutes later, I was staring at the corpse of young Frank Converse.

The last time I saw him, Green's attire was not of his usual style. Although I was looking at only his reflection, I noticed the limp. There is never any disguising that.

In this very moment, with his mind in a flurry of activity, William realized he had been shaving Edward subconsciously, yet still in his gentle manner, even while distracted by his thoughts. His straight razor hovered over Edward's crooked form in one hand as he pulled his neck taut with the other.

He thought, *Should I harden my grip and seek vengeance for the deacon's son? My end would be in the gallows, no doubt, or lynched in the street.*

No. I must allow the white man to dole out his white justice. There is no justice for black folk—slavery or servitude in the South, and just a sort of indifferent tolerance in the North, if we are lucky. I must mind myself and my family, first and foremost, though I'm disgusted by this man and his sins, which are many a hue darker than the darkest of my brothers' complexions. If there is justice, his punishment in the next life will be far darker than any shade of one's skin. It is not the outside darkness but the inside part that damns a man. Will these white men ever understand? I pray they will.

After the shave and haircut were complete, William held Edward's blood money in his palm, in exchange for his honest toil. The barber's mind was tormented with worry that he had been tainted by his proximity to this man's sins. Was his very silence a greater transgression than any he could otherwise commit in his life?

The postmaster's lips were moving, but all William could hear was the thudding of his own telltale heart. He felt faint. Was he safe? Would he ever be? The next sound William registered was the bell ringing once more, and he was alone, mostly—guilt and uncertainty, like the murderer's hair on his clothes, remained tethered to him; they refused to depart from his being.

William's barber pole cast an elongated shadow over the postmaster as he staggered away. Edward was several feet into the street, but the darkness continued to linger on him. William was transfixed by the silhouette as he imagined the red and white stripes outside his view blurring and extending, transforming into a noose, and then hanging from the end of the pole, high above the street.

Like an apparition, the figurative noose swayed in the breeze, and William worried his own neck could be placed into it just as easily as Edward's. He had committed no crime, let alone one as evil as Edward had, but William feared the murder might be pinned falsely upon him, nonetheless. He could not fully trust the whims of these men; they held all the power and he possessed none.

Edward was on the street, out of the barber-pole shadow's reach, and heading toward the depot. William pondered whether Edward was outside the law's reach as well. Watching him but pretending not to do so, William heard part of Edward's song as the postmaster limped farther into the distance: "Over the hills we go, laughing all the way."

Did the postmaster note that his exit from the bank around the time of Converse's murder was observed by the barber, even with his disguise? William took a deep breath, calculating that if Edward held any definite suspicions, the postmaster would have confronted or killed him already. William conceived that Edward's ignorance, or even a mere doubt about what the barber could have seen, would protect him, at least for the moment.

William willed this thought to be true. *Another murder so quickly, no matter if the victim was just a Negro like myself, would draw eyes clearly to the postmaster because of the neighborhood and brazenness of the crimes. Yet, I am aware my prayer for some sort of sanity on his part is just a small bit of refuge from such a dangerous man.*

He has murdered once for money and so is more than capable of doing so again to safeguard his bounty and, of course, his own neck.

The barber turned his eyes away from the street and cleared the murderer's hair off his person and his chair. Gathering it in its entirety, he swept it from his floor and into the street, far away from his establishment. William wished to rid his shop and himself of any part of the postmaster's sins. The coins he earned from Edward, he decided immediately, would go into the donation box Sunday at the First Baptist Church, where Elisha Converse resided as deacon. This was a small solace for the loss of the man's son, but he hoped it would absolve him of any involuntary connection to Edward's sin.

William sat in his old pine rocking chair by the window and gazed out on Malden Square as more questions rattled through his mind.

Where will the postmaster's path lead him to next? What are Green's plans? What are God's plans? Do they include my playing a part in this drama? Could my bearing witness to Green's crimes be the end to the postmaster's story, or will it just place me and my family in grave peril?

William had slept little since the murder, and after this tense interaction with Edward, he pondered if he could ever close both his eyes again. He would have to stay more alert than usual and continue to play the fool that all the townsfolk expected, but he realized from now on he would have to put on a grand performance for the postmaster.

Chapter Three

TWENTY-SIX YEARS EARLIER, while returning home to East Malden from working as a barkeep at Waite's tavern on Salem Street, Reuben Green discovered his wife, Lydia, strewn motionless beside their child like one of his misplaced toys. Their baby, Edward, stared into the abyss of her unseeing orbs. Lydia's limbs stretched out toward her son, unable to reach him, to hold him, to answer his call, his anguished need for her. A gash on her forehead darkened her hair. *Did Lydia trip and fall?*

Observing more blood on the side of the well, where her head must have struck, confirmed Reuben's suspicions. Her blood had seeped from the wound and pooled around and below Edward in a sea of crimson. Reuben lay beside her, tried to stir her, to revive her—but Lydia was cold to the touch. Reuben wept and said a prayer for his wife, then turned to his son.

"Edward, I will take care of you, my son. I promise. Your mother loved you so much"—he paused and kissed Edward on the cheek—"but demons plagued her, surrounded her, and finally it appears they have pounced upon her. I tried to help her through her melancholy, Son. I wish I could have done more."

Reuben sobbed uncontrollably. However, his son was not crying; Edward seemed content, as if mesmerized by the gazing yet unperceptive husk his mother had become. Where once Edward had swam in her womb as she nurtured him and brought him into this world, he now floated in her essence again, the very blood that had once sustained her life and his. But her life was no more.

An empty pail lay behind Lydia in a small puddle of its former contents. Reuben picked it up and retrieved more water. He wiped the dried milk off the boy's lips and attempted to clean the blood off his son, but the mark was stubborn. It took several minutes of scrubbing and more trips to the well for the stain to no longer be visible. He held his son close to his chest, but the infant's head strained to gaze upon his mother. Reuben twisted Edward in his arms so they could both see Lydia and mourn together. He knelt, still holding his baby, and said another prayer, then kissed his wife on the cheek one final time. Reuben looked at Lydia, glanced skyward briefly and then back down at his wife, and spoke to her pleadingly.

"It is now just me and the boy. Lydia, what am I to do?"

All his life, Edward Green wished he could remember his mother, that she could still be with him, comfort him, bestow upon him the love he always lacked. But he felt that, before he lived a single year, she had abandoned him forever.

These longings to be loved would remain unfulfilled in Edward's soul. He would never know the circumstances of her passing because Reuben never spoke of it, and Edward would never allow himself to inquire about it, although he longed to do so. The truth was that Lydia had suffered tremendous difficulty as a teenage bride and mother and began drinking heavily, pilfering bottles from the tavern when Reuben was out on errands or busy with a customer. At the time, it was decided that it would be best for their two sons, George and Rufus, to live with Lydia's parents on their South Reading farm. Reuben and Lydia were both surprised when a third son came along. Reuben held great hope and faith that Lydia had overcome her demons. But when he found Edward soaked in her blood, Reuben decided he must seek another profession to shield his son from the evil habits that had led to his mother's demise if he possibly could.

When Edward was nine years old his father married again, coincidentally to another Lydia. Reuben was forty years old when he wed Lydia Gove of Portsmouth, New Hampshire, on January 25, 1846. She was much younger, just twenty-four years old, so Edward couldn't help but think that his father was just trying to replace one wife named Lydia with another of the same name. And so, the first Lydia, his Lydia, vanished further into a void and he could never resurrect her.

This strange woman professed to be his mother, but Edward believed she could never be so. She was just a mere child herself when he was brought into this world, and no matter the effort Lydia exerted, Edward could never accept this imposter as a replacement for his dear mother.

A stepmother was not the last great challenge to alter his life that year. Edward was afflicted with a scrofulous disease of white swelling in one of his knees. It started with a slight pain which annoyed him for a couple of days. But as the pain worsened, Edward, like a dog that had stepped on a thorn, curled the injured leg upward so only its toes scraped the ground as he walked. A blushed-red inflammation spread across the infected knee, and the tumor beneath it grew puffy with immense, protruding purple veins. The pain gnawed at him. Leeches were used to alleviate this torment, and a large amount of pus was discharged by the doctor. The glands around his groin also swelled. Edward was bedridden with a fever and drifted in and out of consciousness for several days. Once he awoke, the doctor advised amputation.

"Father, let me keep it, please!" Edward begged. "Even if my leg is damaged, it is a part of who I am, a part, even if bad, I do not wish to abandon. I want the use of both my legs. Let me keep it. Please! Please!" Reuben agreed to his son's wishes, and for a short period, Edward assumed he had fully recovered. However, through the long rehabilitation of this leg, the muscles shrank and then the tendons contracted. Edward Green would be lame for the rest of his days, in body, psyche, and spirit.

The following summer, while Edward was still bedridden, Charles Reuben entered the world, both to Edward's fascination and bewilderment. Where once his father and his stepmother concentrated solely on him and his weakened condition, now their attention was completely fastened upon this new creature instead. Reuben, Edward knew, had to focus on the future, his new wife and this child. He felt like old news, like a misplaced remnant of the past. Edward quickly grew resentful of his half brother for having to share his father with him. He also became jealous because Charles still retained his birth mother, whereas Edward had lost his mother and had barely known her, and any recollection of her had long ago disappeared. Edward, through most of his teenage years, could barely leave the property, while he witnessed his younger sibling grow and move about as he pleased.

His father was consumed by his work running his tavern. Reuben still wished to change trades but was unable to find one which would support his family as well as tending bar. One spring day in 1850, an unfamiliar man sat down on a stool at the bar as Reuben stood behind it wiping beer mugs with a cloth.

"What's your poison, mister?"

"Hello, sir. Thank you, no. I am not a drinking man," said the stranger, placing a King James Bible on the bar.

Reuben frowned and thought, *One of these temperance people coming here again to tell me about the evils of peddling alcohol?* He placed the mug he was cleaning on a shelf behind him and thought, *Though, perhaps he's right.*

"My name is Elisha Converse. I have just moved to town." He extended his hand.

Reuben shook it, introducing himself.

"I'll take a lemonade, please. I saw how you looked at the Bible," said Elisha, the newly appointed deacon to the First Baptist Church, "but worry not, I am only here to get to know you, my new neighbor. In my experience, the tavern is as important a place to meet townsfolk as the church. Though of course, you are always welcome at the church." Elisha smiled, for he believed the barstool was, unfortunately at times, a replacement for the pew in many a man's eyes, so he would seek out these men where he knew he could find them. Elisha would not imbibe, but he would not judge either; that was for the Lord, and the Lord alone. "This is a fine town," he said.

"It is, sir. I have lived here all my life."

"Do you know of any homes for sale?"

"There is one on Linden Court. The owner has business concerns out west. I could make inquiries for you."

"I would be most appreciative. Now, Reuben, please tell me all about yourself and this town."

After an hour of conversation and another lemonade or two, the two men grew to know each other quite well. Usually, Reuben, as barkeep, found himself listening to his customers' problems and concerns, yet the tables were turned; he felt such a strong comfort level with the deacon that he unburdened himself of topics he would never think to speak of to his most intimate friends, never mind someone he was meeting for the first time.

"I make my living selling ales and spirits, but I have a personal cross to bear, Deacon."

"I am not here to judge, but I promise to listen with intent and care."

Reuben poured the deacon another lemonade and then one for himself. He walked around the bar and sat on the stool next to Elisha.

"I lost my beloved to the demons in the bottle."

"I am sorry to hear."

"Thank you." Reuben paused and then took a sip and placed the glass back on the bar. "She was just a girl when our first son, George, was born, and he was quickly followed by Rufus. Motherhood as a teen was just too, too difficult for her. She began to drink heavily. We sent the boys to live with her parents on their nearby farm. Then Edward came along and neither one of us was expecting him."

Reuben told Elisha of his second marriage and the son that had come from it.

"Since then, George has passed on, leaving Rufus, who, at this point, is more the son of my dead wife's parents than he is my own anymore. So, I have Eddie and I have Charles. Charles will be fine, but I often worry about Edward."

Reuben informed Elisha about Edward's surgery and how he had remained weak and bedridden for several years. Elisha felt empathy for Reuben with his invalid son as the two men talked about their families and the loss of Reuben's first wife. Elisha could not imagine a life without his Mary.

Elisha, through business and real estate, would, within two years of his arrival, transform into an affluent man with growing influence in Malden. He remembered Reuben's kindness when he had presented himself as a stranger in town. When Reuben grew to know Deacon Converse over many conversations at the tavern and at the church, where Reuben and his family joined the congregation, he became aware the deacon held great ambitions, and the talent to reach his aspirations while assisting all those that were close to him.

When the office of postmaster became vacant in 1852, Elisha help Reuben attain it.

"Thank you so much for your assistance, Deacon!"

"Reuben, God has already blessed me with so much. Your appointment is an act of God's grace; I am merely his instrument."

Reuben nodded; he was proud of having been named postmaster. "I will always be grateful for God's grace as well as your friendship."

"And I, yours," replied Elisha.

"Elisha, I am just trying, with God's will, to live a simple life, to be a provider for myself and my family."

"And you will do so. The delivery of the mail is important to the running of the country, a vital means of communication for family, friends, and the business of the day."

Running the tavern, Reuben had weathered financial ups and downs. Now with the steady guarantee of a government check, Reuben secured a mortgage with a loan of $1,323 from the trustees of the Shoe and Leather Dealers' Loan and Fund Association of Boston. A *Boston Herald* advertisement described the property as "a certain parcel of land situated in the easterly part of Malden called Maplewood together with the buildings thereon standing . . . about 8 acres. Upon this piece of land is a Dwelling House; the land is well stocked with fruit trees; and agriculturalists will realize from its deep rich soil, bearing trees, and favorable location, a sure and perfect harvest for their investment."

Charles was overjoyed at the larger expanse in which to run and play. Edward fumed from his bed, feeling he was now a smaller fish in a bigger pond. Edward's stepmother appeared to love him and seemed to endeavor to treat both him and Charles with equal favor, but Edward continued to view himself as an outsider. Having few means of amusement, he would sometimes trick Charles into believing in false things like the moon was made of cheese or the clouds were the hanging laundry of the Almighty.

Over a couple of weeks one spring, Charles gained the trust of a stray cat and left out a bowl of milk close to the home for it to drink. Edward, bored and exhausted in his convalescence, regarded the creature with disdain.

Day after day, the repetitive lapping of its tongue as it drank increased his annoyance. He snuck up behind the cat. Picking it up suddenly, he choked it with both hands while it scratched his arm seeking to escape. As he snapped the feline's neck, Edward fixated on the mixture of white and red below him, a few droplets of his blood from the abrasions on his arm mixed with the milk spilled on the ground. He limped into the woods and discarded the carcass in some vegetation.

It wasn't until age sixteen that Edward Green was able to walk with only marginal pain. The leg had set, and he could use it; it was not perfect, but it would have to do. Refusing to be bedridden anymore, Edward's quest was to make up for lost time. His youth was spent, and manhood awaited. His mother's death was forever a mystery to him. Fear of the unknown and his own mortality overtook him, occupying Edward's thoughts.

From the very moment Edward took his first awkward steps outside, after being mostly confined to his bed since boyhood, this quest remained in the forefront of his mind. He possessed a second chance. *I have retained both my legs through utter determination. I'll have to struggle, while my peers travel around with carefree ease, blessed by their Maker, but I will show Him. He shall truly see who I am.* One of Edward's legs attempted a confident stride; the other was propelled forward by pure spite. Soon, through repetition and conflict, his gait became a little smoother. The balance between the two appendages was uncertain, and yet a tenuous arrangement was reached. Each leg despised the other for the predicament they shared but resigned themselves to their coexistence as a means of their very survival.

Chapter Four

April 30, 1850
Boston Evening Transcript
The town of Malden is now fast increasing in population and business. Even with North Malden being set apart as Melrose this year, the town has grown to 3,500 souls. It is exceedingly well situated, has an abundance of water, and is in every respect a healthy and pleasant place.

Several factories and different branches of business exist and others are about to be established there. There is already a railroad depot in one village, and another is being built in the southernly section adjoining Chelsea.

A new public highway is about to be laid out directly to the ferry service, so the facilities for getting to and from Boston are everyday becoming more numerous and beneficial to the community.

At no time can land be bought cheaper or on better terms in this flourishing place than present; and every person who can secure a lot at the current prices in Malden, where inhabitants take both pride and pleasure in encouraging newcomers, new enterprises and companies, will be pretty sure to make a handsome sum on his purchase money.

October 23, 1850
The Boston Daily Atlas

The Edgeworth is an incorporated land company, the property being located in Malden, about three-and-a-half miles north of Boston. It is intersected by the Boston and Maine railroad, and is furnished with an elegant and commodious depot. The trains pass between forty and fifty times a day.

The whole property consists of eleven million feet of land. About half the territory is high land, commanding one to the finest prospects in the vicinity, and is beautifully wooded. The other half is a plain and is admirably adopted to manufacturing purposes.

With rail connections now throughout New England, New York and as far as Canada, those far-sighted individuals who invest in Edgeworth or any other lands upon the lines of railroads leading from Boston can expect great returns.

November 7, 1853
Boston Herald

Among the many pleasant spots that environ our metropolis —and Boston can boast of as pretty a circle as any other city in the world—is the quiet and cozy town of Malden. One should take an occasional ride from the city, and look about him, for he will find himself lost—a stranger in his own land, so rapid and many are the improvements constantly going around and about us.

A flour mill is now in full tide of operation, turning out one hundred and fifty barrels of superfine flour each day.

Very beautiful dwellings have been built in this place during the past year or two and many more are under construction or planned.

Yes, Malden, with its little bud of a mountain, which overlooks the proud metropolis of Massachusetts, and of which its denizens are so justly vain; its pretty country roads, thick and umbrageous trees, its pleasant bye-ways, streets and lanes; its purling streams and running brooks; its goodly meadows, fields and gardens; its pretty women and children—well may you hold your head high as any of your sister towns; for by your faith, I do think you are hard to be outdistanced.

Elisha Converse stood atop Waitt's Mount, which he had just read in the morning's *Herald* described as "a little bud of a mountain." Strolling along its highest peaks, which he judged to be a couple hundred feet or so, Elisha surveyed miles of panorama. To the north, he saw the town of Stoneham, where he had dwelled before moving to Malden three years earlier. To the west lay Medford, to the east lay North Chelsea and the sea, and south lay Boston. As Elisha's eyes scanned to the right, he focused on the roundness of the Blue Hills and strained to make out Needham, the town of his birth, farther inland toward the southwest.

It astounded him; from this locality, he regarded all the places he had been, his whole past. *If I really squint, I imagine I can see all the way down to Connecticut, where I met my Mary.* Thinking of his younger days caused Elisha to smile. However, he remained certain his future lay in the town beneath his feet. He scanned it from left to right. The spire of the Baptist church, where he acted as deacon, drew his attention first, and then all of the square. He gazed intently upon The First National Bank, or, as it was commonly known, the Malden Bank, where he was president, and then upon the many other properties and interests of the town in which he was involved. He took pride in what he had read in the newspaper, but Elisha's heart truly swelled in the satisfaction that he had chosen to move to Malden by his own research and enterprise. It was the place for him, so close to Boston and the commerce of the city. Elisha owned a home on Linden Court, which his friend Reuben had told him about during their first meeting. Elisha recently joined the board of the Boston Rubber Shoe Company, its large factory and smokestacks easily seen from anywhere in the town.

Sure that Malden would put its stamp on him, it was every bit Elisha's intention to put his stamp on it as well. Elisha was instrumental in establishing the Edgeworth Company, which purchased nearly forty of Malden's rural lots in 1849 at one to two and a half cents per square foot. Those lots were then planned out as streets and homes and now housed hundreds of workers, who toiled for Elisha and the Boston Rubber Shoe Company. His investments were paying off handsomely, and each year his family was growing more prosperous.

The Converses had two children, Frank, seven years old, and Mary Ida, an infant. Elisha gazed to the heavens and said a prayer. "Lord, you have been very kind to me. Through your good graces, I prospered in business at an early age and now am a family man with a wife and children and pray, hope ardently, that more children will fill our home . . . if you feel fit to further bless us." The warm air brushed against the whiskers Elisha had just begun to sprout, fully and successfully. He inferred this to be a sign of his Lord's blessing. He was in his early thirties, but it had taken this long for the stubbornly slow patches of growth on his face to catch up with their flourishing brothers.

After a deep breath of fresh air and another prayer of thanks for all he had been given and a devout promise to his Lord that he would endeavor to return his good fortune to all those around him, Elisha stood up from his knees. It was time to finish up the last appointments of the day so he could gleefully return home to his wife, his young son, and his baby. Whereas the townsfolk journeyed to the Baptist church weekly for counsel, Deacon Converse visited the Mount. It became a sacred place where he could pray and confer with the Almighty on an elevated, secluded plane, a place to collect his thoughts and clear his mind.

As the years passed, his visits to Waitt's Mount became less frequent, but he strived to climb its summit at least once a month. He thought of himself as a Puritan, like the first European settlers who had reached the very shores almost within his eyesight. Elisha wondered if one of the Natives had stood in this spot and spied the *Mayflower* back in 1620. *No,* he thought, *the distance is too vast.* Elisha, always a diligent and curious student, possessed great knowledge about the history of the town he now called home and reams of details about his own family. When his ancestor Edward Converse had arrived in the New World in 1630, the English possessed harbors in both Boston and Salem, where many Native tribes were clustered, led by Sachem Nanepashemet.

Cotton Mather, an early Puritan leader, estimated that nine-tenths of the Native population had soon perished by the scourge of smallpox, which had been brought unknowingly by those immune to the disease. Mather claimed with vigor it was the "hand of God" which cleared the way for the Puritans. The Great Sachem escaped the sickness but was slain in a battle with a warring tribe at nearby Mystic Pond. Defeated, with their numbers made sparse by invaders seen and unseen, his widow, Squaw Sachem, along with a neighboring tribe, surrendered their lands to the inhabitants of Charlestown in 1629. At the close of the deal, the Natives gave the English twenty-six fathoms of wampum and received five coats of red cloth and a potful of wine in exchange.

One can think now, as in many other bad deals, there was just one drunken night and many years of regret to follow, thought Elisha, a teetotaler, and then he pondered this transaction for a few moments. A little over ten years later, a part of this acquired territory was settled as Mystic Side. In 1649, it was renamed Malden and officially incorporated as a town.

After looking through a full 360-degree view, Elisha once more focused on the town below. He could barely imagine how the land and the people might had been some two hundred years prior, but he recognized the modern progress which had occurred in his short residence in the town. The community had prospered since he first cast his eyes upon it from this high spot, one which afforded him a view of its many changes. Elisha was humbly aware his arrival had initiated a ripple in the pond, which had transformed into a gathering wave.

Early in 1855, Elisha was appointed treasurer and chief buying and selling agent of the Boston Rubber Shoe Company, granting him sole direction and control of all its operations. His positions with the shoe company and the bank, as well as his various real estate investments in the town, catapulted Elisha into becoming a richer man than he ever could have imagined possible.

Chapter Five

Enough time had elapsed since Edward Green left his convalescence so that both his pain threshold and his mobility improved, enough so that he could join his father at the post office. Reuben, hopeful the youngest son of his first wife was on the mend, focused on teaching Edward as much as he could about his vocation. When Reuben worked at the tavern, he was reluctant to show his boys a business which could lead to such folly for some, as it had for Edward's mother.

Because Charles was able-bodied, Reuben was not worried about his future, certain that he would secure more opportunities in life. Edward, on the other hand, was not, and Reuben knew he never would be, so he would require extra assistance from his father.

Maybe, Reuben thought, *Eddie can be groomed to follow in my footsteps. It would be a reliable profession for him where few exist.* And so, Reuben took Edward on as his apprentice.

Edward noticed the joy his father exuded as Reuben demonstrated to him the mechanics of managing the town's post office. Although Edward was thrilled to have his father's attention once again, he couldn't help but feel that it was only out of pity. So Edward was determined to prove that he could run the office as well as his father could do, perhaps even better, in spite of his limp. Edward attempted to ignore the persistent ache in his leg and began taking sips of whiskey to help settle it, to steady himself. Oftentimes, this drink would lead to another and another, until he lost count. Occasionally, he suffered from blackouts. The rotation of the sun in the sky would seem to pass him by in but a single blink. When the alcohol was not enough, Edward would also take morphine to quell the throbbing.

But the ache in his limb was only part of Edward's misery. He still harbored resentment and loneliness from losing his mother and for missing out on his childhood due to being bedridden. To prevent these circumstances from overwhelming him, he began to dabble in opium to experience the euphoria of living another life.

He surmised that God had fashioned him as a cripple, and his fellow man had only mocked him as a result. Few were vocal in this matter, but Edward always sensed their pitying eyes upon him and heard their comments plainly, even if they were unspoken. Many referred to him as "Eddie" instead of "Ed" or "Edward," and he considered this a sign of disrespect from anyone outside his immediate family or close friends. He knew what they were thinking, how they viewed him and his malformed body. They looked down on him; he was not their equal, and Edward knew he would forever be a step behind everyone else.

Edward despised the Creator for all his afflictions. He was certain God had stolen his mother from him as an infant, then tried to abscond with one of his legs as a child. But even when rendered somewhat useless by disease, Edward refused to relent. God had taken too much and given him so little. Edward desired to enjoy life. Some of his pleasures were simple, such as riding in carriages, where instead of depending on his uneven legs, he could trust the horses with their four good legs to convey him. This was exhilarating. Once he started earning some money at the post office, his pleasures became more extravagant. He loved to go to the theater and to any fancy balls he could attend, usually accompanied by his friends John Chapman, who was apprenticing to be a merchant, and Marshall Shedd, who had been working for a short time as a baker.

Their evenings together often began or ended at one tavern or another but mainly at Hill's in Malden, and it wasn't long before Edward discovered the joy of visiting the North End in Boston, the neighborhood where almost a hundred years earlier, Paul Revere had toiled as a silversmith and partook of his famous midnight ride. By this point, several years after the potato famine, tens of thousands of Irish immigrants were living crowded in boardinghouses within the few blocks that comprised the neighborhood wedged between the center of the city and the ocean that separated them from their homeland. They had traded starvation and Victorian oppression for American squalor. Disease and poverty were equally rampant. A section of the neighborhood, close to the docks, was sometimes referred to as the "Black Sea," a red-light district of the city, crammed with scores of brothels and gambling dens.

When Edward drank a bit too much, which was becoming more and more frequent, John warned him to moderate. But John usually left earlier than the others. He was content to have a couple of ales with his friends but was not interested in their late-night activities. John had to wake early to begin his day's toil and liked to start the day well rested and clearheaded. Marshall also had an early morning job but chose to stay since he quite enjoyed a game of dice and felt a duty to keep his eye on Edward and accompany him home. Marshall never complained; he was able to limit his own consumption and stand by while Edward continued to drain one bottle or another.

Marshall worried Edward manufactured conflict where none existed. He considered it his responsibility to make sure that Edward wasn't drawn into too much mischief. The task was often difficult since Edward would occasionally get into boisterous arguments with other patrons at taverns or with the women he solicited. A few of these altercations escalated into fisticuffs, where due to his size and physical limitations, Edward wouldn't often fare well. Marshall was growing weary of his friend's behavior since a couple of errant swings from those fighting Edward, and more than one from Edward himself, had landed on his person.

"Eddie, maybe that's enough for tonight, what do you think?"

"Damn it! Marshall, I will get what I can out of life while my time remains. I seek to have fun."

"There are plenty of nights ahead for us to enjoy."

"Poppycock," said Edward, losing his balance for a moment, and then steadying himself with a hand grasped to the back of his seat. "My mother died before I truly knew her. There are no guarantees in life. Marshall, consumption or even a bout of diarrhea can kill you. Some people start with a simple cough, and in a week, they are down in the ground, mere worm food."

"Such dark thoughts."

"After surviving what I have suffered through all these years, I now instead desire to bathe myself in immense pleasures. Booze, brothels, and bedlam." Edward swayed in his seat. "A toast to all of these! I work all day; I consider this my night shift. Let's go have another drink. The night is far from over, and the day will approach only when I wish to allow it. The owl and I share the night. I have viewed the sun set many a time but rarely have I witnessed it arise."

Marshall drew the reins, and the team trotted forward toward Hill's Tavern while Edward took a pull from his flask.

Marshall secured the horses, and Edward stumbled out of the buggy and braced on a nearby post for equilibrium. He straightened himself up and focused on the paper posted on the wall before him. He was furious.

"Again with this nonsense. Marshall, hurry up. Take a look at this!"

His friend stood by his side and read the advertisement aloud.

"The Sons of Temperance and the Bell Rock Lodge declare that the following members of our lodge have fallen from their pledge of the abstinence of liquor and ales and must be 'taken in hand' to keep them sober." Marshall paused and scanned down the list of a dozen men or so. Third down, alphabetically, was "Edward W. Green."

A moment after Marshall had read his name, Edward lurched forward and ripped the poster from the wall. But his attempt had only been partially successful. The section that contained his name remained pasted firmly to the wooden surface. He scratched at it frantically with his fingernails to banish it from his sight but to no avail.

"These bastards! I don't appreciate being called out as a drunkard. The Lord has already called me out with my limp, which, of course, is plain to see for anyone looking. Why insult me further?" Edward began to cry.

Marshall shook his head and silently attempted to hold Edward up as he leaned over, intoxicated with a potent cocktail of alcohol, anxiety, and anger.

"If I can't hide in my drinking, where can I hide?" Edward stammered.

The intense focus of others on his being, on the very life he had been burdened with living, incensed him.

"Marshall, these Templars say of me, it is necessary to 'push him forward to keep him straight.' But all this pushing forward is useless. The path before me always appears crooked, no matter how firmly I try to keep myself straight."

Edward looked spent, his soft crying turning to profound weeping.

"Eddie, let's go sit in the buggy for a while."

Edward agreed and Marshall lifted him awkwardly up as the horses whinnied with the unexpected disturbance. Soon, after more complaints and a few choice swear words directed at particular temperance members, as the two sat in the scant moonlight, Edward leaned against Marshall's shoulder and began snoring. In the darkness, Marshall guided the horses back on the road toward Edward's home, trying to derive some comfort in his loyalty as his friend's weight pressed harder against him.

This was not the first time Edward had been expelled from the division and lodge for the violation of his pledge, even though he professed temperance earnestly in the meetings he attended. On another occasion, when a party drove from Boston to take part in a dance in Malden, Major James C. Loughton had caught Edward stealing a bottle of whiskey from the sleigh. "Trouble will find you," warned the older man.

"I am easy to find," Edward said, and giggled in response.

Loughton admonished him, "The devil is in the bottle, Mr. Green. This road will lead to nothing but bad choices that will affect your relationship with God and your fellow man. I myself am a man of temperance."

"Lucky you," Edward said as he walked away.

Edward thought, *I can't abide, but I can always imbibe*, and snickered at the wordplay. He enjoyed a much more rewarding relationship with the bottle and whatever devil it held than he ever did with God or any person.

One Saturday around noon, with Marshall and John at Hill's Tavern, Edward, frustrated by seeing another temperance advertisement with his name on it outside, said, "Normally, I know drinking throws off my balance, but my balance is uneven to begin with. Depending on the night and the circumstances, I imagine myself either straightening out or completely losing my equilibrium and falling over. I would freely admit to my fellow temperance fibbers, some of whom we all know disobey their oaths without being called out in these handbills as I am so blatantly"—Edward took a sip of his ale—"that it's surely a mixture of both and mostly the latter. But with each sip, I'm always searching, almost praying, for the former, an odd gamble to transform myself to be as even-footed as everyone else."

John and Marshall had endured such gripes from Edward so often that they rarely responded to them anymore. John stood up and walked away. A minute later he was back at the table.

"Sorry, fellows. Was just checking the town clock. You'll have to excuse me, please. I have a young lady to go visit." He nodded at Marshall and walked over to Edward, placing a hand on his shoulder. "Hang in there, Eddie."

"Thanks," said Edward, but he rolled his eyes as John exited the tavern.

"John thinks highly of himself, don't you think?"

"He is doing well," said Marshall.

"Everything has been handed to him." Edward raised his hands in exasperation. "Anyway, as I was saying before he walked away . . ."

Marshall ordered another round as Edward continued talking. "I have to play a game of chance, not worrying about the long-term consequences, or the short-term ones for that matter."

Edward edged to the left and grasped his stool to center himself once more.

"Consequently, sometimes I've fallen, and I have hit my head hard on the ground more times than I can count."

Marshall shrugged and took a sip of his beer.

Edward continued, "I am able to gain the trust of the fools by stating that I will pray to God and stop drinking tomorrow. Every meeting I promise them I just need a drink to get me through this one day and I will be fine. They are gullible and always believe me."

As more and more time went by, the temperance committee discovered there would always be another tomorrow when it came to Edward Green. One day was never enough, the days stretched on without end as did the empty platitudes. There was always a bottle and a promise, but the promise got Edward nowhere and the bottle, he believed, provided so much more for him in the moment. Edward did not care; he would not care. He would numb himself, sleep, and repeat when the sun reappeared or disappeared, so frequently he sometimes was oblivious to how the whole day had vanished. The fiery orb had traveled from one end of the horizon to the other without so much as a glimpse from him.

Elisha frequented the post office and would eventually bring along his eight-year-old son, Frank. The boy had many questions for the assistant postmaster.

"What's it like to be eighteen? I can't wait to be that age. Are you going to be postmaster too one day, like your dad? Is that your plan? Is that what you are going to do?"

"I don't know. Perhaps so." Edward, at first, felt a bit taken aback by the rapid-fire questions of the child and offended by the insinuation that he could do no better for himself than procure a job only through the assistance of his father. But he could not help but to have a genuine admiration for the boy and realized that his inquiries were only a result of his childhood innocence, openness, and curiosity. There was no need to be insulted. Edward did not feel belittled by Frank and sensed that there was something special about him; he was the son of the benevolent Elisha Converse, after all. Frank seemed to have inherited his father's personable nature and to possess an intelligence beyond his years. Edward was pleased to meet him.

As a reward, Edward showed the boy a magic trick, guessing he had never witnessed such a thing before. "Frank, do you have any money on you, perhaps a coin?"

The boy looked flummoxed for a moment. He stared intently at the older boy, then smiled and began shuffling through his pockets. "Here. My father gave me this lucky silver coin on my birthday. He told me it was minted from a set of just thirty." Frank willingly placed the coin flat on Edward's open palm.

Edward covered his left hand with his right and then removed it. The coin was still there. He covered it again for a few seconds. Frank stared at his hands and then into Edward's eyes. When he looked back down, Edward revealed his opened palm after removing his upper hand, and the coin was gone.

"My goodness!" exclaimed Frank. "Where has my coin went?"

Edward smiled. "I wouldn't take anything that valuable from you, Frank. What your father, the good deacon, has bestowed upon you is yours and not mine." He lifted the empty hand toward Frank's right ear and pulled it back, opening it again to reveal the coin. They both laughed. The laughter of a child and of a man who had lacked a proper childhood mixed as one sound.

Elisha, who had been conversing with Reuben on the other side of the room, reacted to the glee in his son's eyes. "Thank you for keeping Frank entertained, Edward. I get so wrapped up in my business and the needs of the church congregation, I sometimes forget to take the time for playfulness with him."

"I didn't always treat my younger brother with such kindness, Deacon, so maybe I can make up for that by taking Frank here under my wing."

"I would be forever indebted to you, Edward. I had two older siblings myself, so I know how important it is to have good mentors and role models. I would be honored if you, as someone who has clearly overcome obstacles and persevered through adversity, could fill that role for my Frank."

"Well, the bank is just across the street, Deacon, so feel free to bring Frank by anytime you have business to attend to there. I'm here every day, and I have plenty more magic tricks up my sleeve." He smiled and winked at Frank.

The promise of more magic tricks made Frank laugh. "Will you show me how you do it?" he asked Edward.

"A good magician never reveals his methods to the audience. But perhaps if you become my apprentice, I will share some of my secrets with you."

Chapter Six

Deacon Converse began bringing his son around to the post office frequently, and a special brotherly relationship began to develop between Edward Green and Frank Converse. Just as the deacon and Frank were leaving the post office after their latest visit, Edward was surprised to see his friend John Chapman stroll through the post office door in the middle of a workday, with no sign of a package to deliver.

"What can I do for you, John? Shouldn't you be stuffing mattresses or curling feathers right now?"

"Very funny, Eddie. You know very well that I don't have anything to do with the wig side of the business, or the mattresses either. I'm a salesman. I'm actually here for two reasons. One is to see if you'd care to join me for a drink at Hill's tonight. I haven't seen you out in a while, and I have some good news to share."

Edward frowned. "Actually, I've been trying to steer clear of the tavern for a while. The deacon has asked me to take his son under my guidance. He sees me as just as much an important man as you've apparently become. I suppose I should set a good example for young Frank and show the deacon how trustworthy I am." For the first time in Edward's life, he sensed a feeling of pride and responsibility, that he could accomplish something on his own terms. He genuinely enjoyed spending time with Frank, and he didn't want to disappoint him or the deacon.

"Well, that's good to hear, Eddie. You realize how I feel about your drinking habits, so I definitely don't want to hinder your progress toward temperance."

"Thank you, John. I can't say it's been easy, though. I still keep something close by for emergencies." Edward tapped the drawer in his desk, where he kept a bottle of whiskey hidden so his father could not find it. "And while the urge is still there, I'm doing my best."

"In that case, I suppose I can just share my good news with you now. The first is that I've been offered a promotion at the mattress company, which means more pay."

"Well, that is good news, John. Perhaps they will soon change the name from Manning, Glover, and Company to Manning, Glover, and Chapman!"

John chuckled. "It's not that big of a promotion, but that leads to my second piece of news. You remember the girl I mentioned a couple months ago, Clara Allen?"

"Vaguely."

"Well, I've been courting her since then, and now with this promotion along with the strong support of my father, I will have the means to ask her to marry me! It will be a bit of a long engagement due to her age."

Edward wanted to be delighted for his friend, but his old feelings of jealousy and resentment resurfaced, and he found it difficult to articulate the words to congratulate John. "Well, that's a big step. How well are you acquainted with this girl?"

"I've been visiting her every Sunday in Cambridge, and I am confident that she is the one. In fact, why don't you join me on my next visit so you can meet her? Come on, you love horse and buggy rides, Eddie, and I firmly believe that you will concur with me that Clara is worth marrying."

Edward could not resist the offer of a carriage ride, especially a long one, and he hoped for pleasant weather. Most of all, he was curious to meet this Clara Allen and find out what John Chapman was all worked up about. So, he agreed to accompany his friend.

"Oh, and that reminds me of another reason for coming here. Could you please mail this letter for me?"

Edward accepted the letter addressed to Clara. "Why do you need to send her a letter if you're going to see her in a matter of days?"

"I thought starting up a written correspondence would be another way to get to know each other, and a way for us to keep in touch when we aren't able to meet in person."

"Sure," said Edward, who took it and set it in the outgoing mail stack. "Thank you, Eddie. See you on Sunday."

On the ride to Cambridge, John filled Edward in on the history of the Allen family. Agnes, age twenty and Clara's oldest sister, was born in Windsor, Nova Scotia, to Agnes (her namesake) and Ebenezer Allen. Susie, the middle sister, and Clara were born in Massachusetts when the family lived in Taunton. Soon after his wife died, Ebenezer married an impoverished widow named Olive Cowden. Her daughter, Sophia, was a year older than Susie. Olive and Sophia had been living under the gracious charity of the town of Taunton when the reverend of their church proposed a match between Ebenezer and Olive. Within a few years, the newly formed family was living in Cambridge, where Ebenezer worked as a printer and painter.

Their late mother had doted on her three girls, and with her passing, Ebenezer expected his new wife to do the same. Olive attempted to comply but found it difficult to do much after a recent stumble down the front steps of their home, so all her household tasks had fallen to her daughter, Sophia, who cleaned the house, prepared all the meals, hemmed the clothes, and generally tended to every need of the three Allen daughters, including dressing them, bathing them once a week, and trimming their hair when needed. With all her new duties, Sophia rarely left the property.

"I think Clara's father, Ebenezer, is quite fond of me," John shared with Edward. "And I think he is happy that one of his daughters is being courted by someone from a respectable family. They're suffering through some financial difficulties now, as the heavy snow damaged their roof last year. So, it must be a relief to know one of his daughters will be taken care of."

Hearing that there were two other Allen sisters, plus a stepsister, intrigued Edward, and for the rest of the ride, his thoughts wandered to prospects of courting one of the Allen sisters himself.

Meanwhile, at the Allen household, the day was fraught with mixed emotions for each one in the family as they awaited John Chapman's imminent visit. As Sophia was inside toiling away at her daily chores, the other three Allen sisters were standing on the porch, waiting for the hoof steps of the horses drawing the carriage. Ebenezer came out and stood behind them, joining their gaze down the street. Though it was only early fall, he rubbed his arms and said, "A tough winter's on its way, girls. I can feel it in my bones."

"Don't worry, Daddy, I will knit you a new sweater. In fact, I'll get started right now." Agnes went inside and gathered her knitting supplies, then went to sit by the edge of the veranda, content to have a task to busy herself and to be doing something to comfort her father, given the family's financial hardships weighing on his mind. Agnes was especially concerned since she knew her father's income had almost completely disappeared since the relocation of one of his main clients to Providence. She worried the family would be in dire straits if she and her sisters did not marry soon and marry well.

"Thank you, Agnes, that will be wonderful to have a new sweater." Ebenezer put his hands on Clara's shoulders and said, "And it's simply marvelous for you to have such a fine suitor. He is a real gentleman through and through, and being from a family of means makes him even finer." Clara was still impatiently staring down the street but smiled to hear her father's blessings of her courtship. His comment, however, made Agnes cringe, as she furrowed her brow and began knitting more aggressively.

Ebenezer went back into the house, and Susie, who had grown weary of waiting, followed him. Agnes continued to wield her needles fiercely as she gazed at her youngest sister with contempt. Agnes thought it was her divine imperative to wed well to make sure her father was cared for as he grew older and to bear him fine Christian grandchildren. She perceived Clara as overly sweet, a bit fragile, and just a child focused on romance and the foolish whims of a girl. Her sister also naively always assumed the best in people. She didn't comprehend why her father allowed Clara, who was only fourteen, to be courted by such a fine suitor as John Chapman, while the two older sisters lacked admirers of their own. The answer, Agnes suspected, was found in her deep belief that Clara was, without question, her father's favorite child.

Agnes made it a point to be on the porch each Sunday, hoping she could exchange a few pleasant words with John. Agnes prayed she could also one day find a man exactly like John Chapman and considered it unfair that Clara had succeeded in doing so first.

Agnes's thoughts were interrupted by the anticipated sounds of the horse and buggy. Clara was fidgeting. Agnes sensed her sister yearned to leave the porch and run out onto the street to meet her suitor yet restrained herself for the decorum and respect of their father.

Agnes and Clara looked on with equal fascination as the tall, handsome, well-dressed John Chapman and his unfamiliar companion lowered themselves off the buggy. *Alas,* thought Agnes as her animosity grew, *John is here to court Clara, not me.*

After a longer-than-appropriate stare toward John, Agnes glanced for a moment at the other fellow, who was tying the horses to the post as John approached the house. Then she turned her attention to Clara, standing on the cusp of the top step, willing her body to calmly walk and not run down the stairs toward the walkway, though she clearly longed to do so.

Agnes suddenly realized that the long needles in her hands were motionless, and she was staring at the young couple drawing together. She resumed knitting and glanced over again at the stranger. He was new to her eyes, but she thought him quite forgettable. He tentatively approached the walkway. It seemed to her as if an invisible rope were holding him back. He was far shorter than John, and unlike his friend, who had a tidy mustache, this man sported unwieldy whiskers, and his large lips appeared to twitch a bit.

Edward Green stared at the beauty before him. John had spoken highly of Clara Allen, raved of her charms and her appearance, but Edward had not expected to be so immediately flabbergasted, so completely overwhelmed by her on first sight.

She had a lithe figure in a lovely pale-blue dress. Her lips were prominent. Her cheeks tapered down to a delicate, rounded chin. As she spoke to John, Edward detected three vertical lines develop just above her nose and then fade as he walked closer. Her eyes were blue with a small cloudiness about them, as if a storm were approaching. Edward immediately imagined himself capable of being her hero, like in the penny dreadfuls he often read. He conjured in his mind how he would rescue her from any dire situation, hold her, love her, protect her. But she was John's girl, not his.

"Clara, you look very lovely. An absolute vision!" John said. He stood below the portico, his eyes lingered for a long moment, and then he looked toward the back of the porch and paused. "And Agnes, it is clearer and clearer to me each and every week, that the Allen sisters are all very fetching. Do you have any young gentleman courting you?"

"I do not," Agnes said curtly. She pretended to go back to her needlework, but then raised her eyes again toward her sister's debonair beau and, after a pause, said, "At the moment."

"Well, Miss Allen, I'm certain you will have one soon enough, as will Susie and Sophia."

"I'm sure you're correct, Mr. Chapman." Agnes returned to her knitting again, and then glanced back up at the stranger.

"Forgive me, ladies. This gentleman here is my fine friend Edward Green of Malden. His father is the postmaster. Edward works there too and has convinced me he is running the place."

John winked at Edward and Edward winked back. Edward then turned to the women.

"Pleasure to meet you both." His voice, though raspy, was stronger and contained a more confident tone than Agnes imagined could have been emitted out of that malformed body. Edward glanced from the older sister to the one who was closer and more captivating to him. His focus rested solely on Clara Allen; she filled his vision.

Startled, he grasped that he was staring with his mouth agape. Closing it quickly, he cautioned himself to show some restraint. *This is John Chapman's girl,* he reminded himself.

"Are you courting anyone, Mr. Green?" Clara moved a little closer to her suitor and his companion as she spoke.

"I am, right at this moment."

Clara was astonished by this immediate, confident response. Edward perceived those three lines above her nose again for but the briefest of moments, and his heart soared at the sight of them for he was certain he had elicited them. *They were for me,* he thought, *not John.*

Was he referring to me? wondered Clara. *No, of course not. He is John's good friend.* John seemed oblivious to his friend's suggestive words, although it appeared obvious, if not completely brazen, to her as to what Edward's intentions were.

"She must be a lucky girl," said Clara, meaning to shrug off any possible insinuation. She was smitten with John and was almost angry at how his friend was taking liberties, but she was also intrigued by Edward. She tried to deny that feeling, restraining a blush from blossoming.

"More than she knows," said Edward Green.

Perhaps not spoken in a bold manner, Clara thought, but she believed he was confident in his tone. Edward was an interesting and unexpected man, one not to be judged on his appearance alone. *He is not bad-looking,* she admitted to herself. But by all means, he was not John Chapman, she was sure of that.

Clara glanced back at her sister, whom she perceived was just pretending to concentrate solely on her knitting. Clara was aware that Agnes was instead intently focused on John. Many times before, she had caught Agnes's fleeting looks toward her suitor. This mildly concerned Clara. John was closer in age to both of her older sisters and her stepsister, yet Clara firmly hoped that all the Allen girls were pleased that she was being courted by John Chapman.

As the three of them continued with light conversation, the idea of stealing Clara away from John persisted in Edward's mind. He strained to quell the terrible, sinful notion, but it would not go away, and he found himself consumed by it. There was no denying it: he coveted her. John was unconcerned by the look on Edward's face; he innocently assumed that his dear friend was thrilled for him and approved of the young lady of which he was so enamored. He had no way to guess the ulterior motives of his friend, but the gears were already furtively starting to revolve for Edward as he fantasized a way, any way, to obtain Clara Allen for himself. While the inner workings of Edward Green were in a flurry, his outward manner was austere and unassuming: his words could be charming, and no one ever suspected the complicated, sinister thoughts contained within him.

"Well, now, shall we go for our usual ride, Clara? It will be a good chance for you to get to appreciate Edward better." Clara knew John's family in Ipswich, but Edward was the first of his friends she had met. John had warned her of Edward's limp so she would not be put off by it and informed her that his close friend was outgoing and fun, but he had not mentioned his other various charms. Clara thought, perhaps as a man, John was unaware of them. Clara instantly recognized Edward's look of interest; how could a young lady not? She mistook it for something flirty but not serious. But subconsciously or otherwise, she stored it away. It was always flattering for her to be made to feel special, to feel pretty.

They walked to the buggy, and Edward seated himself, feigning not to show the pain and difficulty it caused him. John then hoisted Clara up with a hand from Edward. It was the first touch he had of her, and he nodded coyly. He would imagine for the rest of the day what it would be like to touch more than just Clara's hand. But it would suffice for now. It was a start.

As they journeyed through the countryside chatting, Edward sensed in Clara a kindness, a purity he himself lacked. Also, she liked him, it seemed, for who he was, looking beyond his outward visage. Maybe then, she could also love him. It was possible, he speculated, and he deeply hoped it could be, and then that hope blossomed into a firm belief in his mind. *I will not have to put on airs. It will be effortless to attain her. It will all be worth it, no matter the means by which I may need to reach into myself and destroy a part of my conscience and my earthly being.* He scratched his hairy cheek and thought, *I can't be concerned with the matter of my eternal being, which seems damned already. Any sacrifice will be worth it to acquire the love of Clara Allen.*

Chapter Seven

AFTER RETURNING TO Malden, Edward's obsession with Clara Allen consumed all his thoughts—of the present as well as in the future. *Maybe one day I can be a family man. If we have a son, perhaps my boy could grow up to also* be *postmaster of Malden, as I will one day become myself. Three generations in a row of Malden postmasters. That's how legacies are born,* he thought, and was quite proud of the idea. Scheming against John Chapman created a moral dilemma for Edward, but his needs and wants were great, and having Clara was now the largest of them all. "I must possess her," Edward said aloud to himself as he grasped Clara's soft, pale-blue handkerchief, which he had poached from the carriage before John dropped him off at his house. As he observed the carriage drive away, Edward held the handkerchief and stared intently while John and Clara disappeared from view. She was out of his sight, but he still retained a remnant of her. He squeezed the fabric in his palm. He would, must, possess her entirely.

"If Malden is a new Garden of Eden, as I've heard Deacon Converse tell me and my father more than once, then Clara is the forbidden fruit. It is a great sin to desire the love of my dear friend's girl, no doubt. But sin or not, the temptation is too great, ripe within my very grasp. I am compelled to reach for the fruit on the vine, and I will pluck it!" Edward went to the outhouse for privacy and pleasured himself holding Clara's handkerchief in his other hand.

The expanding turmoil inside Edward's head was too much to bear. He abandoned any promises of remaining sober and decided to have a night out with Marshall. After attending a ball together, Marshall secured the horses to a cherry tree close to Mrs. Lake's brothel on Endicott Street in Boston's North End.

"His house lies yonder," said Edward, pointing up the street. "Paul Revere had his midnight ride and now I am about to have mine."

Marshall had heard this joke so many times, but he feigned laughter, nonetheless.

Edward began, "Mrs. Lake should rename this place 'One if by Hand, Two if by Puss—'" Before Edward could finish, Marshall burst out laughing. This was a new joke, and he enjoyed it but then frowned, ascertaining that his positive reaction guaranteed that Edward would now repeat it several more times in the nights out to come.

A preacher stood in the street. "Sinners, come to Christ!"

"That is not to whom I have the intention of coming this night," said Edward to the man who resembled the son of God with his long hair and beard.

Marshall snickered.

"Glory to God," stated Boston Corbett, who, though born with the first name of Thomas, had renamed himself in honor of the city of his regarded salvation.

"Use me as an example. I encountered much temptation in these streets, this Black Sea," he said, spreading his arms wide, "but I have ceased my drinking and whoring. In fact, I am now a eunuch. Gentlemen, I cut my very balls off with scissors after being tempted by two harlots. Repent or follow in the damnation that was once my intended path!"

"This is not the Red Sea, as you say, but a black one. I still have my balls and I am guiding them with my staff to the land promised. It will be an absolutely jubilant exodus," said Edward, rubbing the front of his pants and then pointing to the brothel. "However, thanks to you, I will now keep a wary eye out for any scissors when my trousers are past my ankles."

Marshall laughed as they continued down the street.

Corbett called after them. "Repent! A traitor to God, country, or his fellow man will face judgment and I will gladly be the Almighty's instrument and carry out his just punishment if called upon."

After a group of sailors passed them, entering a similar nearby establishment, the friends stepped into the parlor house. One of the residents of the home, Harry, a policeman, was seated in an armchair close to the door. A small black dog with rust coloring lay curled up by his feet. Edward always felt intimidated by the man because of his profession and his size, well over six feet and stout. Marshall had recently informed him that the cop was also a boxer, which caused Edward to become even more uneasy. "Hello, sporting men."

"Hello," said Marshall, and Edward nodded.

"I just bought this dog from a German woman named Ada who brought her over from her country; named her Violet." Marshall knelt down to pet the dog.

"Hi, Violet. She's sweet," he said as the dog licked his hand.

"The lady said she was a pinscher, a miniature sort, but cute nonetheless. A bit of a mouser as well, which is quite good for us with the vermin being plentiful in the Black Sea." Harry looked lovingly at the dog and then up to his friend. "A game of dice, Marshall?"

"Sure, Harry," said Marshall, opening his palm and accepting the bone dice. The two walked to a corner of the room in conversation while Edward ventured farther into the next larger room, where he was first greeted by piano music and then the madam of the house.

"Good evening, nice to see you once again, fine sir." Dozens of men walked through her parlor each day, but Edward always stood out to her. Mrs. Lake recognized him the moment he ambled into her lobby. She rang a bell twice, and in a few moments, three ladies appeared, each smiling broadly at Edward. Two of them seemed similar, but one drew his attention. The madam twirled her index finger, and the women sashayed and spun about in their petticoats as Edward regarded each of them. Mrs. Lake then directed them to twirl in the other direction. Usually, Edward enjoyed this spectacle and dwelled on making his choice, but after mere moments, he pointed to the one in the middle. She winked at him, appearing thrilled to be chosen. Bowing, she turned briskly and climbed the ornate staircase. The others' smiles now seemed forced with fatigue as they curtsied and exited the room.

Edward sat in an armchair by the fireplace. He projected a dollop of saliva into the nearby spittoon. The madam handed him a clay pipe, and he filled it with tobacco from a jar on a side table and then lit a match and took a long inhale. He looked at the piano player, but she was turned away from him and he could not discern her face. She was singing, and her voice held a true lament. *She sings sad songs for the dirty lovers,* thought Edward, and he chuckled.

Edward delighted in attending balls, but while he could charm ladies there, the events were of the "look but don't touch" variety and only tended to stimulate him without an avenue for release, so he often ended his night at an establishment such as this. Prior to his apprenticeship, Edward could only afford to visit common streetwalkers. Now, with some coin in his pocket, he preferred the parlor houses. There were lots to choose from in this part of the city, but Edward, before his recent attempt at temperance to impress the deacon, had been drawn to frequenting this one. Plus, Marshall preferred gambling to waiting in the carriage for Edward to return from some random alley and had become quite friendly with Harry in recent months.

Mrs. Lake motioned to him, and Edward approached the stairs. How he wished there weren't any stairs at all. The carpet before him swirled as if he were entering a whirlpool. Clinging to the railing with both hands, one of his legs climbed, braced, and hefted its brother up equal to the next level, then paused and began the process once more. Upon reaching the second floor, Edward winced in relief and turned to the open door on his left. He felt overjoyed.

Hi, Clara, I'm home, thought Edward, and he closed the door behind him as he entered the room.

"Hiya," an Irish accent greeted him, and he wished the woman had not spoken. It was ruining his illusion of being with Clara.

After obsessing about Clara nonstop all day, Edward desperately craved a surrogate for being with her. He hadn't the pleasure of seeing Clara's naked form as of yet, but in his mind, he superimposed her lovely face, with those three lines indented above her brow, onto the naked prostitute before him.

The woman had mentioned her name, perhaps it was Mary, but Edward cared not to hear it, and could not recall it, as only one name held his attention.

"Shut up." At this, her lips hardened and tightened into a horizontal line. She lay on the bed facedown, her dress, bonnet, and other clothing scattered pell-mell on the floor as Edward had demanded.

Edward had chosen her because she had somewhat the same hair color as Clara, though she was shorter and heavier. Only the act and the thought of his infatuation mattered. It was as if the other woman were not there at all; she was a mere vessel to the fantasy Edward intended to make real. There was a strong smell of vinegar mixed with other chemicals. Looking away from her backside, he noticed syringes with remnants of what he assumed was mercury as well as fine combs at her bedside. Then he closed his eyes and thought of his beloved, Clara. He felt moments of ecstasy, but the finality of the undertaking lacked the passion he sought. It wasn't nearly enough.

"Stay that way until I leave and don't say another word." She remained silent and motionless as he dressed. Edward peered at the hair spread out along her upper back and then eyed the bare form of her contours down to her toes. She was not Clara. Regrettably, he could not transform her into Clara. *If only this soiled dove had not uttered a single syllable, the illusion may have worked for me, but she* had *to go and talk with that foreign sound of hers,* he thought. "You are useless. You are not Clara or even the imitation of her I desired, that I actually paid for you to be!" he shouted. The impulse to grab the spittoon by the door and slam it on her head while she was prone and vulnerable was powerful. But there was the matter of the tough police officer downstairs playing craps, the man's small dog, and Mrs. Lake herself. The madam regarded him just as all others did. Edward had detected the heat of her eyes upon his back as he shuffled gingerly up the stairs. It was strenuous to rein himself in, but he succeeded in doing so. Edward Green was aware that his limp would betray him in leaving any crime scene, by immediate arrest or eventual accusation. So instead, he exited the room and edged back toward the stairs, hoping the descent would be less excruciating than the ascent had been.

Walking back to the carriage, Marshall was jovial, having outplayed his opponent and leaving with more coin than when he had arrived. In contrast, Edward pondered if this visit had gained any value for himself. He had spent his money and expelled part of what was building up within his insides, but he still lacked the satisfaction of being with his infatuation; this activity was just a charade, experiencing it only compelled him to desire, need, Clara even more. *I suppose I should be happy for John and Clara. After all, John's a good, loyal friend, so how can I injure him by desiring the woman he loves? And yet I feel I have no choice but to do so.*

Chapter Eight

"EDWARD, I HAVE attained her father's blessing, but I must make sure she is of the right age, which she should be soon. I could really see myself marrying her. Such a lovely girl. I think about her from morning to night and once more when I awake. The cycle starts and spills over into my dreams. Do you know what that feels like, to be so smitten?"

Edward did, but he could not confide in his friend. He was positive whatever John was experiencing could not possibly equal what he held in his own heart for Clara, utter and complete infatuation. No, he corrected himself, this was not infatuation, this was fate. Edward Green and Clara Allen were meant to be together; he was certain of it. Unfortunately for his friend, John had fallen in love with the wrong girl. Although, if John had not, Edward concluded he never would have encountered Clara himself. It was the greatest moral conundrum of his life, and nothing could ever surpass it, he supposed. But Edward had made his decision, or should he say, the decision had been made for him. *Well, yes, that is easier, much easier for me to think, to believe, it has been chosen by fate and not solely by myself, yet it surely has. Being with Clara is my constant, often only desire,* he thought.

John clasped a new letter from Clara, pressed it against his heart, and said, "We have engaged in some heavy petting, but I, we, have decided to wait until our wedding night to make love. We will consummate our joining in God's eyes as it is intended." At this, Edward envisioned himself alone in a passionate embrace with Clara. He nodded as John proceeded to speak but paid less attention to his friend's words as they were eclipsed by the vivid but not quite tangible images of Clara in his mind. After Edward initially met Clara, he had only encountered her once or twice more, and both times he needed to insert himself into John's business to do so. He realized John preferred to be alone with the young lady, but he also knew that John could not act rude to his dear friend if he was in need. The last time, Edward asked to share a carriage to take him to a destination where he really did not need to go. He desired to enter Clara's orbit somehow, and his ruse was using John as the means to do so.

A man like Edward Green was always searching for angles to gain an edge, always scheming and plotting for any personal gain. Since those of privilege and ability did not require that kind of advantage, they were oblivious to the machinations of men like Edward. John's visits to the post office were becoming more frequent, as the written correspondence between him and Clara increased. Each of their letters passed through Edward's hands, and he would watch with derision John's gleeful reaction every time he arrived at the post office to pick one up. John would smile at the romantic missive from his beautiful girl and walk out the door as if his steps did not for a moment touch the ground.

Whenever Edward spotted an envelope with Clara's handwriting, he would pause and fantasize that the letters were intended for him. One time, he thought he could smell her perfume through the paper, and an impulse came over him to rip open the letter. But his father had compelled him to take an oath before God and country to uphold the sacred trust of the U.S. Mail. After several deep breaths, Edward was able to show restraint.

However, the frequency of the correspondence between John and Clara concerned Edward, and the thought of not having Clara to himself continued to vex him. Because John was his friend and confidant, Edward assumed a good extent of the contents of John's letters to Clara; but to Edward's regret, he had no idea whatsoever of what Clara was writing.

One late morning, when a delivery from Cambridge and Somerville arrived, Edward was alone in the office. He threw all the letters on the floor, got down on his haunches, and desperately sought for the name of John Chapman on any envelope.

He wished he was John, for his good looks, his easy manner, his pure soul—but mostly because he possessed the love and attention of Clara

Allen. Edward Green would gladly sacrifice all the former if he could only possess the latter.

The light was growing a bit dim since the day was stormy, so Edward reached for his lamp and held it close as he scattered the letters left and right, not discovering what he coveted. In his excitement, he knocked the lamp. Panicked the flame would spread, Edward caught it before it tipped and gently moved it aside. He started to heave, unable to breathe.

His eyes traveled to the large plaque that hung prominently above his father's desk—the Ten Commandments, which all government offices were required to display. Flustered, Edward considered how many of these commandments he was breaking in this very moment. Once Moses had stared into the burning bush, searching for divine answers from God. In comparison, Edward gazed, probing in the dying embers of sunlight scattered across the floor for his answer. It was his ardent desire to smother the deep passion between these lovers so he could satiate his jealousy and satisfy the lust burning within him; but he was shocked that his desperation had almost inadvertently ignited an inferno in the post office.

It was not my intention to use these letters as tinder and burn down this place of business, my father's livelihood, myself, or most importantly, any letter addressed to John Chapman from the girl I love, he thought.

The private expressions of Clara Allen were valued above anything else in his life from the first moment he had made her acquaintance. He longed to consume her admiring, loving words, even if they were not addressed directly to him. But there were dozens of letters before him, and none of them were from Clara. Discouraged, he sorted through them, picked them all off the floor, and reluctantly went back about his business.

The next couple of days, he went about his normal tasks, but his constant thoughts of Clara and the desire to read her sweet nothings and imagine she was writing him instead of John gnawed at him. Whenever the mail arrived from Cambridge and Somerville and once his father was out of the office, Edward repeated the same tactic, keeping the lamp at a safe distance, from where it emitted dim illumination but would not ignite a letter addressed to his dear friend John Chapman.

Finally, after three days, he saw it, a letter with "John Char" poking out from a stack of other letters. He nudged the pile and reached for his quarry.

Lifting it to his eyes, a narrow beam of dying light crept in from the direction of the train depot, the faded illumination of the setting sun. He admired it carefully, considered it. A part of Edward, like a predator capturing its prey, wanted to tear the missive open and devour her words all at once, to consume some inner part of Clara herself without her permission; it was intimate, it was obscene. He felt both these qualities equally, yet each struggled within him. He steadied his hands and delicately unsealed the letter.

Her words penetrated his eyeballs and swirled in his brain. Edward became lightheaded as he imagined they were composed directly from Clara's heart to his own.

> *I miss you, I love you and I cannot wait, as we have*
> *discussed, to one day be your wife for I know in my head*
> *and heart that a life with you is utter joy and a life without*
> *you is dismal and full of longing. One day, our lives will*
> *lead us to a path of marriage and bliss.*

> *Love Clara*

After allowing her words to ricochet around his mind for several minutes, Edward hesitated and resealed the letter. He cleaned up the mess he had created and placed Clara's letter back in the outgoing mail.

Edward began to read letters from John to her as well but just glanced over them, mainly scanning for pertinent details, but in contrast, each of the syllables in Clara's hand were dear to him and were savored as he scanned her words over and over.

After the initial interference with the missives of the two sweethearts, Edward's hesitation declined, first slowly and then quickly and then entirely.

He discovered another letter from her and again opened it painstakingly.

> *John, my father and whole family adores you and all are*
> *thrilled that we are courting. Well, mostly they are, it*
> *seems. Agnes has been sterner with me than normal and*

*appears quite agitated often for little reason. I am unsure
if she is upset that I possess the joy of going out riding with
you while she is just left to her knitting. She is not spinning
the wool, but to my mind, she's concerned that she is seen
as a spinster nonetheless. This is far from true and will
matter little once we are wed, my love, and so I will put it
out of my mind.*

Love Clara

*Agnes fancies John and is jealous of Clara. I should consider this and
what it means, how I can benefit from this knowledge,* thought Edward. He
carefully resealed this letter but set it in the bottom of a drawer instead of
mailing it.

Days later, after opening another letter from her with the same tender
care and preparing to reseal it and put it back as he had found it, Edward
paused. He no longer wanted to close Clara's words away once they had
finally been revealed to him; they were precious, they were delicate. He
wanted to swim in them and claim them as his own. His ears were deaf to
these voiceless expressions, but in his mind, they formed an orchestra, this
single thought turning into a cacophony.

The more he became knowledgeable of her innermost affections toward
John, the more Edward found it increasingly difficult to uphold his oath
and not take advantage of the obviously direct access to her feelings. And
yet he felt guilty and unsure. So far, he was just a bystander to her prose,
but he ached to be a participant with her in a love affair as John was. If he
could just find a way to get rid of John, his mind convinced him that Clara's
loving words then would be dedicated only for himself.

*Should I destroy the budding romance of my dearest friend and the woman
he loves, just to acquire something I desire for myself?* thought Edward. There
was no hesitation—his answer was yes.

Edward found himself in an enviable position. He could consume the
whole conversation between their two hearts, and they no longer could.
Unbeknownst to them, they were now prisoners of his whims. The avenue
of their romance flowed right through his hands and before his eyeballs as

they darted from left to right, and back again. Each letter from John would be read and then thrown in the fire. Those from Clara, Edward would read numerous times. Then he would cross out John's name and mark his own in its place. He would then write his name and address on an envelope and place the altered letter inside.

Edward found himself constantly opening the latest letter and reviewing it. It did not quite come across as real enough, not like it was written by Clara and meant for his eyes only. So he transcribed the letter, carefully mimicking her handwriting. This new letter appeared legitimate. The same sentiment she emoted to John was now sent directly his way. He studied this letter, very impressed by it, and put it in the envelope he had been carrying around addressed to himself, sealed it, and placed it in the bag of the outgoing mail. The next day, Edward was ecstatic to receive his very first letter from Clara Allen, informing him how much she loved him. He scanned it over and over, each and every word, feeling complete euphoria, then took some time to ponder how he would respond to her.

> Clara, reading your loving feelings toward me makes me happier than I ever thought I could be. My soul is so elated! My life's been arduous at times, but your kindness and devotion will be my salvation. I'm honored you want to be my wife and that the most blessed of days is in our future, I assure you!
>
> Love, Ed

Edward read Clara's letter and his response back and forth for an hour or so. Eventually satisfied the correspondence was becoming more and more genuine to him, Edward burned both missives, one addressed to her and one to himself. He then waited with anticipation for her next letter to John, which Edward would rewrite and then place in an envelope addressed to himself, then put in the outgoing mail, excitedly awaiting its arrival. He continued this letter charade for a week or so, sometimes adding details about himself that Clara couldn't have possibly known, as he imagined their relationship flourishing.

Reuben noticed the letters arriving for Edward with more frequency and also the upswing in his son's mood and reckoned both were a good thing. He suspected Edward might be courting a young lady but didn't want to intrude by asking. Reuben was convinced his son would tell him if a relationship grew serious.

Edward observed that the usually unflappable Chapman was quite distracted as he entered the post office one week later. "Eddie, have there been any letters for me?"

"No."

"I sent a letter to Clara, but she has not returned one for a few days, which I find quite unusual. Are you sure there are no letters for me?"

"I am."

John exited the office, and Edward noticed him wander away, walk in one direction, and then, unsure, abruptly change course. Still peering out the window, Edward opened his desk drawer and removed an envelope that had already been sliced jaggedly along its top. He pulled the letter out and read it:

> *Each time we part, in the very last of those moments, I try*
> *to dwell in them, to burrow as deep as I can into them with*
> *my heart and my mind, hibernate there peacefully until*
> *the very next moment, the next time I am blessed to be in*
> *your presence. Clara, the boundaries to which you have*
> *stretched my heart with your love are as endless as the*
> *starry sky.*
>
> *Love John*

Edward then read a passionate letter from Clara to John, which, like John's to her, had arrived only hours before. It was the first one she had written after a considerable pause.

After no more letters arrived from her for several days, Edward came to the conclusion that Clara had ceased corresponding with John, and indirectly with him. He was so disappointed, he didn't even bother reading John's letters anymore, just scanned them briefly and put them directly into the fire. Edward had to remind himself that this was his plan all along, to interrupt John and Clara's correspondence and so end their courtship. It appeared he had succeeded. After reading the last letter he had rewritten from Clara to himself once more, Edward walked over and threw it into the fire and watched as the words disappeared in flame, never to be read again. He then added the latest two of John's. The correspondence written with white-hot passion between two sweethearts was consumed completely by the flame of Edward Green's envy and connivance. It was too much of a temptation, his attraction to Clara was too difficult to resist. Remorse, if it existed at all for Edward Green, became null and with his continued guidance, he was certain John and Clara's romance would burn in flames, forever undelivered and unrequited.

Chapter Nine

EDWARD KNEW DESTROYING the lovers' correspondence was only part of the actions required, so he was prepared when John came to him seeking advice about how he should react to Clara ignoring his correspondence.

"She is young, John, maybe a bit flighty, perhaps not mature enough for a serious relationship."

"I care deeply about Clara. She is in my thoughts all the time, but perhaps you are right, Eddie. What right do I have to question it if the Lord has deemed it to be so?"

"True. He makes the choices and we live by them. It would be a sin to try and go against his heavenly wishes."

John sighed. "We are but pawns on the chessboard."

"You may be, in this case, John."

Edward scratched his leg, glanced down at the floor, and then looked John square in the eye and continued, "Clara is lovely but, as you say, she has stopped responding to your letters. You haven't stopped by to visit her, have you?"

John shook his head no, and Edward Green expelled possibly the largest breath he would ever exhale. But John, distracted in his thoughts, had not noticed.

"Perhaps, you should consider her older sister. Agnes is closer in age to you, anyway. She's more a woman than a girl. I see how she looks at you."

John paused, rubbing his chin, mulling over this statement. "Is that what you think?"

With no hesitation, Edward said, "I do!"

John was silent for a long while, considering this information. Edward allowed him as much time to process it as he needed, not wanting to disturb him in this pivotal moment. "She is a fine woman, and perchance you're right that she is more the marrying kind than her baby sister. Clara's really just a mere child, I suppose." John frowned.

Edward almost jumped up and wanted to do a jig, to shake a leg; either appendage, bad or good, would suffice at this point. His plan was working precisely as he had hoped. And Agnes was not a bad consolation after all for John, but Clara was the true prize of the Allen sisters, no question. John would probably agree with this as well if he were aware of all the facts and contained the knowledge that he, indeed, was but a pawn on the chessboard Edward Green was controlling.

His friend's head bowed. Edward was surprised when an emotional John reached out and grabbed his arms, saying, "Thank you, Eddie. You really have my best interests in mind."

"I do," said Edward Green, and part of him believed he did, but he acknowledged to himself that his own interests and needs always came first, no matter the painful costs to any others, near or close.

Reuben Green was working at his desk when an attractive but distraught-looking young lady walked into the post office and asked for Edward Green.

"Eddie is across the street at the bank, probably chatting to his pal Frank. The two are like brothers, the way they get on. He is sometimes gone quite a while. You may want to go over there or come back sometime later, miss."

"I'll wait, thank you, sir. I wish to speak with him privately," the young woman replied with composure, though it looked to Reuben like she was about to burst into tears.

Before Reuben had a chance to respond, Edward stepped through the door and froze when he beheld a vision he had only fantasized of for the past several months—Clara Allen was standing before him in the flesh. The stars were aligning, Edward thought. The letters exchanged between them were not merely conjured by his libido but were indeed real; his thoughts were not only possible but were now being realized.

She must love me, he thought. *Why else would she be here before me in this very moment?* While overwhelmed and distracted by his fantasy come true, Edward retained a cool demeanor. He understood he would have to answer questions about John, which was the reason Clara believed she had come to his place of business. But Edward knew the real reason, and seeing her there in person was proof enough to convince his mind that Clara was mainly there to see him again, to be alone, completely alone with him—no John, none of her family. There was just the matter of his father.

"Father, do you mind if I converse with Miss Allen?"

Reuben nodded and smiled. *I wonder if she is the one he has been corresponding with,* he thought. *If so, Eddie has done very well for himself.*

"Of course, Son," said Reuben. "Perhaps the fresh air would be good for the stubborn coughing I've been suffering. Maybe I'll even stop by and see what the deacon is up to."

Once his father was out the door, Edward smiled at Clara and said, "Miss Allen, what a surprise. How can I assist you today? Do you have some parcels for your father or some correspondence I can help you with?"

"Mr. Green."

"Please, call me Eddie"

"Okay."

"And can I call you Clara?"

"You can," she muttered but appeared distracted. Edward noted she was staring down as she spoke.

"Sorry for the dusty floor. Wilbur doesn't do as good a job as his little brother, Amos." She looked up but seemed to be glancing past him. He knew not at what; there was nothing behind him but the street and the bank, where he had spent the previous half hour talking about books with Frank. Not really talking, mainly listening and asking an odd question if and when he didn't quite understand the concepts the boy genius was conveying.

"Eddie"—she paused, feeling the new syllables in her throat—"I have some questions about John. Can you help me, please?"

"There is no one who knows John better than me, Clara." Edward had no problem saying her first name as it had been a long time on the tip of his tongue, never uttered before. The two syllables articulated aloud sounded wonderful to him. Not just a sound but a declaration.

"I'm glad to hear that. I seek your counsel then, if you please."

I do please, thought Edward, but he said instead, "How can I be of service?" He wanted to finish that sentence with the sweet sound of her name once again, but he held the word back. In time, he thought, he could say it so often he might even get sick of doing so. But that would not be possible, he believed.

"Has John been distracted in some way? He seems different. Is he feeling fine? Is he having trouble in health or business?"

Edward placed some parcels down, including another book he had borrowed from Frank. He went behind the counter. He really must get Wilbur to clean up better, or perhaps implore his father to fire him and hire Amos instead, especially if his visitors would include Clara Allen going forward. He glanced around at some of the clutter and then he looked Clara directly in the eyes. He took note that tears were ready to flow on her orbs' corners, the consternation in the rest of her face and her whole body straining to dam her melancholy up. "John seems the same to me as when I first met him." Her expression was one of disappointment. *It is I that have changed since I first glanced upon you, sweet Clara, and I have changed everything between you and John as a result,* Edward thought, but instead he said, "Is there something else you would like to ask of me?"

She was silent, her head bent toward the floor. *Lead her on the path you would intend her to follow,* Edward thought, but he maintained his outward ruse. "What has put these thoughts into your head? John's a fine, upstanding citizen of Malden, and besides perhaps young Frank Converse and my old pal Marshall, he's the very best friend I've ever encountered." Although Edward believed this to be true, he stated it merely for effect.

Her body quivering, Clara said, "I have a sensitive question to ask you as both his friend and as the assistant postmaster, Mr. Green."

"Eddie. Please call me Eddie."

"Eddie," she said. She averted her eyes to the floor again and then brought them up, looking directly into his.

"Yes, Clara." Edward was happy to address her this way once more.

"John and I, as you probably know, have been exchanging at least one letter a week each. Often many more."

"Have you?" feigned Edward, aware of each and every letter addressed to either Clara Allen or John Chapman and each and every word they contained.

"We have. And for the past two weeks, I have received no letters from him. Unsure, I paused as well, not wanting to appear too desperate. But I desired to know why he had stopped writing me. I sent him a letter a few days ago to inquire why his heart had grown absent toward me, and there was no response." She placed a hand over her mouth and turned away to disguise her anguish.

Edward ran his hand along one of his bushy side-whiskers and then the other. The embers of this letter lay perhaps two yards away from where they stood. "John has not mentioned anything about letters to . . . or from you."

Clara turned back quickly to face him.

"What has he mentioned? I know you are his dear friend. Please give me any insight you can . . . Eddie?"

She was pleading, and Edward was feeling exuberant, although he allowed his face to only express solace and concern in these crucial moments. "I shouldn't say. It's not my place."

But her eyes were large and moist and about to start an equivalent of a forty days rain. "Clara, he is my friend."

She turned away from him, back toward the street.

Edward gathered himself; it was too late to stop what he had put in motion if he wanted to succeed. He bit his lip. "John's a bit older than you, than us." He emphasized the latter part, not sure if he was overplaying his hand. He continued, "And you have two older sisters and that stepsister."

"Sophia?" said Clara.

"Yes, Sophia," Edward agreed and continued, "And surely you have noticed Agnes thinks quite highly of John. It would be no surprise to me that your father would prefer that the oldest daughter be married off first, as there will be an abundance of suitors for the other sisters . . . especially the ravishing, youngest one."

Noticing Clara was blushing, Edward was convinced he had her; he needed to just reel her in a bit more. Knowing the irony of the statement, Edward said, "When it comes to a young girl's heart, one can never trust the dealings of the men involved. Clara, they always have ulterior motives."

She nodded, thinking she understood. Her father, Ebenezer, had expressed that he hoped all his daughters would find fine suitors, and she assumed he was quite surprised when the esteemed John Chapman had started courting the youngest of the three. Now in hindsight, Clara surmised her father must have also been aware that Agnes clearly pined for John Chapman from her knitting spot on the porch. With Edward's insight, Clara began to suspect both her father and her eldest sister had a part in this play. But what of her sweetheart?

"Eddie, does John love me?"

Feeling he had to be delicate with the words to come, Edward thought through all the answers he had rehearsed to her possible queries about John. "He thinks you're a doll. Though . . ."

"Though? What does that mean?"

"He adores you. Really, I shouldn't say anything."

"Say it! Eddie, please say it."

"Oh, well, I shouldn't, but please, if I do, promise you will not tell him, or Agnes for that matter." Edward was trying to cover all the angles, thinking a few steps ahead. His body may not be able, but his mind was taking one steady step after another and reaching the destination long sought after.

"I will. You have my solemn word. Please tell me all you know about how John feels."

Edward possessed more knowledge about John's feelings for Clara than either of the two sweethearts understood. He had read all the passionate letters written between the two lovers, letters sent but never delivered. He was their sole recipient, and so these missives may as well have gone to the dead-letter office. It was not his intent to hurt anyone, he thought. Sure, there would be heartbreak and confusion for a bit for Clara, and John as well, but he rationalized that it would pass in time. John would have Agnes, and he would have Clara; maybe not right away, but if he could move both John and Agnes out of the way, he could eventually clear a path for himself to openly court Clara. As far as Edward was concerned, they would all be winners in the end; he was just rearranging the board.

Edward looked away from her, then begrudgingly confided, "John has told me that he's confused. That he thinks highly of you, but he also has developed, over time, some feelings for Agnes."

"He fancies my sister?" Clara appeared heartbroken and astonished.

"He has told me in confidence, and I am also telling you in confidence. Please, if you don't mind, do not mention I have told you."

Clara's shoulders slouched. "I have sought your counsel and am thankful for your honesty as a friend of John's, and of mine as well, I hope. I will not betray that trust, I promise you."

"Thank you, and I'm pleased that you consider me a friend. I'm delighted I've had the opportunity to get to know you better, even under these unpleasant circumstances."

After Clara left the office, Edward took some time deliberating over the new developments in his relationship with her. Gleeful, he composed a new letter to Clara with great care. It detailed the ways in which he was devoted to her, knowing she adored him, as well as the life he planned for them together. Finally, satisfied with it, he gave it a kiss, threw it in the fire, and watched it burn, staring at the bright flames until it was mere embers. Then Edward limped home.

Two days later, a letter from Clara arrived for John. Edward carefully opened the envelope and read it.

> *Dearest John, we appear to be different people with different desires. Recent events have made it clear to me that the two of us are not to share a future together. Letters sent and never responded to should relay to us that our hearts have clearly wandered from their once unified path. From what I know now, from what I have learned about us and who we are, in my very being, I believe, I feel most deeply, that we are not to marry.*
>
> *With deepest regards and tender regrets, Clara*

It was a letter that, after reading, Edward carefully resealed and was delighted to deliver.

The next day, John stood before him disheveled and forlorn. "Eddie, first Clara stops replying to my letters and suddenly, she finally writes and tells me she no longer wants to be courted by me or to become my wife! I'm distraught, my friend."

"John, it's best to realize where her heart is, now rather than later. It's better for all involved, surely." He put his arm on John's shoulder to comfort him and forced himself to frown.

The two friends stepped out onto Pleasant Street and turned right on Main Street, past the town house, which housed the board of selectmen and the local seat of government.

At the corner of Irving Street, they found themselves at Hill's Tavern, also known as The Rising Eagle, a public house John and Abigail Adams once frequented and where the Sons of Liberty had plotted the seeds of independence from Britain less than a hundred years prior.

On May 27, 1776, Malden became the first town in the colonies to support independence from Britain. Its inhabitants wrote a letter to their representative, instructing him that if the Second Continental Congress "should declare America to be a free and independent republic, your constituents will support and defend the measure, to the last drop of their blood and the last farthing of their treasure."

Edward, while not planning an all-out revolution, was conspiring to upset the status quo as he bought an ale for his friend and leaned in close to offer as much comfort as he could muster. Edward's face was austere and compassionate as he listened to his best friend lament about the end of his relationship, but Edward's mind was gleeful and hopeful about how he could benefit from the treachery he had set in motion. Starting a one-man revolt, Edward appeared to have been victorious, the opposition not knowing of the battle he secretly waged.

The following Saturday, Edward took a carriage ride with Marshall. They had intended to go to Boston, so Marshall was surprised when Edward took a sharp turn toward Cambridge.

"Marshall, enjoy the sun and the fine breeze. Just a little detour; we have plenty of time to get to the ball and other places afterwards." Edward smirked.

Marshall complied, as his friend suggested, and sat back in the seat a bit, pulled the brim of his hat slightly over his eyes, and enjoyed the day.

Falling into a doze, he was startled when the carriage drew to a halt. Marshall drowsily lifted the hat from his head.

"Just stay here. I will be back shortly."

With considerable care, Edward lowered himself from the carriage and ambled down the walkway to the familiar house. Past the portico was a young woman knitting alone and eyeing with some suspicion the figure gradually approaching her. Marshall pulled his hat back down and covered his eyes.

Some time later, Marshall was startled awake when Edward climbed back on the carriage.

"Did you have a nice chat with Clara's sister?"

"I did."

"And how is Clara?"

"Agnes said she has not left the house or ventured outside at all in almost a fortnight."

"It's a shame how her courtship with John ended."

"It is. But these things happen sometimes."

"I suppose it is out of our control."

"Perhaps, you're correct in that." Edward hesitated. "But Agnes informed me that she, while sad for Clara, thinks John is a fine suitor, and I told her that John has often spoken very highly of her."

"I don't recall him doing so."

"He has, very often, to me—very often. They will make a fine pair."

"Eddie, do you think that it would add to poor Clara's heartbreak if her sister was to be courted by the man who had, up until recently, been wooing her?"

"Clara can have any man she wants, and she will find the best suitor she can imagine shortly; I am sure of this. Meanwhile, John and Agnes should still be allowed to find some happiness of their own. It is only fair, don't you think?"

Marshall made no reply. Reaching inside his coat, Edward removed his flask and took a long pull and then offered it to his friend.

"Have a drink; we're celebrating."

"What are we celebrating?"

"Life itself and all its possibilities."

Marshall, pondering the reason for Edward's immense smile, took a swig, and Edward held on to the reins tightly as the pair rode away from the Allen home.

Chapter Ten

THE NEXT DAY, Olive Allen nestled in her armchair, close to the fireplace, a shawl covering her lap, as was her custom. Agnes and Susie sat nearby on the couch, with Agnes leaning forward. Sophia stood beside her mother. A short distance from Olive, Ebenezer settled himself into his large, ornate chair, a line of gold tassels hanging from its seat.

"Where is Clara?"

"She hasn't left our bedroom for two days, sir," said Susie. While the two youngest Allen sisters shared a corner room, Agnes resided in her own chamber and Sophia slept on a cot outside her mother's door. Ebenezer mostly stayed in his lavish master bedroom, which lay in the home's upper chamber, and Sophia would always notice when he crept past her cot to stay the night in her mother's room. But since the roof damage, he had been sleeping primarily in Olive's room, falling asleep long before Sophia finished her chores.

"Susie, you and Sophia go talk to her and tell her to come down here at once!"

The stepsisters left the drawing room and climbed the stairs silently. Sophia only ever spoke with the Allen sisters and her stepfather in snippets of conversation, never engaging in any small talk whatsoever.

Taking a left at the top of the stair, Sophia followed Susie into the bedroom she shared with Clara.

Susie plopped down on her own bed, her palm and elbow supporting her head. Sophia idled at the door, just past the threshold, and then took a single step back into the hallway. They both stared at the heap of blankets which contained Clara.

"Father wants you downstairs," said Susie.

Silence.

"He, Agnes, and Stepmother are all waiting."

More silence, but Sophia spotted brief movements in all the fabric before stillness joined the silence as a team once more.

"John wants to court Agnes, and Father approves."

Sophia was in awe as all the heavy blankets disappeared at once and Clara sat up in bed, disheveled but quite alert.

"He does not!" shouted Clara.

"He does," Susie assured her.

Clara stared at her sister, mouth agape, arms akimbo, for a full minute and then glanced toward Sophia. Moments later, with much effort, Clara was again covered in many layers, an impenetrable mountain of fabric. The former silence of this enclave was replaced by her muffled sobbing.

"Clara?"

There was no verbal response, but the pile of blankets heaved and sank, heaved and sank. Susie exited the room, passing Sophia, and the two descended the stairs.

Returning to the drawing room, Susie sat by her older sister, and Sophia again stood by her mother's side.

"Clara is not feeling well," said Susie, and Sophia, surprised by this charitable remark, nodded in agreement when Ebenezer glanced at her.

"There are great matters to discuss, and if she will not be a part of it, we shall proceed without her. Isn't that correct, Father?" said Agnes, standing up.

Sophia observed as Ebenezer contemplated this question. She noticed him staring at the ceiling. She imagined her stepfather was straining to hear the persistent drips emanating from the top of the home. She knew he hated rainy days like this, when the water seeped into his abode.

Since early in the year, Sophia had placed many cans and buckets on his bed in the morning to collect the water and stem the continuing damage to the floor. Later in the day, she would carry them all outside one by one and toss the rainwater into the garden. The work was arduous and repetitive, and the buckets and cans heavy, but the flowers on the edge of the home had grown nicely as a result in the summer months, which brought Sophia so much joy, for she possessed so few pretty things in her life.

Ebenezer said, "We shall proceed as you say, Agnes. You mentioned that John's friend, this son of a postmaster, came to speak with you about John's growing feelings."

"Yes."

"Well, Green spoke to me as well. He seems an odd yet somewhat sensible fellow. I suppose I shall reach out to John's father, Mr. William Chapman, and discuss how we can alter, yet continue, the arrangement we settled upon months ago. Instead of Clara, John can wed you if he wishes, and I can get my roof fixed as the elder Chapman has promised me."

Shock at this announcement stirred the women in the room, all except Agnes, and Olive, who rarely moved anyway.

Clara's courtship to John was arranged? Sophia thought, and then allowed her mind to travel back to the early-spring day the strange older man, who must have been John's father, had joined her stepfather in the parlor.

On that morning, after preparing breakfast, like every other day, Sophia was dusting and sweeping. Ebenezer approached and said, "I need you to run out on a special errand for me."

"Yes, sir."

"Take this." He handed her a cloth bag filled with coins, heavier than she expected. "This will be a partial payment," he continued, "but the man will surely require more from me."

"Yes, sir."

"Nothing is more vital to me than impressing my guest who arrives today." Sophia thought he was conveying this to himself as much as stating it to her, for he was staring at the floor and appeared out of sorts.

Regaining his composure, he looked directly at her, took a letter from his breast pocket, handed it to her, and said, "Take this as well and follow the Western Avenue Bridge across the Charles River into Brighton. A left and then a quick right will lead you to the home of Mr. Bigelow. It is a red house, which I have recently painted for him; you will know it by the large hedge which leads from the river directly to his front steps. Give him the letter and the bag of coins, and return back to the house posthaste with the object you get in return. Do you understand?"

"I do."

"Good, on your way then."

Sophia arrived at the home described and banged with the heavy brass knocker three times. After accepting the money bag and reading the letter carefully, the burly man with reddish hair and a matching complexion stated to her, "Make sure Mr. Allen is aware how very dear this bottle was to procure. I had to reach out to numerous contacts. He is out to impress, no doubt, whoever his visitor may be. He has been in my debt many times before and repaid what he has owed. Recently he has taken longer to do so than is my like. You tell him I expect him to make additional amends tomorrow or no later than the day after. Do you understand me, girl? Will you repeat these words exactly to him?"

She nodded. He handed her a paper bag, and she went on her way. Sophia allowed herself just one glimpse inside the bag she carried to spy the word "cognac" printed on the bottle's label. She recalled hearing her stepfather mention drinking the rare spirit while traveling in France.

Stepfather is out to impress his guest indeed, thought Sophia.

When she returned, Ebenezer removed the bottle from the bag and gazed at its shiny label for a few moments and then placed it delicately on the table between the two main armchairs in the drawing room. One of these chairs was where his wife spent most of her days since her infirmity. But Sophia knew her mother would not be allowed to convalesce in it today with the important company that was arriving.

That morning as Sophia returned to her cleaning, she watched her step-father out of the corner of her eye fidget and rearrange the chairs and table several times, often by mere inches before moving them once again.

A knock came at the door and Sophia opened it. A large, dignified man with auburn hair and a beaming smile stood there.

"Are you one of the Allen sisters?"

"I am their stepsister, sir."

"Oh, well," he said, passing her as she closed the door behind him.

"The man of the house is awaiting you in the parlor, sir. I will gladly show you the way."

She led the visitor into the interior of the house. Ebenezer stood to greet him, and the two men began to chat as if they were old friends; but in reality, they were just recent acquaintances. This meeting was but a mere arrangement, for each man was in search of what the other possessed.

Agnes, Susie, and Clara stood in a line, with Sophia positioning herself a bit behind them.

"So, these are your daughters, Ebenezer?"

"Three of them are."

"Come to me, girls. I have sweets for the sweet." The Allen sisters stepped forward in their birth order, and the visiting man let each of them carefully choose two of the brightly colored confections from his palms. He had one remaining, so he motioned Sophia forward and dropped it nonchalantly in her eager hand. She curtsied and stepped back.

The sisters each consumed one sweet and then the other, scattering the colorful parchments that contained them onto the floor absentmindedly. Sophia eyed hers with care, pulled the colorful paper containing it to one side and took a nibble. The taste was so wonderful, so unexpected, she wanted to experience it over and over, let the sugar cascade along one side of her tongue to the other endlessly.

However, unlike her stepsisters, Sophia knew how to be patient and savor nice things, for in her experience, they appeared so infrequently. She tightened the exposed corner, convincing herself she had not opened the treat at all. She wanted to believe it was a brand-new one the next time she unwrapped it, so she could imagine it was yet another flavor. She tucked the remaining delicacy deep into her pocket, anticipating that the sweet confection would brighten her mood if she needed it to break up the expected monotony of the next day.

She bent down to collect the paper her sisters had discarded and let the empty wrappers join the partially eaten candy in her pocket. Olive had already called the sisters out of the room, and Sophia stood up and followed them.

As Sophia entered the adjoining room, she saw all three of them brushing their hair, each angling to get the most flattering view of the long mirror before them. Olive fidgeted alongside each of them, checking the hems of their dresses and making certain they were free of both lint and wrinkles.

"Sophia, attend to your sisters, please." Olive handed her a brush, and Sophia began primping the girls' dresses and then their hair as Olive left the room.

After speaking into her husband's ear and cupping a hand to her own as Ebenezer responded, Olive returned to the room and sealed the door behind her.

"Okay, you all look very pretty. Stunning, actually." The three girls blushed, and Sophia smiled, for she agreed with her mother's assessment. "This gentleman visiting your father is a very important man. Mr. Allen wants to impress him, and the best way he can do so is to show off the beauty and refinement of his daughters."

Agnes appeared serious at this statement, but her younger sisters giggled.

"I suggest you smile and exhibit your best behavior for this gentleman."

Olive gazed at them all but let her eyes linger on Agnes a moment longer. To Sophia, the expression Agnes offered seemed mostly grim. Her oldest stepsister must have also been aware of this since she took a few deep breaths before collecting herself. Soon, a forced smile filled her face. In contrast, Susie and Clara chatted among themselves.

Olive opened the door slightly and, after catching her husband's attention, he motioned toward her and she said, "Ladies, it is time. Keep your posture upright and answer any queries directly and respectfully."

Olive opened the door, nodded at her husband, who nodded back, and said, "Now go, go and present yourselves well!"

Agnes, who was at first farthest from the door, skipped ahead of her distracted sisters, leading the way. Clara followed her, and Susie went last.

Sophia strained to join them and said to her mother, "Can I go and present myself as well?"

"No, but you should follow carefully what transpires so you can learn for the future. Like Cinderella, you are not going to this ball."

Sophia was unsure of what this meant, but her mother patted her head and smiled at her. Olive closed the door, leaving it a bit ajar so Sophia could peer into the parlor. Olive sat down on a stool and leaned on a nearby wall for additional support, missing the comfort of her armchair, which was currently occupied.

"Take a look, dear."

Sophia positioned herself as close to the door as possible and peered through its crack as her three stepsisters stood before their father and his guest.

The stranger leaned toward Ebenezer, speaking muffled words Sophia could not perceive and made a twirling motion with his index finger.

"Spin around for the gentleman, girls," said their father, and they did so.

Again, the gentleman leaned toward Ebenezer and spoke while whirling the same finger but in a counterclockwise manner. "Now, spin the other way."

They complied. Their twirling dresses, red, green, and blue, reminded Sophia of the candy wrappers in her pocket that the sisters had discarded onto the floor.

The gentleman considered the girls before him, then took a puff of his cigar and a long sip of cognac.

Sophia said, "Mother, please can I go out and twirl for the gentleman as well? It seems like so much fun!"

"No, dear, and it may or may not be fun. It depends. There are a lot of considerations and consequences."

The gentleman stared at the sisters, took three long puffs from his cigar, and then, discarding the ashes into the tray beside him, said, "Allen, which one of these is your youngest?"

Agnes frowned.

"Clara. She's in the center," said Ebenezer.

"I would like to speak further to her. You can dismiss the others, please."

Sophia took a step back and was glad at the timing of that choice since Agnes threw open the door, exiting the parlor in a huff, as Susie followed her. Agnes stormed toward the stairs and her bedroom while Susie meandered and then headed outside to the porch to hang in the swing. Olive stood to close the door, leaving it slightly ajar as she had done before.

Meanwhile, back in the parlor, Clara remained standing before her father and the man who, without her knowledge, intended to be her father-in-law.

"What is her name?"

"Clara."

"Hello, Clara. I wish to learn more about you."

Ebenezer spoke up: "Clara, answer the gentleman's questions and maybe he will give you another candy."

The man nodded at Ebenezer, and Clara smiled. "Child, what do you think about getting married one day."

"I think I would like it very much, sir."

"Good, and do you wish to have many children, as our Lord desires?"

The wording of this question perplexed Clara. Wishing to please this visitor and thinking only of the additional candy promised, she said, "I do, sir."

"Good."

Sophia was leaning so far forward through the crack in the door that her mother cautioned her, "Step back a little, my love."

Sophia did so but stretched her ear to hear what she could. The sound, however, was muffled.

She took a chance, realizing how tired her mother was, and leaned farther forward again. She saw Clara approach the man as he beamed at her step-father. The stranger turned back to Clara and reached down deep in one of his coat's side pockets and retrieved one last sweet. Sophia noted it was far larger than any of the others given earlier. It seemed like the prized pumpkin grown for the local autumn fair, as it was the most immense sweet she had ever gazed upon. Sophia watched in astonishment as Clara received the candy, unwrapped it, and placed it entirely in her mouth.

"Allen, dismiss her, and let's talk terms."

"Clara, go to your room."

Clara tried to respond but was unable to do so. Instead, she nodded, bowed, and strolled past Sophia and Olive as she headed to the stair, chomping on her reward as she did so.

Olive, straining to rise from the stool, said to Sophia, "I can't get up; attend to the gentlemen, please."

Entering back into the parlor, Sophia curtsied. The two gentlemen were jovial, and Ebenezer looked at his stepdaughter and pointed toward the empty glasses. Sophia poured more of what seemed to her a strange liquid with a strange name into their two snifters. She admired how gleeful her stepfather appeared, thinking whatever bargain he had offered for the bottle seemed like a wise investment, for his guest was jubilant.

The two men raised their glasses for a toast. "Cheers to the combined futures of our children," they said in tandem.

"And to my dry, comfortable bed," said Ebenezer as they both sipped from the contents of the vessels they held. The men laughed at this, and Ebenezer, dismissing Sophia, who had no idea what any of these words meant, reached for the bottle again himself to top off each of their glasses once more.

This is how Sophia remembered that day, and now she was aware that the visiting gentleman had been John's father. *On that occasion, Clara appeared so happy and Agnes so upset. Now their roles are reversed,* thought Sophia. She knew that everyone in the house except Clara would be quite content if John started courting Agnes. Her father would be thrilled to have the roof repaired with funds from Mr. Chapman. *I feel bad for Clara,* thought Sophia as she watched Ebenezer composing a letter, with Agnes looking over his shoulder as he did so. *I hope she comes out of her sadness, but there is a small consolation for me, for if Agnes weds John, she will leave this house, and she is by far my least favorite of these three sisters.*

A week after attempting to coax Clara from her bed with Susie, Sophia answered the door, and a familiar gentleman walked by her without saying a word. He knew his way to the parlor. Sophia cut through two rooms so she could again stand at the crack in the door, as she had done months before. Mr. Chapman was seated next to her stepfather, and Agnes stood before them both. There was a brief discussion, and soon she saw Agnes approaching her with a genuine smile upon her face. Sophia was not sure she had ever seen this expression before on her eldest stepsister. She flinched and stepped back from her position, and Agnes, with but a careless motion, opened the door and passed Sophia as if she were not there at all.

Later that week, John entered the post office and Edward handed him a letter. After reading it, John looked up, a bit astonished. Edward, already knowing its contents, was not surprised by John's reaction.

"Eddie, it's from Agnes. She says she wishes to speak with me. It seems one way or another, my father wants me to court an Allen sister. I am a bit nervous about riding out there so soon after Clara ended things with me. Do you think you could join me, keep me company to calm my nerves, please?"

Edward rose from his chair and grimaced. "Well, John, I think you should go, yes, but I can't join you."

"Why not?"

"My leg is feeling a bit tender these days. More sore than normal. You go. I'm sorry, and frankly, I have to get back to work. A lot of letters and parcels were delivered within the last hour. Good luck, my friend."

Edward limped to his storeroom, and John exited the post office, confused by the letter from Agnes but even more confounded that Edward had declined his invitation to join him. He had never heard of Edward Green refusing an offer to go riding. Edward's begging off, saying his leg was bothering him, was peculiar, for John could never think of a single time that Edward's leg did not torment him.

John journeyed alone to call on Agnes, and soon he was visiting her frequently. On each arrival, he was oblivious to the youngest Allen sister who, from the shade of her second-floor window, was wiping tears away as she glared at him appearing alone in his buggy and departing with Agnes beside him in the seat in which she had once sat so happily.

Finally, Clara gathered the nerve to confront her sister after Agnes had returned from one of her dates with John.

"As my sister, how can you allow yourself to be courted by John when I had pledged my heart to his?"

"I have been informed otherwise. You wrote him a letter telling him you wanted to end it. Is this correct?"

"It's more complicated than that." Clara took a step back.

"How so? Seems pretty clear-cut to me. You had your chance and now I have mine. You wrote that letter with your callous pen and admonished John and rejected him."

Clara stammered, "I have not, well, I suppose I have. I, we, no longer saw a future together."

"You have plenty of future ahead of you, Sister—you are only fourteen!"

"Almost fifteen."

"Still, fourteen, nonetheless. John is twenty-one, and I am, by your powers of reckoning, almost the same age. Clara, I am a woman. You are a mere girl."

"But I love John."

Agnes sighed. "You are too young to know what love is. John is handsome, yes, successful, and he can afford many servants. This is so wonderful. I will have the proper attention for my needs. Not just the meager talents of Sophia scurrying around to take care of three sisters' requirements. All the attention will be on me and what I desire. As for love, I hope to perhaps grow to love John one day. Who knows, whatever God wills. But my duty as the oldest daughter is to marry well and marry first. I did not like it that you sought to rob me of that honor."

Clara retreated further into herself as her sister continued to scold her. Her body shook and her lips drew tight.

"Love, oh dear, fragile Clara. Love is secondary to our divine purpose as women. It is selfish. Love of God must be our absolute focus and dedication. A young girl's fancy like yours is trite. You will most certainly better understand one day. I recommend ardent prayer and constant reflection. Don't be a sinner with lust in your heart and some foolish notion of romance. Forget John Chapman, and love the Lord instead. As I have said, it was unseemly of you to want to wed before I did. You'll have your time. Susie should be next, and perhaps even Sophia. Have the patience and serenity only God can provide. But don't beg him for it. Be prudent and he will bestow it if you are deserving."

Clara remained shocked and silent as Agnes strolled away. She stood motionless for several minutes. Stuck, unsure. Weeks ago, she had been so happy. She loved John and John loved her. Now there was just emptiness and her sister's bitter condescension.

She retreated to her bedroom and shut out the world, only staring out her window when she heard John's buggy arriving and departing. Eyeing the pair riding off together, again and again, Clara was concerned with her growing melancholy. Illness in childhood had confined Edward Green to his bed; heartbreak now did the same for Clara Allen. Her body was not broken as Edward's had been, but her heart was shattered, its ability to heal, uncertain, and her desire to let it do so, barren.

To the surprise of many in the town, John Chapman and Agnes Allen were engaged and then married.

Maybe Clara's youth confused her feelings, John sometimes reflected as months turned to years. *It was wiser for me to marry a woman who is more of a prudent adult rather than one who was but a flighty girl.*

John tried to focus on his marriage to Agnes and not dwell on the mystery of why his courtship ended with the younger Allen sister, yet occasionally it flittered into his mind: *I loved her and a sad part of me knows I always will.*

John, Clara, and Agnes, unbeknownst to the others involved, had relied solely on the counsel of Edward Green for advice in the matters most vital to their hearts, each of them thinking Edward had only the best intentions in mind. But as Edward would prove again and again, what benefited him the most directly was the only thing about which he truly cared.

Chapter Eleven

WHEN WILLIAM FIRST opened his barbershop, the deacon offered him sound advice on how to design it and gave him an interest-free loan for the renovations. William spent endless hours making sure the shop was ornate, deserving of his customers' business. The position of the large oval mirror was determined by William lying in the barber's chair once for several minutes to make sure it afforded his customers a pleasant view, one they were accustomed to, both of themselves and of the barber attending to them.

He never allowed himself a second perspective from this angle; once was enough. It was certainly a more pleasing view from that position for the client, although William was not thrilled with his own dismal appearance as he performed his enterprise behind them. Yet, he considered it a small sacrifice on his part as long as these men were happy and not belligerent toward him, so William catered to his clients, ignored himself, and prayed himself invisible.

The barber's chair was smooth, red leather, cleaned and shined by William at the end of every day and the start as well for good measure. There was a spittoon on the right side and also an ashtray, for most of the gentlemen smoked or drank as they sat for a cut, reclined for a shave, or waited for their turn as they scanned the daily newspapers. The only man who just read the papers and neither smoked nor drank was the good Deacon Converse, his mentor, a man William admired and respected above all in the town. For the others he would pretend to do so with different degrees of truthfulness in his heart. Outwardly, he hoped these men had no way of ascertaining this fact.

The elegant men expected an elegant parlor. It was part of the unspoken arrangement. A Negro could shave them, style and cut their hair, custom design them a wig if need be, all of which they deemed tasks beneath the dignity of a white man to perform. But they must be surrounded by gentility, as that was what the white man of means naturally expected, and this was the assumed duty of the black barber to provide, William believed, or at least forced himself to believe.

He worried these men could perceive even a modicum of doubt on his part. William never stepped upon a stage, but he considered himself a great actor; he was not performing for applause or adulation but purely for his survival and the well-being of his family. It was a needle he threaded carefully. To survive and benefit, he perceived he must be deferential and act like he understood his place. While doing so, he could make his living and be respected himself as best as he could, as much as *they* would allow him to be.

William had mastered how to use a straight razor at age twenty, with the tutelage of his uncle, Lewis, who learned the trade from a friendly German immigrant. Many men had trouble shaving with one without nicking themselves on its sharp edge. It was also delicate and had to be cleaned and stored properly. Knowledgeable about a variety of oils and creams, William always gave a first-class shave. His business was prospering.

On this day, Reuben was sitting in his chair for a haircut while the deacon was reading a newspaper, waiting for his turn.

William was snipping the small hairs along the postmaster's forehead when the man began convulsing in a violent cough, projecting some blood, which landed directly on William's shirt. The barber took a cautious step back.

"Reuben, how long has your cough been that bad?" asked the deacon, very concerned.

Reuben attempted to collect himself and then another round of coughs ensued. He wiped his mouth with his shirtsleeve, wheezed, and said, "I don't know, Elisha, off and on for a couple of weeks."

"You should see Dr. Sullivan. I can reach out to him to come see you if you like."

Reuben straightened up and thanked William as he handed him a cup of water.

After he took a big gulp, he handed the cup back. William placed it on the counter and stood behind his customer and resumed trimming his hair.

"I'm okay, Elisha, take no heed, please."

Elisha stared at him a moment considering and then returned to his newspaper.

William spotted a few scant hairs in the mirror still jutting down from Reuben's forehead but would leave them there since he had no intention of being coughed on with blood and spittle once again.

This postmaster is not well. He is quite pale. It is not my place to tell him and he is not even sensible enough to listen to his friend's advice to see a doctor. The deacon, a fine man, is my friend as well. Mr. Green is somewhat decent. His son, Edward, is another sort altogether—his figure is malformed, but his temperament is even more so.

I can do very well in this town if I continue to provide a superior service. These men can seek me out for my skill, but I do have to mind myself as best as I can so they don't seek me out for any other reason; even a frivolous one could lead to disaster for me, thought William as he swept his floor before closing shop for the day and heading home.

Reuben's cough persisted and grew more constant. Soon, he was confined to bed. Edward assumed all the duties at the post office and replaced the older Tenney boy with his younger brother Amos without informing his father. The deacon visited Reuben frequently and prayed with him. Lydia and Charles huddled in a corner as the postmaster's condition worsened.

"Elisha, you've been a dear, caring friend, and it's a great solace to me that you spend some of your precious time to attend to me in my convalescence."

Holding a handkerchief before his mouth, Elisha said, "Think nothing of it, my dear Reuben. You were the first to greet me, welcome me in this town, with such kindness. I've always been grateful to you for that." *And now sadly, it looks like I will return the favor as you depart this town and our earthly sphere,* thought Elisha, but he said instead, "It's my pleasure to comfort you any way I can with God's grace."

"Deacon, my heartfelt thanks for your prayers and your friendship. I ask that you please give comfort to my family"—he nodded toward his wife and youngest son and his meek hand grasped Elisha's—"and my Edward. He will have a tough road to travel, and he travels it poorly sometimes. Help him, please, if you can, so he doesn't wander too far off God's path." The postmaster appeared to grow drowsy. Soon, Reuben was snoring, and the deacon released himself from the wispy palm and then bid adieu to Mrs. Green and her son.

After suffering with consumption for nearly a year, Reuben Green died on December 2, 1859. Elisha, Mary, Frank, and Mary Ida Converse attended the burial. It was the first dead person Frank observed in an open casket, and it affected him, so much so that he did not know what to say to Edward.

"Frank, why are you so quiet?"

"This is new to me. I am sad for the loss of your father, but his death causes me to think of the future loss of my own father for the first time. I know it is not right to think of myself when you are in so much grief." Frank bent his head. "I'm sorry for being selfish."

Edward comforted him. "Frank, don't fret about your father. The deacon is so full of vigor and life. My guess is that Elisha will live a very long time."

This seemed to ease Frank's anxiety, but Edward's grew more intense as his mind searched for any answer to what he was going to do now that his father was gone.

Edward's father died poor. The family's home and property had been auctioned off in the summer of 1858 for breach of mortgage conditions, though the Greens were allowed to continue living on the property as tenants.

With Reuben's passing and no further income from the post office for the family, Edward moved into a small apartment with his stepmother and half brother, closer to the square. Incapable of doing physical labor, Edward hoped for an official appointment to the office of postmaster and the steady paycheck it supplied, unsure of what other profession he could pursue if this was denied him.

The townsfolk, including Elisha Converse and John Chapman, took pity on Edward because of his situation and recommended he assume the open position of postmaster. Known as a happy and reckless youth, many mentioned Edward was prone to living outside his means. He liked to go riding a bit much and enjoyed other luxuries generally considered beyond the reach of young men with small incomes. However, Edward's honesty and integrity were not questioned by anyone.

Elisha offered his support, saying, "He will do no harm. God has found it fit to give Edward Green a purpose, and it is to take on the tasks of his father as postmaster. Let us all consider his circumstances and his need to find a way to make a life for himself. He's more qualified than any other for the position. Edward has been an apprentice, and I see no reason why he should not attain the office his father held. The post office is a vital means of conveying communications for our town; we should have no interruption in it."

Elisha was thinking of Edward and his promise to Reuben, but he was also considering his growing business interests and wanted no cessation in the mail which would stymie commerce.

"Let Edward Green have the place, he is capable enough," others repeated. The postal commission agreed and so the position was his. On January 16, 1860, Edward W. Green became postmaster of Malden, filling the vacancy left by his father's passing.

Edward's first act as postmaster was to remove the Ten Commandments plaque from the office wall. Rules were not Edward's prime calling, and he did not desire to stare at them and be reminded of them each and every day. Edward replaced it with a mirror, for he always wished to look his best in case a young lady was passing by.

Edward convinced himself that the town's view of him had altered now that he was their postmaster. The men would no longer mock him for his limp and small size, and the women would regard him as the important man he had become. Clara, mostly a shut-in since her sister married John, rarely, if ever, ventured into town. For a while, Edward still coveted her and thought of her often, but he had needs to satisfy and he believed there were so many women for the taking now that he was postmaster.

He loved to flirt. One morning, as was his habit, he spied a group of young maidens in their frilly dresses walking by, one of them being quite familiar. "Miss Hammersley, please stay there. There is a parcel for you in the office."

Edward ran into the post office and scurried through the bins to retrieve the package, returning as swiftly as he was able.

A bit out of breath but with a broad smile, he handed her the package and said, "Here you go! Think of me as your knight in shining armor. Night or day, I am at your service, my lady." Steadying his arm on the nearby horse post, he attempted as deep of a bow as he was capable.

The young lady was blushing at his attention, and her friends giggled. "Why, thank you, Mr. Green. The town is lucky to have such a charming postmaster as you!"

Such politeness and attention to detail made him more admired among the fairer sex than Edward's physical and financial status would lead others to believe him capable of being. He relished the attention and his new standing in the town. Attaining this position convinced Edward he could feel able, like a man of means, like a man of substance.

While Edward was working at his new job, and trying to adjust to his new status in town, he was overjoyed to see Marshall approaching the post office. He expected Marshall must be coming to congratulate him on his appointment. But Edward was a bit perturbed to find out that Marshall's visit was for other purposes.

"Eddie, I am putting some handbills out for Mr. Lincoln. Do you wish to join me?" Although the Republicans had placed both his father and then him in office, Edward took no part in the great Lincoln campaign, being too easy in conscience, or wholly lacking one. "No. I was fine with Buchanan, though I think it strange that the man doesn't have a wife. Lincoln, I can take or leave. Seems like, to me, he has too many ideas. Any of the four candidates will do, as far as I'm concerned, as long as I can retain my position as postmaster." Edward laughed.

"I am thrilled to see that doughface Buchanan gone. The Dred Scott decision was disgraceful. Lincoln's a great man. You should think more about his campaign. I want very much for him to get elected. There are terrific concerns about the Southern states and if they will rebel against our country."

"It is of no matter to me, Marshall. The picking of cotton and its economy is not my fight. The South is so far away, and I am not, by any means and have never been, a traveling man." Edward looked down at his legs, paused, and then looked back up at his friend. "When you are done with this foolishness, would you like to join me in heading to the city later? Have some fun and forget politics and the part of the world which doesn't concern us. Marshall, look in the mirror. We are slaves to no man, only our fates. Again, it is not our fight."

Marshall frowned, shrugged, and said, "I should be finished with the handbills by six. I can meet you at the stables then."

With his new occupation and steady income, Edward could now attend even more balls, concerts, and festivals than he had managed on his apprentice salary. He visited Boston to meet women, usually with Marshall, but sometimes alone. Having never a need to work or provide for himself before, he did not possess the greatest concept of money or how to manage it. The futility of his languished youth troubled his mind so Edward lavished himself in any pleasure he could stumble upon as proof of his freedom.

His expensive habits led to financial embarrassment, but not of a serious nature—his reputation remained fine among the townspeople. He was popular as postmaster. Although not an influential man in Malden, people felt he was respectable enough and trusted in the title he held, and they knew he possessed powerful friends. They had respected his father and understood Edward was not fit for the other more physically demanding professions of labor in the town. His was simply a clerical job for a man who had no physical means to make a living.

Later, weeks after Lincoln was elected president in November of 1860, Edward fell into deep financial distress, and there were concerns about his drinking once more. The Templars were seeking Edward's removal from his postmaster position, and others in the town were beginning to agree. Elisha considered the situation from many angles. First and foremost, he remembered his promise to Reuben before his passing to look out for his son and guide him as best he could, which he deemed a sacred vow. He thought about how Frank cherished his friendship with Edward and how it was prudent to have each near by to look out for one another. There was also the matter of a possible war between the North and South now that Lincoln had secured the presidency. If conflict ensued, Elisha knew that it would be vital to allow letters from the front to return home to families and friends, and for business in the town to proceed as normally as was possible.

Elisha excelled when presented with obstacles in his life. After weighing all these factors, Elisha decided the best course of action would be to defend Edward and keep the mail flowing. "All young men ought to be allowed to raise some Cain. Edward will mature, and I believe and will argue that retaining the responsibility of this office will be the best thing to happen to him," stated Elisha to other influential members of the town.

The deacon trusted in God's plan and prayed he would be one of the many instruments to help Edward realize the righteous path in which to travel, by offering him another chance, a chance of redemption.

When civil war erupted the following spring, Elisha felt, without reservation, that he had made the right decision.

Edward appreciated having a second chance, but that did not improve his dire financial situation. To relieve his stress, the physician next to his office, Dr. John Burpee, prescribed opium. Sitting at his desk one May morning, he placed a tincture of the narcotic under his tongue. As Edward agonized over his ledgers, his attention was drawn to a commotion outside. Union troops had mustered in the square, near the post office, and a sergeant was barking out orders as the soldiers marched in drills, crossing from the north side of Pleasant Street to the south side and then back again. Edward imagined the formation growing smaller and smaller as more soldiers faded along the southern side, their numbers dwindling as the consequence of war.

Letting go of this distraction, Edward peered down at the page below him, where he fought one endless battle after another with the amounts in the columns and found no obvious path to victory; the ledger was becoming a continuous conflict of incongruent figures.

His temper burned in frustration. His funds were in arrears. He held his eraser above the numbers, wanting to obliterate them, yet instead pondered the army of able-bodied men outside. This gave him an idea: he could be like the sergeant and secure a way to rearrange his forces. Like his personal battalion of troops, some of his soldiers could switch sides, crossing from one column to another, thus wiping out the trails of his debt.

He reached for a blank piece of paper and sketched out the entries on it to appear as he wished they would, in a manner that if someone skimmed over them, his debt would appear camouflaged. But this task was difficult. The deacon had granted him another chance, but Edward sensed his status would be tenuous if his superiors became aware of his mismanagement.

As long as no one notices, I will continue my attempt to skew the numbers like this, yet I'm aware I'll eventually be found out. For no matter my efforts, the simple math will reveal my deception. What then? I have no idea. Whatever choices I make at that time might be quite drastic. For now, I can only continue to conceal my debts, he thought, but held a more immediate concern as his anxiety bubbled to the surface. Edward wished to further dull his thoughts in his usual manner but due to his lack of funds, he was running low on whiskey.

To clear his mind, he walked over to visit Frank, who was just arriving at the bank after his school day had ended. Edward eyed the troops as they continued their drills.

Outside the entrance of the bank, Frank leaned on one of the Greek columns that supported the portico of the structure, and Edward leaned on another. They watched as a burly man in a dark-blue uniform rode by them in a flurry on his horse, sword raised, the hat on his head held tight by his chin strap. The regiment of about four hundred men, all dressed in a lighter shade of blue, quickly assembled at their sergeant's urging in tight formations. Within a minute, the soldiers, led by their captain on horseback and a color guard, passed by the two friends, drums banging, trumpets blaring, marching off to the railroad depot and then to some unknown battle.

Edward watched them go by as he would any other strangers in the street. *These able-bodied men can have their self-important displays if they desire. Their fight amounts to a hill of beans for me,* he thought, *I possess my own problems.*

The first time troops had assembled in the town, it caused quite a commotion as everyone gathered to observe the spectacle. But it had occurred so often a month into the war that it had become commonplace.

The day was overcast. Frank glanced at the procession but returned his attention to the open book in his hands once it had gone by. Edward was gazing upward intently. He knew behind where he stood lay the accumulation of all the town's wealth, which the cashier, Charles Merrill, kept locked safely away. Across the street, at his office, was his own ever-mounting debt. Edward gazed skyward, his anxiety building. "Looking at clouds makes me a bit nervous, Frank, especially the big, puffy ones. I imagine them reaching down and smothering me."

Frank closed his book. He noticed one of Edward's legs shaking and the postmaster leaning farther into the column for support.

"You all right, Eddie?"

Edward exhaled and inhaled many rapid breaths. His forehead was drenched with sweat, which was sopped up by his facial hair as it dripped down his nose and cheeks. He stared at Frank and wanted to respond but discovered he was unable. Lightheaded, he worried he might vomit. His vision drifted back up to the clouds and his body grew tense, only feeling relief as they moved on, revealing the blue sky once more.

"I'll be all right, I think. Thank you. Sometimes, I reckon being postmaster has more responsibilities than I supposed it would." Regaining his composure, he forced a smile toward his friend. "I should get back to work then; please go back to your book. I will be fine."

"Are you certain?"

"Nothing is certain, Frank, my boy. But you know Edward Green will always find a way in or out of some mess or another. It is my modus operandi."

The two laughed.

"Come back across the street any time if you need anything from me, anything at all."

"Thank you. I will remember this kind offer; you can be sure of that."

Frank entered the bank, sat down at a reading table, and watched with concern as his friend returned to the post office in his usual slow manner. When Edward arrived at his desk, he opened his favorite drawer and pulled out an almost-empty bottle.

Angry, and blaming it for the bottle's low level, he threw the ledger spitefully to the side. It befuddled and infuriated him. He could find no answers, no comfort in it, so instead Edward drained the remnants of the whiskey. Unsure if he retained the available funds to purchase another bottle, he convinced himself he would acquire one either by hook or by crook.

Edward dwelled on the fact that he had shared his fear of clouds with Frank. Edward wished he had not revealed this weakness to his friend, and he was determined from that moment on that no one else would ever glimpse that side of him.

Chapter Twelve

FEW PEOPLE HAD seen Clara since she ended her engagement with John Chapman. More than five years had passed, and although Edward still fixated on his desire for her, he had not yet acted to attain her even after all the subterfuge he had created to end her relationship with John. By this time, John and Agnes had three sons, Willie, Arthur, and Walter. Besides his work at the mattress firm, John was also involved with the school committee and was studying for a law degree.

What is wrong with me? It has been so long but I can't stop thinking about her. My finances and my life in general are such a shambles. A wretch like me doesn't deserve Clara, Edward thought.

Taking a deep swig from a new bottle, acquired from the tavern in trade for the free postage of several parcels, Edward shifted from one account to another in his ledger, attempting to round the figures to the best of his ability. Everything was a mess. Tinkering with the penciled, the erased and rewritten numbers confounded him. Edward assured himself it was wise to bide his time and try to get his financial situation under control before approaching Clara.

Edward was overwhelmed with the stresses of the job and terrified that someone would discover his altered ledger. And now, he found himself always staring at clouds, fearing they would fall on him, smother him, and yet he could not look away, no matter how anxious they made him feel. Plus, he was still embarrassed that he had admitted this fear to Frank. So how could he try to court Clara when the sky was threatening to collapse on him at any moment?

Leaving his bottle and modified ledger to deal with later, Edward went to the stables to pick up a carriage and then drove to the Cambridge post office to deliver some parcels. He had only intended to stay for a minute, as he also had errands at the main office in Boston and then planned to wander along the taverns and brothels of the Black Sea.

"Hey, Eddie, I have a piece of information that I know will certainly interest you," said Chester Hodges, the Cambridge postmaster.

"Chester, I am sure it can wait; I have places to be," said Edward as he turned toward the door.

"Clara Allen has received a letter for the first time in a long time."

Edward forced his bad leg to stop its forward motion and, pivoting back toward Chester, he grimaced and said, "She has?"

"Yes, I remember all those years ago when Chapman was courting her. Letters were coming in and out of this office and your father's two or three times a week. Until he married her older sister instead." Chester snickered.

"Where is the letter from?"

"Some gentleman all the way from California."

"It was addressed to her directly, not to her father?" asked Edward.

"Yes, maybe it takes a man from plain across the other side of the country to coax that reluctant beauty out of that house. The few times I've seen her, she is so pale. She will get plenty of sun out west if he weds her." Chester laughed.

Edward offered a weak smile in return, saying, "Chester, you appear pretty comfortable in that chair. I could, if you wish, deliver it—it's on my way, and I know the family well."

Chester considered. "I thought you were in a hurry?" Then, grinning, he said, "But if you wouldn't mind. I was going to go out in a little bit, but if you want it, here it is." He picked up the letter from a small pile on his desk and handed it to Edward.

Edward bid Chester goodbye and returned to his carriage. Sitting there for a moment, he stared at the letter displaying the fancy cursive of Clara's name and address. He had no intention to travel to the Allen home. Instead he pulled at its seal to reveal its contents.

Edward read it and, to his dismay, discovered Clara did, indeed, possess a new admirer. Edward determined it was finally time to act and secure her as his own before this man traveled east and undid all the hard work he had wrought to make sure Clara had remained without a suitor. Worthy or not, it appeared it was now time for him to pounce.

Leaving Amos in charge, Edward began visiting the Cambridge post office every day, if possible, and brought a bottle of watered-down whiskey to share with his counterpart.

"Hi, Eddie. You're becoming a common sight."

Lowering his head and hoping his disdain was not obvious, Edward said, "Hello, Chester."

Chester, who was wise to Edward's affectations, stated, "Come on, Eddie. I'm not complaining. Did you bring the bottle?"

Edward, straining his lips to appear content, said, "Of course."

"Good, I'll go get my deck of cards. Up for poker?"

"Sure."

"Great. We can head to the back room. I might need to go to the desk and deal with customers occasionally, as you understand. That's okay, right?"

"Sure, that is fine with me."

Chester dealt out the cards, and the two sat across from each other sipping whiskey and eyeing the hands they held.

"Eddie, I know you have been interested in Clara for a long time. Why wait so long and let her be courted by another? Those remaining Allen sisters, every eligible bachelor in Cambridge and"—he paused and let out a loud laugh—"a few of the married ones as well would love to take them as brides."

Edward shook his head. "I suppose you could say I was just waiting for the fruit to ripen on the vine a bit," said Edward, smiling, for he held a straight flush.

Day after day, Edward and Chester would play poker and drink. Whenever the bell rang on the office door and Chester exited the room, Edward would search for and then pilfer any letters from California addressed to Clara Allen. He had no cares about their contents, only their destruction.

Time passed and the letters ceased, and so did Edward's visits to the Cambridge post office. Edward then began his courtship plan with Clara in earnest. Having once moved heaven and earth to separate Clara from the loving arms of John, it was now the right time to act to secure her as his own.

Edward actually made an effort, with difficulty, to curtail his drinking for a time to focus himself on this quest. He kept his eyes firmly on the ground and avoided looking upward as much as possible.

Years had passed in a haze of alcohol, opium, and bad decisions, not all of which Edward could recall, but one thought which never wandered far from his mind was of how he felt in Clara's presence from the very first moment he encountered her.

The compulsion to eventually have Clara at his side had never relented. Put off, it now needed to be satisfied, and he didn't want to confront the threat once more that she would be taken by another. *At least I knew and liked Chapman. This Californian interloper doesn't deserve her in the least, especially after all my hard work,* Edward thought. *Clara should be mine and mine alone.*

Edward drove a buggy to the Allen home. As he walked up the path to the house, he was greeted by Susie, who sat lounging on the porch swing.

"Hello, Mr. Green. Father and I were just at the post office yesterday. Mr. Hodges mentioned you, knowing you were familiar with our family. He said you visited him quite frequently for a bit and now he hasn't seen you in a while."

"That is true, Miss Allen. I have become very busy in my own office." He scratched his chin. "Is your father home? I would like to have a discussion with him, please."

Susie stood up and walked toward the front door. "Sophia, fetch Father and see if he agrees to meeting Mr. Green."

Edward saw the door crack open a bit, and Sophia's head poked out. She studied them both and then shut the door and disappeared back into the home.

Sophia returned, opening the front door again.

"Mr. Allen will see you. Please follow me."

"Hello, Mr. Green," Ebenezer greeted Edward. "It has been a very long time since you used to visit this house with John."

"It has been."

"Please have a seat and state your business."

Edward grasped the armrests as he lowered himself in the armchair beside Ebenezer. He had gone over and over what he would say to this man but felt uncertainty in his stomach. He had to quell the shaking in his bad leg as he reclined farther into the plush chair.

"Mr. Allen, when you made my acquaintance, I was just a boy and my father's apprentice. I have been postmaster of Malden for over two years. I think now that I am a man of means, it is time for a wife, and I have always thought well of Clara's charms and beauty."

Ebenezer lit a cigar, inhaled and exhaled a long puff, and contemplated Edward through the smoke. "A lot of eligible bachelors are off fighting in the war. And I suppose you, because of your condition, will not be called."

Edward grimaced, readjusting. "If you are implying I am not able-bodied, you are correct, sir. My legs are in constant battle, nonetheless. But because of their internal fight I will not be conscripted."

Ebenezer chuckled. "I'd forgotten how charming you are, Green. You have that, your position of postmaster, and the fact your lame leg will prevent my daughter from becoming one of the many war widows." He took another long pull on the cigar, exhaled, and paused a few moments to consider Edward more clearly. "I accept your proposal. You can begin courting Clara with my blessing."

Ebenezer stood and reached out. Several moments later, after using all the strength in his arms and straining on his good leg, Edward stood by his side and shook Ebenezer's hand.

"Yes, you will not die in battle, Green, for it certainly appears you have enough difficulty in fighting off the embrace of chairs, never mind Rebels charging with their bayonets!" Ebenezer laughed so loud that Sophia rushed into the room.

Edward sensed his face grow red and his right hand curl up in a ball, but calmed himself, forcing a smile. "You are correct, sir. Oftentimes, furniture is my greatest foe."

Ebenezer let out an even louder laugh, and Sophia exited the room. Edward released his grip from their handshake and thought to reach toward the table and grasp the heavy glass ashtray that lay full of Ebenezer's ashes and bludgeon again and again the laughter out of the man mocking him.

He breathed deep, thinking only of Clara, and said instead, "Mr. Allen, I am honored that you will allow me to court your daughter."

"Green, she has been locked up in her bedroom for so long, I was afraid she would have no further men courting her. I have a colleague in San Francisco with a son just started out in business, and we had corresponded about his courting Clara. There were some letters between them, but strangely nothing came of it. Perhaps he found a young lady he fancied without the need of such travel. Clara held such promise from a young age, but no one else has come aknocking, so at this point, you'll do." Edward was furious at this statement but convinced himself the end result was worth all the barbed words of Clara's father.

"Thank you," he said. "I promise I am able to do so."

"You'll take one daughter off my hands and pay me in mirth. I know you have no father to compensate me, as John's father did. But lucky for you, my daughter's been a caged bird and no one else seems to want to set her free!"

As Edward walked away from the house, his eyes caught some movement in a second-floor window, but when he looked closer, there was nothing. He wondered if it was just the wind blowing through a curtain.

The next day, Edward returned to the Allen home. He carried with him a bouquet of irises. Sophia showed him into the house, and he entered the parlor to see both Ebenezer and Clara awaiting him.

"Hello, Green."

"Hello, sir."

Ebenezer turned to Clara. "Greet the postmaster, my dear."

"Hello, Mr. Postmaster."

"Remember, Clara, you once called me Eddie. You can call me that again." He stepped forward, smiling broadly, and presented the flowers to her. "I recalled the color of your eyes and searched for the proper flowers to match their beauty."

Clara had only intended to be obedient to her father's wishes and meet with Edward, but she discovered herself blushing. There was a feeling surging within her that felt strange, one long dormant. She realized she was happy. "Why, thank you, Mr. . . . . Eddie." She took the bouquet and held it up to her nose and exalted in its fresh scent. Things had been so stale for so long, her senses dulled in melancholy, and the postmaster had now ignited some life in her heart; blood pumped feverishly in her veins. "They are lovely."

"It is you that are lovely, my dear."

"It is very kind of you to say."

He smiled and nodded, then turned to Ebenezer. "Sir, with your permission, I request to take Clara on a buggy ride and get reacquainted."

"Yes, Green, it would be terrific if she could get some fresh air."

Edward turned back to Clara and offered his hand. "Clara, the day is fine, and if you join me the company will be finer."

The next moments transformed into a whirlwind for Clara. She was exiting the front door of her home, a threshold she rarely crossed in the years prior, and next she was being helped up into a buggy and sitting beside a gentleman who wished to court her as John had once done. Waves of endless loneliness and confusion washed over her, but the sun shone warmly on her face and the look of what she detected as kindness was emitted as well from Edward's eyes. She glanced over her shoulder toward her bedroom window, from which she had gazed so often with sadness at John riding away in his horse and buggy with her sister beside him.

Clara exhaled deeply as she allowed herself at last to escape that figurative and literal self-imposed prison. *I deserve to be loved. I have always deserved to be loved.*

The horses trotted past Harvard University and entering a straightaway along the Charles River, Edward lashed his whip and the buggy sped forward with the galloping team. The ride was exhilarating. The wind blew through her hair. The sun shined on her neglected skin, and Clara felt her soul warm for the first time in a very long time. The river was teeming with sailboats and Clara was mesmerized by the sparkling sunlight as it danced upon the water. After crossing the river to Boston, they picnicked in the Public Garden among many other young couples. This was the sort of romantic adventure for which she had been longing. Edward was good company, and Clara realized she was having so much fun.

Later that evening, Edward returned her home and walked her back up to the front steps.

"Clara, did you enjoy our day out together?"

"Oh, yes. Thank you, Eddie."

"You are a wonderful, beautiful, young lady, and I am honored to be able to court you." He reached out to shake her hand, and she offered hers. He held it and gently kissed the back of it. His touch, his affection, allowed her to recall the feelings she had not felt since she was a girl being courted by John.

Lying in bed late at night, she heard her sister's sheets rustle.

"Susie, are you awake?"

More muffled noise.

"Yes," said Susie as she yawned. "I suppose you want to discuss your buggy ride with Edward?"

"Father wants me to be courted by the postmaster, and so I will. We had such a fine time today."

"Yes, you seem happier than I can remember for quite a while."

"I surprisingly am. I didn't think I could be again. What I've really yearned for and which has been sorely lacking, is a man who's attentive and who will answer all my letters. I have a great fear of being ignored or abandoned. I'm trying to convince myself that Eddie, as postmaster, will be more vigilant than most since the mail is his business. It's at his command since all of it travels through his hands. If he doesn't respond to my letters, then I wonder if I'll ever find a man who will. Men are so casual and noncommittal, in my experience and opinion."

"Open your heart, Sister, let your guard down some. What's the worst that can happen? Agnes has her husband and family . . ." The thought of this caused Clara to frown in the dark. "And it is time for us to have ours as well."

"I just hope Eddie won't break my heart; it can only stand so many fractures." Clara sighed.

"Think positive thoughts. Sweet dreams, Clara." Susie yawned and then turned over.

"Sweet dreams," replied Clara, and she wished them for her sister but mostly desired them for herself.

Clara had no need to be concerned about this next suitor. Edward Green was not going to play coy. He was well aware of how his scheme was working, and he was out to win her and would do so with utter attention and devotion.

Visiting Marshall at his bakery, Edward took a large bite out of a fresh loaf and said, "Clara's a young woman who believes she's been spurned twice," then he thought to himself, *And though I'm the party which caused these illusions in both cases, I now intend to benefit from these deceptions by winning her heart with my directness.*

Marshall opened his oven, considered the condition of the bread, closed the oven door, and wiped his brow. "You will make a fine pair, Eddie."

"Thanks, my friend," said Edward, reaching for the butter. There was only a small bit remaining so, instead of using a knife, he dipped his fingers directly into the bowl, licked the butter off his fingers, then took another bite of the warm bread, exulting in the mixture of the two upon his taste buds.

Edward knew Clara hungered for affection and devotion, and he schemed the best plan was to dole it out to her in ever-increasing morsels like one would when trying to win the trust of an injured animal. *Soon,* he thought, *she will be eating out of my hand, and she will see that I'm the only man who loves her.*

Edward was correct. With some misgivings initially, Clara was soon caught up by his affection and dedication. Having been abandoned twice, she was comforted by his attentiveness and his letters, which affected her in ways she had never expected.

Sitting upright in bed, caressing her hair and reading the latest missive from Edward once again, Clara had a wide smile, but as her thoughts wandered from the page to letters in her memory, her mouth furrowed to a frown. She confided in Susie, who was also reading a letter from her own suitor, "Even after five years, it perplexes me why John would suddenly stop writing me with no explanation. We were so in love, and it still bothers me that he's my brother-in-law, married to our older sister."

Susie had heard Clara lament about John so often that she answered indirectly. "Yes, it is hard to tell if Agnes is truly happy. She is a mother and a wife, but she appears most content when she is deep in prayer."

"I'm glad we both have suitors of our own now, Sister. To be honest, when my last admirer stopped writing me, I was quite defeated after allowing myself to get my hopes up. So much time elapsed, and then I was disappointed once more."

"But now you have Edward, and I have Charles." Charles Nichols, who worked as a craftsman, had begun wooing Susie shortly after Edward started seeing Clara.

"Yes, I hadn't planned on being courted by the postmaster, but Eddie Green has my attention and I am well aware, I certainly have his."

"And Charles has my heart. His writing is so polite and sweet."

"I can't say the same. Eddie's writing is more forward, far more candid than John's ever was. Listen to this. 'Our bodies merging, our souls intertwined. Tongues, fingers. I would gladly let my spirit be damned, my dear Clara, without equivocation, for a moment of your tenuous touch. I hang on everything, awaiting the next time I can be with you.' His letters are more profane, less gentlemanly than John's, but since John deserted me for Agnes, I appreciate Eddie's directness. Maybe it's less poetic, yet it's simple and right to the point. I desire honesty in a man more than anything else, and Eddie is nothing if not forthright."

Chapter Thirteen

FRANK WAS READING outside the bank when Edward sat beside him. "Hello, pal."

Frank closed his book. "Hi, Eddie."

"It's a fine morning."

"The weather has improved since yesterday."

"Yes, the clouds have parted somewhat. The sky is clear and that brings me great joy."

"You do seem in a merry mood."

"I very much am. I have some news to share with you," Edward said, smiling at Frank.

"Don't keep me in suspense; what is it?"

"I have raised my share of Cain in my day, but I truly love Clara. I have captured her heart, and we are to wed."

"That is simply wonderful news! I am so happy for you, my brother." Frank's face lit up in a smile that prompted many a schoolgirl in town to feel a fluttering in her heart.

"I have a young lady I am interested in as well. Her name is Dorothy, and her father is one of the directors of the bank. We talk about books, and I'm thinking of asking my father about how I should go about courting her, but I thought I would seek your advice first."

Edward smiled and jabbed his finger into his friend's temple playfully on one side of his head and then the other. "Frank, my boy, do you love her?"

Frank stepped back a bit. "I do not know what love is at this point, Eddie, certainly not the kind of love as powerful as you possess for Clara, which you have stated you would do anything on earth to attain and keep. And congratulations, my dear friend—you're about to attain it. As for me, I just want to get to know this girl a bit and see how things develop. Don't forget, I've only just turned sixteen. I've all the time in the world."

Frank winked at Edward, and Edward winked back twice.

To his bewilderment, John Chapman heard the news all over town that the postmaster, his once best friend, Edward Green, was now engaged to Clara. The two had kept out of each other's way since John's breakup with Clara years before—partly because Edward was immersed in running the post office, and also because John's business concerns had him traveling by rail across the country, and so he was often gone for weeks at a time. But the main reason was because John held a hunch that Edward had played a part in ending his relationship with Clara. And now Edward's engagement to his former beloved further cemented this belief for John.

Susie and Charles were soon engaged as well. After conferring with Agnes and Ebenezer, it was decided that both couples would be wed in a single ceremony in the Chapman home in a northern section of Malden known as Oak Grove. Although a sense of unease permeated his thoughts about how Clara was marrying Edward Green, John understood it was the honorable gesture for him to host the double wedding of his wife's sisters.

Saturday, November 29, 1862
Boston Daily Advertiser
At Malden, Wednesday evening, Nov. 26th, at the residence of
John W. Chapman, Esq., Oak Grove, by Rev. J. T. Greenwood,
Mr. Charles H. Nichols, a brass finisher, to Miss Susie Everett
Allen; also, Mr. Edward W. Green, Postmaster of Malden, to
Miss Clara Richardson Allen—both daughters of E. K. Allen,
of Cambridge whose occupation is a printer and painter.

Frank stood in the corner chatting with Edward, while Mary and Olive were conversing on a nearby couch. The father of the brides, after consuming two glasses of cognac, was beaming and started giddily speaking to the deacon without introducing himself.

"I went from a man with three young daughters about marrying age to having the oldest married first, as I believe important since if a woman gets close to twenty-five without a husband, she has a severe chance of being viewed as an old maid. It's taken my youngest a while to find true love; there have been a couple of misfires. I've always thought well of Chapman and believed he would be a fine son-in-law, and it turned out that he certainly would be, not wed to Clara, but rather to Agnes."

"John is a good man," said Elisha, but Ebenezer continued as if the deacon had not responded.

"It was a turn of events neither I nor anybody else, really, had seen coming. Agnes and John have two sons, Walter and Willie. They lost one child as well, poor Arthur. The lad passed away just at the beginning of this year. Now in this dual event, my two remaining daughters are being married off as well. Chapman and Nichols are fine men, and Green, though a cripple, has a respectable position at the post office, and I have to confess I'm charmed by him."

"I've always had a rooting interest for a man like Edward Green. It's the Christian thing to do. Green's had a tougher road than many, but he's made something of himself. Taking his father's position of postmaster—that's no small thing," said Elisha.

"Agreed. I know Clara loves him, and Green treats her fine. My main happiness as I approach old age is that all my daughters have now married and married well. They, and my grandchildren, and hopefully the grandchildren to come, will tend to me in my remaining years."

Elisha nodded and said, "Congratulations, Mr. Allen. By the way, my name is Deacon Elisha Converse, and I know both John and Edward well. Charles also seems like a fine man."

"Sorry to ramble on; hope I was not being rude."

"No, sir. All is well, and again, I am overjoyed for you on this day."

"Thank you, Deacon." Ebenezer walked over to the table to fill his glass once again, emptying the bottle.

John forced himself not to stare at Clara. He wished to talk to her, but she was not his bride as she was once meant to have been. Clara had stood to the side as he married her sister, and now he would do the same for her as she married the man who was once his best friend. *I've a strong impulse to sweep her up in my arms at this very moment as she prepares to wed Eddie instead of me. Clara and I shared something that I fear has been lacking in my marriage to Agnes. I cannot find the proper words to describe the feeling but it was a special, unique bond. I must constrain these urges which have stirred just below the surface before emerging so prominently on this day. I am a family man and a devoted husband, and God has divined that I marry one Allen sister and not the other. I will trust in his will.*

Clara also held confused feelings and confided in Susie as the two brides stood in the foyer of the Chapman home in the minutes before they prepared to walk down the aisle on the arms of their father. "Years ago, I always assumed my chastity would be given over to John in God's eyes. I felt assured of it since the moment of our intended engagement, and shortly before, to be quite honest," she said to Susie.

Susie rolled her eyes. She loved Clara, but she was a bit furious at her sister's ruminating about the past since this was her wedding day as well. *I am the only Allen sister never engaged to John Chapman,* she thought but said instead, "Clara, Eddie loves you as Charles loves me. Focus on the man who will soon be your husband instead of the one that is married to our sister."

Sophia, quietly attending to both her stepsisters, almost laughed but stifled the noise in her throat as she bent down to make sure the hems of their dresses were not creased. Olive had instructed her to see to it that the brides' attire and hair were perfect. This was her remaining stepsisters' joint wedding day, but it was also a joyous occasion for her since all of the Allen sisters would leave the Allen home and she would only have to attend to her stepfather from now on.

Clara was so caught up in her thoughts that she had not heard Susie's words. "But now I'm about to be the wife of the postmaster, and so it will be for Eddie Green to take my womanhood from me," Clara continued. "Our stepmother told me it is a gift a young lady can only give once, and it should only be given to a husband in the conceiving of a child, if God wills it. So be it." Clara sighed as these thoughts lingered.

Susie, annoyed, was about to respond that Olive had given her the same talk, but then Ebenezer entered the foyer and held out his arms for his daughters. Sophia left to go stand by her mother, sitting in the back of the room.

Ebenezer started walking with his daughters clutched at his sides. He appeared even more joyous than they were, as one daughter was distracted and the other remained perturbed.

The whole ceremony from that point on was a blur to Clara. There were murmured words between Susie and Charles and she thought she heard Edward speaking as well, but her soul existed elsewhere. In a daze, she was startled when she realized Reverend Greenwood was staring at her.

"And do you, Clara Allen, take Edward Green to be your lawfully beloved husband, to love and to obey him until you two shall part?"

Clara, in her continued haze, thought to glance one last time toward John and have him gaze back toward her with loving eyes, but she buried that longing deep inside her forlorn heart. A section of it contained a great fissure that would never heal. Yet, their love affair was in her past, and John had chosen her sister over her. She convinced herself she deserved to be happy, to feel loved. And it was long overdue. So Clara instead searched profoundly within the face of the man she was marrying and sought for the love and devotion there which she felt had always eluded her.

Eddie has rescued me from my despair. He is truly the man I should love, and I will put forth all my efforts to do so, she thought and then said, "I do."

Clara waited patiently in a guest room for Edward. Susie was in the adjacent room waiting for Charles. Edward was downstairs, drinking and celebrating with his fellow groomsman and their new father-in-law. Clara was certain that John had already turned in after showing out the other guests, knowing he was an early riser who spent many of his daylight hours striving to succeed in business. She recollected that on John and Agnes's wedding night years ago, all the revelers had departed early and the couple immediately went to bed. Why was Edward now biding his time before joining her, on this night of all nights?

Alone and nervous, Clara anticipated the time when her new husband would enter the bed with her for the first time. She prayed it would be soon. Continuing to await his arrival frayed her nerves raw. She had no idea what to expect from him or from the act she knew they would soon join in together. Clara wished he was there now so they could share some tender moments. Her concern was that their consummation would be both quick and painful without any buildup, whereas her whole life seemed to just swell to a moment of this very magnitude. She was getting somewhat perturbed that he was delaying his arrival, as if what she was offering to him was merely ordinary or pedestrian.

It is not so for me. This moment means everything, all I ever dreamed of, first as a young girl in love with and eventually jilted by John, then as a lonely young woman who felt forgotten by all men. At least until Eddie came knocking and asked Father for my hand.

But now this further waiting for Edward was nerve-wracking. She attempted to speculate about what would happen, what could happen, but it was all new to her. She was certain somehow that Edward would be on top of her, then inside her. There had already been times when they rubbed against each other with their clothes on.

But now with their garments going to be removed, Clara feared complete exposure. *Being naked in front of someone is new and scary. I bathe weekly, but those are brief affairs. I scrub as is my duty for good hygiene and then return to the comfort of my many layers of garments,* she thought.

Her concerns then spiraled to all the heartbreak she had endured and might endure still. Edward was the only sanctuary she could grasp onto; she had wandered in a desert of loneliness for so long, and he had been the first one to offer her a way to quench her dry heart. She clung to the idea that Edward was her oasis.

Why didn't John respond to my letters? Why didn't we wed as we discussed? Why hasn't any other man been as much in love with me as Eddie Green is, and I'm sure in my heart, he will forever be? Eddie's devotion is all consuming and it replenishes my soul, voids the emptiness caused by the indifference of my prior suitors. I wish John held the passion for me that Eddie conveys now so freely.

The past still bothered her. Edward was attentive, always ready to do anything to please her, it seemed. He nourished her twice-abandoned heart. But there was something missing. Clara tried her best to put John out of her mind altogether. But she was aware, in this very moment, he was right down the hall, in bed with her sister Agnes, while here she was enduring the minutes without end which passed by as her new husband drank downstairs.

Why can't Eddie be more like John? Why couldn't John have married me instead of Agnes? Lying in bed and becoming weary in both body and spirit, she exhaled. She was almost in the lull of sleep when the door opened as if Edward had fallen forward into it. He caught himself on the doorjamb and regained his balance after stumbling into the room. He slammed the door and immediately started disrobing.

"Hello, wife."

Clara sat up very high against the pillows and drank in the image. Here was her husband hurriedly stripping off all his clothes after she had been lying in bed waiting for him for almost an hour. "Hello, husband."

Edward jumped in bed and then jumped on her. "Hello, wife," he repeated.

She had no words in response.

Everything now proceeded so quickly. She was in shock. Edward was rough and overbearing. He went too fast. His perspiration cascaded down onto her face, and her mind raced backward in reaction. Clara was uncomfortable with her body in these fresh moments with Edward. She had not been so with John in the limited romantic things they had done together. John had been so kind and gentle. She longed for her new husband to be so as well.

Edward's hand was down along her stomach probing for an entry and then his fingers were in her. They felt like unnatural intruders. There was a pain. She closed her eyes. The room was dark, just about pitch-black, but Clara ached to embrace the darkness completely and hide herself entirely away. She had been told the act was her wifely duty. Maybe having a child would fill the void within her, which so concerned her. She sincerely hoped so. Clara tried to focus on any positives she could grasp.

Eddie loves me, he has a steady, respectable profession, an official government job. And his limp, that injured leg, and his occupation as postmaster will keep him out of the terrible war, which sends more and more men and boys to their Maker each and every day. Eddie will not die in battle. Father has assured me of this. I will not lose my husband, and I will always have someone to love me, as I've desperately hoped, thought Clara.

Clara could feel Edward's extension down along her upper thighs as more sweat trickled off his face and splashed upon hers.

While myriad thoughts bounded through Clara's head, Edward held just a single one as he finished: *Now I've gone where Chapman has never ventured.* He smiled broadly. He was quite content. Clara was finally his and his alone.

Soon after the act, Edward fell asleep and commenced snoring. Clara lay still; all she could think of was motherhood and whatever divine purpose led her toward marrying Edward Green. The cacophony of her new husband's breathing was a roar on every exhale.

Clara stayed awake contemplating how life had turned out this way for her. Apprehensive that she would forever look in the eyes of her future child, or children if God would bless her to have more than one, and search endlessly for a sign of John and never detect it, just a smattering of the creation, the copulation of her and Eddie Green. Clara, now married to another, wanted to forever rid her thoughts of John Chapman, but they remained.

After his marriage to Clara, Edward continued his attempts to avoid crossing paths with John in the street, feeling John's unease at the wedding as well as the weight of his own guilty conscience. However, it was impossible for John, with his business and personal needs, to not interact with the postmaster. When dealing with Edward, John would be courteous but not overtly friendly as he had been in the past. He would not inquire of Mrs. Green, and Edward would not ask of Mrs. Chapman. They would exchange basic pleasantries and little else.

In light of Edward marrying his former sweetheart, John continued to question Edward's motives from that time when the correspondence between John and Clara might have gone directly through his hands as the postmaster's apprentice. *I've absolutely no proof of his possible treachery, just an uneasy feeling,* John tried to reassure himself when he spotted Edward and Clara together. *Yet, I know it would've been so convenient for Eddie to sabotage our loving relationship so he could then steal Clara for himself, so convenient indeed. No matter how many years have passed, I'm starting to believe that it's possible that my once dearest friend plotted against me and Clara as well.*

Now, it was quite clear to John that Edward had not only claimed his former love for himself, but also had replaced him altogether, as young Frank Converse appeared to be his best chum. To confirm his suspicions, he decided to inquire of Frank about his friendship with Edward.

"Hi, Frank,"

"Hello, Mr. Chapman," Frank said as he walked from school to wait for his father at the bank.

"I have a check to deposit; do you mind if I join you, please?"

"Sure."

When they entered the bank, Frank went behind the counter to join the clerk, Charles Merrill.

"Hello, Charles," said John.

"Hello, John, great to see you. Hope you are well. Day is going to be fine."

"I think you are right. I have this check to deposit, please," said John, taking the paper out of his breast pocket.

John watched as Charles went to his money drawer and got out his ledger to enter in the deposit and then began writing a receipt. Frank stood at his side studying the man's every move.

Frank has a bright future. I am not so sure about Eddie, thought John. *Though the pair are a decade apart in age, their bond's not a big shock to me since Eddie will always remain a teen in his manner and attitude.*

"Frank, please take this to Mr. Chapman," said Charles, handing the boy the slip of paper.

When Frank returned with his written receipt, John wished to pose the question on his mind: "Thank you, Frank. Do you mind if I ask you something?"

"No, sir."

"It was very grand to have you and your parents at my home for the double wedding. Are you and Eddie quite as close as it appears?"

Frank's manner brightened. "Yes, sir. I have known Eddie since I was a boy, and besides my father and my uncle, he is the man I most depend upon and admire."

John, speechless, nodded and left the bank, thinking, *Perhaps as Frank matures, he will outgrow Eddie and doubt the character of the man as I do now. I hope he does sooner rather than later since Eddie, after stealing Clara from me, as my gut compels me to see as a fact, is capable of stealing anything he puts his devious mind to.*

This new friendship sometimes hurt John as much or even more so than knowing that his best friend had married his sweetheart.

As the year winded down, the Chapmans, Nicholses, and Greens gathered at Ebenezer's house. Susie tried to act as a peacemaker between her two sisters and their standoffish husbands. Ebenezer, oblivious to any ill feelings, was so overjoyed at seeing all of his daughters married that he had sent Sophia out for a bottle of cognac. Edward had never tasted such a fine liquor before; it was something he could never afford, so he filled his glass more than once as Clara looked on frowning. John played with his young sons as they made a wall of wooden blocks.

As the year of 1863 began and with the holidays passed, the Chapmans and Greens saw little of each other, though each visited Susie and her husband, who lived on Cedar Street close to the Chapman home.

John dealt with Edward when he must but went out of his way to avoid Mrs. Green, the once future Mrs. Chapman, altogether. It was awkward, it was painful. On the rare occasion one saw the other in the street, each would look downward and be silent as they passed.

Chapter Fourteen

WHEN ELISHA CONVERSE awoke on a cool April morning, the sun was barely glimmering in the lower portion of the windowpanes. Mary was still asleep, and he would let her doze. The deacon prayed and praised God for shining his light and love upon him. Opening one of the many large windows, he felt a gentle breeze caress his beard. The house had been built specifically so its master bedroom faced east. Elisha loved the rising sun, and it welcomed him with God's blessing to each new day. The day was young, and there was plenty to set out to accomplish. He stepped into the light along his balcony, which overlooked his vast property. By his reckoning, it would soon be six o'clock and the first of many horse cars to Boston would pass his house and then would continue to do so every half hour until midnight.

Elisha built his opulent mansion along their route on Main Street, on top of Belmont Hill, in 1859. The family had moved in the following year. The horse street railway, a train car pulled by a horse team, connected Malden to Haymarket Square in Boston, a short walk from Elisha's downtown office. The railway would also transport Elisha directly to the bank in Malden Square in a few minutes' time. Elisha was instrumental in bringing the Boston and Maine Railroad through Malden, in close proximity to where the horse rail ended. A connected track also stopped right in front of his Edgeworth factory.

The fare for the horse-car ride was seven cents. Elisha delighted to see its frequency, for it contributed to the growing business between Boston and his adopted and beloved Malden. Its fare and its travel were for the greater good of all, but Elisha did not have to rush to board it to get to either the center of the town or to the other terminus in Boston. His personal chauffeur was patiently standing by for him outside.

Elisha accepted that life was best when you slowed down to savor it. Business had consumed most of his time since his late teens, but now he was able to enjoy a modicum of respite. Elisha planned to look in on his gardens later in the day, relishing the tranquility they gave him after hours and hours of business dealings in Malden and Boston. He would feed the ducks while sitting and contemplating God's grace by his private pond.

David Roy, who supervised the greenhouses and floral arrangements for which Mr. Converse's estate was becoming famous, promised to show him chrysanthemums, which he said were currently in full bloom. Elisha loved walking the five and a half acres of his estate and its adjoining farm, and he did this at least every other week, depending on business concerns. Roy had planted orchids again this year as well as South American and tropical ferns. There were also a variety of lilies, including Easter lilies and *Lilium speciosum*. Elisha eagerly awaited the second annual flower show at his estate. Several hundred people attended the previous year, and it was the talk of the town and surrounding areas.

Elisha walked to the nearest of four doors and opened it.

"Good morning, Mr. Converse." His butler stood holding a tray containing the morning's papers in one hand and an ornate robe in the other. There was a pair of slippers placed neatly on the floor, and Elisha settled his feet into them.

"Good morning, Robert. Thank you." Elisha first grasped the robe and put it on and then clutched the tops of three newspapers and began to scan the headlines as he reached for the golden banister of the half-moon-shaped staircase that led to the main floor. There were twenty-two carpeted steps in all and through habit, Elisha was able to negotiate them as he looked from the printed pages to where his slippers landed on the plush steps. Robert followed behind him in silence, not wishing to interrupt his employer's concentration. When Elisha entered the kitchen, after passing through the library and the drawing room, Robert stood to the side near the window. He peeked out into the distance toward the stable to make sure Jeremy was standing by the buggy and nodded to him. To this, Jeremy started prepping the horses, knowing Mr. Converse would like to depart for the city at his usual time of seven. If Mr. Converse instead wished to visit the bank or his other interests in Malden, Robert would have come out and informed him earlier in the morning.

Elisha sat at the table, where breakfast was already prepared and the chef awaiting. The chef lifted the lid off the hot tray in his hands and placed the steaming plate by the clean linens on the table before his employer. Fresh eggs, poached; bacon from one of the hogs recently slaughtered; fruit canned from the orchards the previous fall; and from the greenhouse, a fresh salad. Mary and the children would awake at their leisure, and their breakfasts of just about anything their hearts desired would be awaiting them, or could be quickly prepared.

After breakfast, Elisha returned upstairs to his private dressing room and then walked into a room which was one of the most modern features of the house. The estate was just one of a handful in the Boston area to be equipped with indoor plumbing. The staff used two outhouses fifty feet from the home, but the Converse family had access to two indoor bathrooms—a half bath consisting of a toilet and wash basin on the first floor, and Elisha's master bathroom on the second floor, which contained a sink, a toilet, and an L-shaped bathtub with cold and hot running water. Placing his undergarments in a hamper, he took a short bath, about ten minutes. On Saturdays, he would allow himself a full half-hour soak in warm water. After putting on his clean undergarments, laid out for him neatly, he returned to his dressing room and, with Robert's assistance, dressed in his freshly laundered suit. The one he had worn the previous day was currently being washed and would join his eight other suits by the end of the day. With Robert trailing a few steps behind, Elisha descended the elegant staircase for the second time that morning. Elisha removed his slippers in the mudroom, and Robert lifted them up without a word. Soon after Mr. Converse's departure, he would carry them up the grand staircase and place them in a cupboard next to the entrance of the master bedroom. Two hours before his employer awoke the next day, which was always at the same time without fail, they would be retrieved and set in the expected spot so Mr. Converse could slip into them without losing a step.

In the mudroom, Elisha regarded his pairs of shoes, all identical, black, and polished, but nothing ornate about them. "Robert, how many pairs of shoes do I currently possess?"

"Six, Mr. Converse."

Elisha eyed a pair he had worn the prior day and picked them up, studying them closely. "Are these the oldest pair, you think?"

He handed them to his butler, who looked at them carefully. "If they are not, sir, they are certainly the ones you have worn the most."

"Robert, please take them to the square on your errands today and seek out a soul who is in need of them. No sense throwing them out; they still have some good in them. I will return home with another pair from the factory sometime this week, and you can place it in rotation. Also, while you are out, bring some of our surplus vegetables to the poorhouse as well; our garden has been quite bountiful."

"Yes, sir."

Elisha selected the pair of shoes which looked the most worn of the remaining group, perhaps a few months old, and after putting on a pair of socks, he laced them up as Robert stood nearby, holding the discarded pair. There were several other shoes arranged on the floor—three pairs each for his wife and his daughter, and four for his son. Seeing Frank's shoes alongside his own filled Elisha with august pride. He often thought of these as miniature versions of his shoes but realized the boy had grown, was almost a man, and the shoes were now about the same size as his own.

Robert opened the door and accompanied Mr. Converse to his horse and buggy. Once there, he and Jeremy pulled out the small stepladder and placed it so their employer could climb and enter the buggy. Robert closed the door and wished Mr. Converse a fine morning. Elisha returned the sentiment and immediately his thoughts turned to the many business appointments scheduled for the day. Elisha Converse was a successful businessman, active in thought, untiring in work, and conservative in method. The citizens of Malden were grateful he called their town home. The decision to move to Malden permitted Elisha to attain great wealth and influence and would provide the town with a center of industry and expansive growth for years to come.

Life was not so easy for many other residents of the town. The working class struggled from day to day. Their ancestors had arrived in later waves of immigration and passed on, in many cases, less to their descendants.

That morning, as she lay in bed next to her snoring husband, Clara whispered to him, "I'm certain of how well you provide for me and how much you love me." She leaned forward and kissed his face, trying to press her lips onto his skin directly while avoiding the unkempt wisps of his facial hair. "And so, in response to your love, I love you. Eddie, I know you'll do anything to make me happy. I cling to and cherish this fact," she said, her voice attempting to rise, as she was growing emotional. Succeeding in tempering it, she then eased herself carefully out of bed, knowing full well that almost nothing could disturb Edward in his present condition.

An hour later, Clara wiped the sweat from her brow as she cooked over the fire in the small, one-and-a-half-room apartment she shared with Edward in a boardinghouse on Pleasant Street, conveniently located between the train depot and his place of employment. Realizing she was closer to the flame than was safe, Clara retreated a few inches.

She would have to remind Edward to gather more firewood; they were running low. The pipe above the stove vented some of the fumes, but not all. Clara wished there was a window to relieve her from the remaining smoke that drifted toward her. This was only a small concern since she was over the moon to share a home with Edward after hiding herself away from the world for so long before he had started courting her.

Following their wedding night, Clara, uncertain about her feelings for Edward, expressed this uneasiness to Susie. Her sister explained that she held similar feelings after marrying Charles, but as time passed, she gained both comfort and familiarity with him as her husband.

Susie then admonished her, "We are now these men's wives and we are in service to them. They will care for us, and we must trust in them and obey always. Father has told us as much, and we should honor his wishes."

And so, Clara focused on this advice and placed her lot entirely with Edward Green. More and more, she found herself dependent on the postmaster for the entirety of both her well-being and her happiness.

Before Clara began cooking, she had swept and dusted both rooms; washed, mended, and folded clothing; and made sure that the lamps were well supplied with oil for the night to come. The apartment was not as charming as her father's house in Cambridge, but it was a fine start for a young couple, Clara assured herself. Rent was only $4.58 a month. Clara's hope was that they could save enough money so that by the time they started a family, they could move into a larger apartment.

Clara was also in desperate need of a new pair of shoes. Her lone pair had completely worn down. Edward had promised to take them to the cobbler on his way to work, but had neglected to do so all week. Edward, Clara was well aware, was not practical in many ways. He always wished to impress her with an unexpected gift, such as fine chocolates, whereas a pair of reliable shoes would be worth more to her than just about anything else. To please her, he hinted that she could purchase a new pair soon from James Howard's shoe shop down the street. This made her grateful to have him as a husband. Edward possessed a single pair of boots himself from the Boston Rubber Shoe Company, but much like his position as postmaster, he had also inherited them from his father.

The pot bubbled and emitted what Clara considered a pleasant aroma. It contained a few morsels of meat her husband had not finished from the previous day and a mixture of carrots she had cut up and some celery and potatoes Edward had brought home three days before. Clara often snacked on raw celery since it was always abundant in the house. Edward ate most of the scant meat they had. In her judgment, he deserved it since he was the man earning the money that supported them both. And she retained no doubt whatsoever he strongly believed the same.

Edward was still out cold, his britches scattered pell-mell on the floor beside him. He was sleeping off a late night at Hill's Tavern. Clara fretted and wished he would wake up to enjoy the morning with her and perhaps assist her with her many chores, but according to her husband, socializing and sleeping late were a man's prerogatives. Edward mentioned time and time again these evenings out were a fine way for the town's postmaster to mingle with other important folk. It was more the consequences of the mornings which followed that concerned her.

Clara often worried that Edward drank too much. Her father partook of brandy, and cognac when he could afford it, but only on occasion and never on the Sabbath, as Edward did. Clara abstained from consuming any spirits herself and questioned why men would drink alcohol at all. She dared not confront Edward directly about this. However, she wished furtively he was more committed to the temperance society. He assured her he was making a mighty effort to drink less, and she tended, truly wanted, to accept this as truth.

Clara devoured his devotion to her and in response had developed an overwhelming, almost complete dependency on and worship of Edward. His love quenched her arid heart.

And so, Clara deemed herself fortunate to have married him and dreamed of starting a family together. *If we have a son, I wonder if he'll continue in the tradition and become postmaster as well,* she thought as she observed Edward sleeping soundly in their bed. Recalling how Edward had attained the post-master position with the help and support of John Chapman pivoted her thoughts toward her former suitor. She fought to expel the joyous memories of being courted by John from her fragile mind.

But how could she not succumb to their call? No matter how Clara and John sought to avoid each other, family obligations fixed them within each other's orbits, and the pull of their shared past tugged at them.

In fact, whenever Clara gazed upon her nephews, she couldn't help but wonder how their features would have altered if she had been the one to marry their father instead of Agnes. These contemplations were relentless; Clara agonized over them.

She was, over time and with considerable effort, straining to convince herself that she was a fortunate woman and that Edward Green was truly the love of her life. How could she have known, or even guessed, that her fate and choice of husband had been manipulated by an envious, scheming man who thought his own life had been thrown asunder by his Creator? Clara lacked this knowledge and was ignorant of the terrible deeds committed by her husband to win her heart, yet she thought it indeed curious how things had played out.

Agnes would often discipline her and Susie, saying, "We are all wives now and with God's blessing, you will give your husbands an abundance of children, preferably sons. The Almighty saw fit to give John and me three sons, though we lost one. Pray and put your faith in our Maker, sisters."

While listening to Agnes's stern words, Clara's mind was instead centered on the image of her sister's husband. She often caught herself staring at John, pondering what might have been if fate had not abandoned its desire for them to be together. Clara would snatch away her look of longing intent the moment before she believed John could detect it.

Many times, she also sensed his probing eyes upon her as well. Clara wanted, desired more than anything else, to allow them to linger on every inch of her very being, no matter how wrong, how sinful the sensation was. To have any part of John caress her once more, even if such a passion resided only in her imagination, it would quench the pain of her still-broken heart. The lack of him, her first love, compounded by his choice of her sister as his wife, continued to destroy her.

Yet, whenever Clara gazed back in these moments, the heat from John's intense look had darted elsewhere, before its lust could fully satisfy her. While their eyes had not locked as one for many years, Clara still felt their souls craved to be reconnected once more.

Luckily for her fragile ego, Clara was blissfully ignorant about how these two unfulfilled hearts longing to join as one had been separated.

Although she had already swept the room, Clara picked up the broom and began sweeping by the bed once more, banging it against the floor a couple of times. Soon Edward rolled over and with one eye looked at her.

"Eddie, are you up?"

"I am now."

She registered his frown. "Sorry to disturb you, dear, but since you are awake, I have a question for you, please."

"You do?"

"Yes, please?"

He yawned. "Okay, proceed, so I can go back to sleep."

"Sorry, well, I, um, saw Mrs. Converse the other day along Linden Avenue, and she said we should come over for lunch."

"Will Frank be there?" Edward sat up a little and placed his head higher on the pillow.

"Yes," said Clara, assuming he would be.

"Great. Inform the deacon and his wife we will be delighted to attend." Edward mouthed a great yawn and turned over. His voice then murmured from the other side of the bed, "Now let me sleep, woman. Attend to your chores."

Clara was overjoyed. She wandered as far from Edward as the meager apartment permitted, her thoughts requiring some space to fixate on visiting the grand Converse estate. First she pondered if the entirety of the Green apartment would easily fit just in the entrance of their lavish home, then she remembered the kindness of the Converses during her wedding. That night, next to Frank, Elisha and Mary Converse had stood serene and proud. Clara was convinced that the deacon and Mrs. Converse were quite deserving in the way the community admired them both. Everyone in town viewed the deacon as the one most responsible for the growth of Malden, with his rubber factory employing many of the townsfolk, and Clara was honored to have such a notable and beloved man present at their ceremony.

Clara also admired the way Mrs. Converse stood by and supported Mr. Converse, and she had fantasies of being the same loving and confident companion to her own husband. *If only Edward's habits and business endeavors were as ambitious and honorable as the deacon's, it would be far easier for me to do so,* thought Clara as she continued her chores.

William Shiloh awoke and began his usual routine, which involved shaving his own face—a bigger challenge than shaving others' faces since he had to avoid opening his old wound while squinting at a skewed reflection through an aged, worn-out hand mirror. He kept his better mirror at the shop, knowing his clients would not tolerate a less-than-perfect view of themselves. But for William, an altered reflection aided in obscuring his scar, though it could not fully erase the painful memory it contained, nor could he ever forget its origin and the agony it caused.

As William guided the blade around the tender protuberance, he contemplated what would befall him if he ever harmed one of his customers. The outcome could be a much deeper cut in reputation and perhaps his very livelihood, far greater an injury than he could ever inflict on his own person. He recalled a recent close call, when he nicked a client. It was a small scratch, minuscule really, but William feared the blood would blossom into a bouquet of bad luck. Fortunately, the man, who went by the self-proclaimed title of the Count Joannes, or also sometimes with the slightly altered spelling "the Count Johannes," especially when signing letters, was oblivious. George

Jones, as others called him, though famous to some as an actor, had recently been but a stranger to William. But now, the man with a whimsical mustache and fine clothes was a constant, almost daily, visitor to the barber.

As the red stain widened in William's vision, the inebriated Count was spinning one of his numerous yarns.

This tale is not a very good one, William thought, but he would never, could never, complain as he listened and served his customers. When the Count revealed the ridiculous plots of the books he personally had written, William grew bored but feigned interest with utter aplomb when necessary. He could see the renowned performer, the Count, gleam at the performance, not realizing that he was just an audience to a superior actor. "Need always surpasses want" was a quote William lived by and imparted to his children. *This white man can pretend for adulation and acknowledgment, but a black man such as myself must pretend solely out of desperation,* he thought. The only stories with which the Count regaled him that were of interest were those in which he quoted another William—Shakespeare.

William squeezed a trickle of oil from a container and wiped it across the softer back of his hand. With a gentle motion he knew the Count could not detect, the blood vanished. The smear was now on William; he wiped his hand against his pant leg and ignored it. He rubbed a small handful of special ointment on the open wound. As a barber, he was familiar with bloodletting and how to stymie a cut if need be.

At the time of the inadvertent slice, the Count had been engrossed in his soliloquy with William as a willing soundboard. Whereas other men in town could disregard or refuse to suffer this fool, William knew he held no choice. In his establishment, the customer was always right, and to the resentment of other Negroes in town, the customer was always white as well.

Back in his apartment, after reflecting on these thoughts, William Shiloh scrutinized his image, tilting his head a bit in the dull reflective surface, so as to glance past the scar on his cheek. Holding up a candle to get a better look at his countenance, he regarded himself as still handsome for his age. His wife, Emily, appeared to agree. She had given him seven God-fearing children. Their first born, William, had died from consumption as a toddler. The grief was enormous, but he and Emily focused on their faith and yearned to bring more children into the world; and they were blessed to do so. William trusted that the future held promise if a generation of their people could just cling to the hope that the Lord would provide. It had been a struggle, and the knowledge that it would persist was not a deterrent.

William held a firm belief that progress was only accomplished with a determined effort. To build, it was necessary to pile one stone onto another to form a foundation, and William prayed he, Emily, and the children could contribute toward this goal for their people. Henrietta was the oldest and starting to become a young woman; she was followed by Caleb, Mary, John, Phillip, and Annie, who had just recently been born. The family had all eaten porridge as they did every morning. William would eat last, whatever was left, in the scant few minutes which remained before he departed for the barbershop.

The Shilohs resided at a boardinghouse on Clifton Street, in one small room, since moving to the town four years earlier. The deacon's friend was their landlord. William and Emily slept on one side with the youngest children, and the three oldest slept curled up on the opposite side of the room. A single door led to a hallway and then down three flights of steep stairs. There was a quarter of a window situated in the upper right corner of the room. It produced a glimmer of light on occasion, but one could never depend on it. It was always closed, and never allowed air in or out. Today was one of those rare occurrences where a fraction of sunlight glistened into the abode, raising all of the family's spirits.

At one time, William reckoned, the light shined on a much larger room of the old house, but over the years, the room had been divided into several living spaces for the freemen arriving from down south. So they all just retained a paltry slice of what was given. All the residents shared access to two outhouses in the yard, a few feet from the building, and so William was quite grateful the family did not reside on the first floor. As William sat barefoot, he looked at the younger children's uncovered feet, then noticed Caleb, who was fourteen, wearing the only pair of shoes the family possessed. William had begun sharing them with his son but would always wear them himself when he was working to appear proper to his customers. Smiling at his son, he contemplated how much Caleb was beginning to follow in his daddy's footsteps. The shoes were even older than the boy. William had traveled a great distance in them, and life had transformed tremendously since he first wore them. William questioned if they had ever been new, but they always had been reliable, with the patching of their wear and tear done piecemeal when possible.

There lay a small bowl of water on the table before him, and he dipped his hand in it and wet his face. William reluctantly leaned his cheek a trifle more toward the image staring back at him. Readjusting the candle, he squinted a little to examine himself. He persevered in attending to the side of his face he preferred not to acknowledge. Like much of his past, William shielded some things from view on purpose. Caleb, pausing from his chores, sat on the floor beside him, mesmerized by his father's steady hand with the sharp razor. Now old enough, he would soon be joining William at the barbershop as his apprentice. William gazed down at his son.

"Caleb, we all have a good side and a bad side," he said. "This is a good lesson to remember about all men, no matter who they are, no matter what shade they project. We can pretend one of these sides isn't part of us. Yet, I'm aware the blurred image staring right back at me is a face all the world can see. Do you understand?"

Caleb nodded and stared at the mixture of water and oil as it made his father's face gleam. William continued, "However, I know, while my scar is blatantly apparent to me, to most of the townsfolk, it's not my most obvious trait or means of identification. A mark is only a portion of our skin, and the skin, as a whole, is what truly sets me and our family apart from them."

Having to shave carefully around the scar was a constant reminder to William of the past he had escaped and to always move with an abundance of caution around white men thereafter. Still, William thanked God he was no longer that fourteen-year-old boy who had received this injury, a child unaware of the tiny place he was allotted in society and who had suffered greatly for this lack of knowledge. He was not sure how it all occurred; perhaps the strange white man on the road just lashed out at him for no reason. There was little memory of the event, and the years which had passed since clouded it further. William had survived the injury, yet the scar remained, a reminder of how he was truly viewed. The mark was deeper than his skin, but how he was regarded was not.

William was elated that his son was not living under the same circumstances he endured at Caleb's age. But there was one thing he yearned for:

that the life his son and his other children lived and would live, while problematic, would still be blessed since they were free from real chains, though invisible shackles remained.

Plus, William prayed with devotion that his profession of being a barber could lead to a sort of acceptance and, perhaps one day, a proper way to make a living for his sons, first Caleb and then the others, as it did for him. Furthermore, with God's blessing, he prayed his position would lead to good marriages for his daughters.

The lighting, while never plentiful in the cramped room, grew abysmal on this morning as the day turned cloudy. So William lit a second candle to compensate for the sudden transition, aware the first was near its end. Low on matches, he used the fading wick to light the new one.

William cherished possessing his own razor; he had earned it. And now there was a brand-new one waiting for Caleb which he would present to him once his son mastered shaving his own face, and soon he, too, would be earning his living shaving the wealthy chins and cheeks of the white folk of Malden.

Distracted by this surge of pride, William almost cut himself, but his adept hand smoothly pulled away from his chin. His concentration was automatically focused on the razor, as it always was, whether shaving his own face or, perhaps doubly so, attending to his customers. William heard the chatter and laughter of his other children and his wife, and it filled his heart with joy.

Emily had been up before him, and the older children had awoken soon after, dressed and tended to their various chores. The two youngest were still sleeping, but he was positive Emily would have them doing their fair share in the years to come. William adored his family and was devoted to them. After all, all his toil, all the exaggerated subservience to his clients was for his family's benefit and betterment, though sometimes he suffered the shame of not speaking his mind directly to the arrogant men whom he waited upon.

William shaved at home for a couple reasons. He did not want to use the same razor as all the affluent white townsfolk he shaved, some daily. Two, they most certainly did not want to know the razor on their paler skin had also neatly trimmed the bristles of his dark face. These men had ceded a little autonomy to him since he was skilled with a razor, but there was a large price to pay. He was not a slave, but they were masters of his destiny and his day-to-day well-being nonetheless.

Lost in these dark thoughts, William stopped shaving and held his straight razor directly below his chin. Emily, closely monitoring her children strewn about the room, tending steadfastly to their chores, immediately noticed her husband's pause and the position of the razor, angled so close to his neck. Concerned, she rushed to his side.

Breathless, she said, "My love, look at me now!"

His eyes lumbered to meet her gaze. Caleb sat motionless.

"Tell me what's on your mind."

He looked at her, at Caleb, and then at their other children, who had all halted their activities and were staring intently at their parents. "I know circumstances will not permit me to talk back to these men whom I serve but, darling, it weighs on me ever so much. They are bullies, and they look down on me." William started crying. "Emily, I am just trying to make my way in this world, just as they are, only with the darker complexion God has bestowed upon me."

"William, the children and I are so grateful for your toil," she said and stared intently at the straight razor he held. "And we love and depend on you."

William looked at her pleading eyes, and his hand lowered the razor, placing it softly on the table, and he then separated it from his palm's clutch and the intent it had held moments before.

"William, these white men do not own your thoughts. Pleasing these fools is just a mere means to an end. You've told me that more than once," said Emily, hugging him tightly as he sobbed.

"Sometimes it weighs on me that I'm not able to serve our people as well. Am I letting them down?"

She patted his head and kissed his wet face, getting shaving oil on her lips, but she did not care about that. She continued to hold him with her arms, just as tightly, but leaned back so she could look directly into his watery eyes. "You are in an impossible position, my love, and you are doing the best you can," she said.

"You're right. I feel a small pang of guilt knowing I do not serve my brothers, but know if I desire what is best for our family, I have to always please these affluent, white customers instead."

"You must, William—the family depends on you."

"You are right. But it's difficult. I know for a fact if one of these men walked in and saw a Negro getting a shave or a haircut in my chair, I would never have another white customer and then we and the children would be destitute and hungry."

"I'm sorry the choice is so repugnant." Emily eyed him with great affection but also a rigid firmness. "But it is an easy one to make, considering the circumstances. These men have all the power," she said.

William knew this was a fact, for on a whim, the patrons could walk out without paying, they could inflict any damage they chose, or get in a fight with another customer or even William himself. He was at their mercy.

"William, as a barber in this town, you've gained an iota of respect you have never held before. Cling to that idea, please! As long as you play by their rules and dote on their vanities, as you tell me you do, you win the battles you choose to fight and the only ones you can be victorious in waging."

"You're right. Part of my strategy is being attentive. I must be a good listener, ask the right questions about stories, compliment and never ask the wrong question, or one that could be misconstrued by a rich, white man as the wrong question from a Negro barber."

Talking with his wife calmed William. His tears stopped, and the children, including Caleb, returned to their chores. He gazed at them for a moment and then back at Emily. "Thank you, my love. I will be fine now."

Emily looked from him to the table with concern.

"Don't worry about the razor. I am fine, I promise." He smiled. "But I do need to carry on shaving."

She hesitated, pondering the intentions showing on his face, and then turned, going back to her chores. "Okay then, but I promise you I will keep one eye on you and the other on the children."

"As you always do. Thank you."

She bent down to scrub the floor, and William stared back into the mirror and picked up the razor. He scraped it against the stubble on his neck softly and then dipped the blade into the soapy bowl of water while contemplating his image.

Chapter Fifteen

IT WAS A short walk from the Converse estate to the old burial ground. Elisha had visited there several times on his own but wanted Frank at his side on this day to experience the town's history as well. "The first European settlers in Malden lie beneath our feet, buried in the ground they once walked upon, and are forever part of the town, Son. Even though most arrived from elsewhere, they dwelled and died right here. Frank, I see them as the very foundation of our town. All of these souls first voyaged across the ocean, then the river from Charlestown to Mystic Side, and then many years after journeyed along the ultimate plane from this world to the next." Elisha wanted his son to grasp the history of their town, and he was also aware he had more to discover about it as well. This was their home. A home he had chosen for his family. There was the river and wildflowers to their left and the beginning of the many rows of graves of the cemetery on their right. Carnations and other trinkets of remembrance were strewn about the earth near the grave markers.

"How's school, Son?"

"I'm doing well, sir."

"That's good, Frank. I've talked to your instructors. They've spoken highly of your diligent and studious nature. I'm proud to hear that, Son."

"Thank you, sir. I'm enjoying it, but I know my high school life is about to come to an end."

"Each end is a new beginning. Frank, soon, when you are ready, we will start to plot out your future." Elisha paused. He discovered the stone he was searching for as they were walking. "Here we are. This is the grave of the Reverend Michael Wigglesworth. Cotton Mather wrote the funeral sermon himself and I can recite the last bit from memory." Frank glanced down at the stone. Over one-hundred-and-fifty years old and it looked like it had not aged a day since it was carved. A skull with wings hovered over the engraved words marking his final resting spot.

Elisha began to speak:

> His pen did once Meat from the Eater take. And now he's gone beyond the Eater's reach. His body once so thin was next to none.
> From hence he's to unbodied spirits flown. Once his rare skill did all diseases heal. And he doth nothing now uneasy feel. He to his paradise is joyful come.
> And waits with joy to see his Day of Doom.

"Day of Doom?" Frank asked.

"Yes, it is a poem the Reverend Wigglesworth wrote about Judgment Day, when our Lord will return and we'll show Him that we have lived a good life of piety and love, fair treatment of our brothers and sisters, while some others have not. I have a copy at home. I will read it to you. It was wildly popular in its day."

"Will the world end then?"

Elisha scanned all the nearby graves and then looked directly at his boy. "One day, yes. In the duration of my lifetime or later in yours, or perhaps after that, I know not, but one day, it will and so, Frank, we have to live our lives piously. We never know when it's our time, so we must be prepared."

Frank appeared to tense up a bit, so his father smiled at him. "Easy now, Frank. Life is doom and gloom, but it is also light and salvation. Don't mention this visit to the graveyard to your mother. She's not as strong as you and I, Son, and she still mourns her father; it's only been a few months since his passing. You possess a bright future ahead of you. I've worked, am working, hard for it. It will be yours—all of what I have—one day. I'm so proud of the man you are growing into. I remember vividly bouncing you as a small boy on my knee. Where do the years go? One has only to blink, and everything is different."

Elisha did just that. The sun, which had been obscured behind a cloud beyond Frank, suddenly came to its full brightness and for a second, Elisha was blinded. His son vanished completely from his sight. When he blinked again, Frank returned before his eyes, smiling at him.

"Father, we should get home to dinner. Mother and Mary Ida must be waiting for us."

"You're right. We must be off." Elisha looked once again at Wigglesworth's gravestone and thought of the last words of Mather's sermon. *"And waits with joy to see his Day of Doom."*

The Reverend Wigglesworth must not have lived a happy life, thought the deacon. Elisha, while God-fearing and preparing his life for Judgment Day, was a businessman and enjoyed the spoils of his labor. He was affluent now and would endeavor to accumulate additional wealth in whatever years were remaining to him so he could pass it on to Frank and his other children. Frank, as the firstborn son, would get the bulk of his inheritance as Elisha groomed the boy to be his heir.

A few days after discussing with his son the future he planned for him, Elisha entered the post office. He held two packages. Edward Green, seeing him approach, rushed around the side of the counter to the best of his ability to assist the deacon in lifting the parcels onto it.

"Thank you."

"You're very welcome. How is business at the Rubber Shoe Company?"

"Busy as always." Elisha scratched his beard and continued. "I wonder if you could do me a favor, Edward. I've decided to let Frank begin working at the bank, now that his schooling is coming to a close. I know you've always been fond of him. Merrill will take him under his wing and teach him the business. But I would be appreciative if you could continue to check in on him, even more than you normally do, please. I don't get to the bank as often as I would like these days. I'm spending a lot of time in Boston on other business concerns."

"Mr. Converse, I'll always be in your debt, just as my father was. Frank's a good kid, becoming a fine young man. It's amazing how he's grown."

Elisha, agreeing with this opinion, smiled. "I know you've had a rough going, Edward, but I hold faith in God that he will lead you on the right path."

"Thank you. I'm honored by your words, Deacon, and indebted to you for your help in supporting me with the post office commission. I don't know if I'd still be in this position if not for you and John Chapman."

"Yes, Chapman's a fine man. A very fine man, indeed. When good people support you in times of trouble, Edward, you know you are worthy of their deeds."

Elisha bid Edward farewell. While Elisha's thoughts moved on to crossing the street to the barber and the rest of his schedule for the day, Edward gazed after him and continued to contemplate the deacon's last statement. *Worthy of their deeds? I don't always feel worthy; have I ever felt worthy?* thought Edward. He certainly felt deserving, believing he had to take what he could, but worried that he had now taken too much, having adjusted the ledger to hide the missing funds. And so, Edward found himself in a quandary, with no real escape from it.

I will lose my position, I will lose the respect I've garnered, and I won't be able to settle my debts. I will lose everything. The thought immediately crossed Edward's mind to run after the deacon and plead for a loan, but he was too embarrassed to ask for further assistance. Edward could not take on any more debts, but it was his habit. He was burying himself. Every waking moment was filled with dread and worry. So, what was there to do? Was there any way out? He did not know. Edward inhaled deeply, held it, and let the air ebb slowly out through his pursed lips.

Once Elisha had walked out of the post office, he did not look back. He would not see Edward Green again for several months. Frank would soon see Edward every day, as he would be dropping off all the letters of the Malden Bank and the Boston Rubber Shoe Company at the post office. Charles Merrill, the head cashier, had performed this task up until this point, as had Elisha occasionally, since he felt a need to check in on Reuben's son. It was the Christian thing to do, but now it would be one of Frank's main responsibilities. Elisha had asked Edward to be there for Frank, and so he knew Frank would also be there for Edward; the two would be connected.

Elisha noted the twirling blend of red and white on the familiar pole outside William's barbershop. There was an important dinner coming up with the board of the bank, and Elisha wanted his hair and beard to be styled and cut, to be presentable. Elisha thought there was only one man in town to do it properly. He was also a good man, and one Elisha admired. William had no need to be saved, as Edward did. He had already prevailed over his circumstances, ones more dire than God had ever seen to trouble Edward Green with, in Elisha's opinion.

There was no remedy for his limp, but Edward's poor money management and his tendency to drink too much could all be overcome and forgiven if he followed the path God laid out for him. However, the burden William Shiloh had been born with was unacceptable to the deacon. Slavery was abhorrent to Elisha and Mary. They held many a discussion on it as well as the great ongoing war that was partly based on its being an institution in the Southern economy. There were not a lot of colored folk in Malden, and few possessed such prominent jobs as William did as a barber. Although, Elisha was well aware, by this point in time, many of the barbers in the North were Negroes. Still, Elisha had never been as satisfied by a single haircut than the very first time William Shiloh tended to his hair. He knew then he would be the only barber for him. Elisha could always depend on the man.

"William, did you ever hear the reason the barber's red-and-white pole came to be?"

"No, sir," William said, though he was well aware of why.

"In Germany, many of the barbers were also doctors and sometimes bloodletters. They wrapped a bloody rag around a white pole so others would know they offered that service."

"Sir, my job, for the customer's sake and certainly for my very own, is never to shed a drop of blood in this shop!"

Elisha laughed, and after a moment, William joined him in doing so. Around most of the men who walked through his door, William was a bit nervous, though he feigned not to be. The barber admired Elisha as a man of knowledge, a man of charity, a man of doing, and a man to emulate. He was the most powerful man in town, but he was not a tyrant. Like George

Washington, he could become king if he chose to do so, not of the whole country but of the whole town. Although Elisha lived well, he mingled with all the commoners as if he were one of them. Elisha Converse turned up his nose at no one, regardless of station, nor, William also trusted, at the color of one's skin.

He even sometimes called William "sir" at first, whereas none of his other customers called him that. The Count actually referred to him as "boy," and although William sometimes felt youthful, he had not been a boy in many, many years. So, he was quite taken aback when this man of prestige had offered him so much respect. He also felt a bit uncomfortable since he was not accustomed to it; though being called "boy" was not something William particularly liked, it did not surprise him.

William had been cutting Elisha's hair since the day he opened his shop, and soon after he began cutting his son Frank's hair as well. The boy reminded him so much of Mr. Converse. Strong, intelligent, kind. Children can be taught to be kind, he thought, to at least look kind, sometimes for a reward of a sort, a candy perhaps, but Frank was kind, pure and simple. William was proud to see Frank growing into such a fine young man and following in the deacon's footsteps, just as he was proud of his own son Caleb for following in his. He would do whatever he could for the lad, but Caleb's future was uncertain. So many things could change, so much was up for grabs.

But for the son of Mr. Converse, the future was much more certain. It had been predetermined. He was the apple of his father's eye. In many ways, he was the apple of the whole town's eye. The young girls were crazy about him. He was handsome and had an air of confidence, which was tempered by inheriting his father's fine manner and sense, and the generous heart of his mother, Mary. Frank was not cocky, but he was sure of himself. His future, like the town his father had been converting slowly from a farm community to a bustling center of industry and recreation, was full of possibility. Elisha had been raising his son with the certainty that he would be his heir and be able to take what he had built to even more unimaginable heights, all that heaven would allow. Trimming Elisha's hair, William thought, *Perchance, the Converse name will one day be known far and wide, and perhaps it will be because of Frank Converse.* William hoped so.

With the tumultuous times in which they lived, Elisha thought it was wise to prepare Frank for his life to come. *The boy is ready,* he thought. *Frank is almost a man, and there are boys younger than him dying on Abraham Lincoln's battlefields.* Elisha had always journeyed up to the top of Waitt's Mount by himself. Now, he trusted that his boy was ready to join in God's presence. Frank would be taking over all his business interests one day, so he needed to begin, to gain a start, to get a feel for all the ins and outs of being his father's son. Life was hard work and sacrifice. Times could be tough, but they could also be glorious.

Elisha walked up the path from Leonard Street. Frank followed behind with a slight bit of trepidation as his father took a turn which seemed to steeply climb to a higher destination.

"Follow me, Son. God has willed it. You are ready."

Frank was a bit reluctant. He remembered the sermon from church the previous Sunday, about an Abraham who was not the president and how he wished to sacrifice his son on a mount since God demanded him to do so. Why had his father finally invited him up here? He was aware the spot was private and personal to him. Frank did not want his father to sacrifice him, but then the thought evaporated as the boy realized from all his experiences that his father was both his protector and guide. They reached the summit, and Frank was immediately in awe of the view. He had traveled a small amount in his life but not too far, and now he could see the town and all its surroundings as if he had grown wings and could soar above it.

From his favorite spot in town, Elisha looked upon Malden. He focused on the town's armory, where many of the young men of Malden had mustered and many had never returned. He was also thinking of the reverend's sermon about the sacrifice God asked Abraham to make of his own son, Isaac. Elisha knew Abraham must only show his willingness to obey the Lord. It was not the deed but the obedience that God demanded. Elisha was a devout man, and his love and devotion to God would, for his entire life, remain above all other concerns, no matter the heartbreak he incurred. Frank meant the world to him, and he struggled mightily with the idea of doing what Abraham had intended to do before the Lord compelled him to hold his hand.

Now another Abraham, our president, is suffering a similar fate as his namesake. Instead of one son being sacrificed, it's tens of thousands of sons being slaughtered for what I strongly conclude is for the greater good, the preservation of the Union and the freeing of enslaved people from their shackles, as God intends, yet the violent consequences are so terrible. Elisha trembled thinking of them and recalled a recent discussion he and John Chapman had about how the gruesome images affected him.

"John, I've viewed and studied with fascination and dread the photos of Matthew Brady from the battlefields of the dead, showing the sacrifice that this new Abraham has made to God. The bodies torn asunder and strewn about like thrown-away toys. The weight on the president must be tremendous, more than one man should be forced to bear."

"Deacon, I have not seen them, but I shudder to think of such a horrible death or being among such carnage myself. Sending these boys into such certain danger must be a burden."

"Agreed. I cannot help but imagine the large top hat of our president filled with heavy stones, and yet the man holds his head high and stands heroically for the very ideals of justice and equality that this country was founded upon."

At the top of the Mount, Elisha eyed Frank thoughtfully. "Frank, are you ready to work, to learn a profession?"

"Yes, Father. I'm ready, God willing."

This succinct answer was all Elisha hoped to hear. "Wonderful! I've decided to have Mr. Merrill train you at the bank. I'm aware you have spent some time helping him and he states you show an aptitude. So now it is official. You'll be his apprentice. He's a tough man, but he's a good man, and you'll learn a great deal from him, my son. You have a good mind for numbers. Later, you can join me at the rubber plant and learn that business from top to bottom. This is just the beginning. You understand, as my son, all I have is to be yours. Also, I have asked your good friend Edward Green to check in on you."

Frank nodded silently. Elisha smiled. Frank was a fine son; he had been blessed to have him. With the right guidance and patience, his life's work would be Frank's as well, and so it would remain in good hands. Plus, Merrill knew the workings of the bank very well, serving as cashier for the past ten years. Elisha was confident Merrill was up to the task of passing on his knowledge and experience to his son. "It's settled then," his father continued. "You start in the coming week. Make me proud."

"I will, Father."

Elisha noticed that, like himself, Frank was first swiveling his head to gain a view of the whole panorama but then focused directly on the town below. "I know you'll do so, Son. I'm proud of you. Take another moment to gaze at the town. I understand the sensation, Frank, I've viewed it from this spot so many times, but it still causes awe for me, standing at this vantage point."

"Father, it's like I'm in the town but removed from it. I can see some townsfolk moving around, but I feel detached from them somewhat, being up here." This last detail was odd for Elisha to hear. He had gazed at the town and its inhabitants from this height many times and, even from this distance, always sensed himself completely immersed in it. It was part of him, he was part of it, and the two intertwined as if they were naturally one. He thought, with age and experience, Frank would feel the same way.

"Take a deep breath, Frank, if you're able, and look again. And if you don't see the town as I do, that's fine. Look upon it as many times as you need to, and make your own observations. I'm a settler here, Son, but Malden runs through your veins, and if God graces you one day with sons of your own, I hope they'll give to this town as well, for they'll benefit from it as we have. It's the bargain we make. God wants us to give if we are to receive, and then to pass it on to our loved ones and neighbors."

Frank nodded and tried to see the town below just as Elisha said he viewed it. Frank was unable to do so but did not tell his father. He simply smiled at Elisha and hoped that, in the years to come, he could perceive Malden as his patriarch did.

It was his first train ride to Boston on his own, and more importantly to Frank Converse, it was his first train ride as a representative of the Malden Bank. Charles Merrill had supplied him with all the details he would need for the day, jotted down in cursive on a notepad. Elisha had instructed Merrill that Frank must attain competence and confidence. The cashier wanted to please Elisha by being kind but also tough on the man's son and protégé. He assumed Elisha would live a long life but also thought perhaps one day this boy would be his boss. The boy would soon be splitting the rides to the city with him on behalf of the bank, and both the father and the cashier wanted to see how strong Frank's mettle was and had decided to put it to the test.

As the train left Malden and headed south, Frank studied his superior's instructions as he had first done while waiting in the depot. He felt a confidence in following them to the letter, so he allowed himself to look at the whirl of trees passing by, to feel the vibration of the train car in which he was sitting, and to take in the sights and sounds of his fellow passengers as they traveled to their chosen terminus. This means of conveyance was miraculous. He was mindful it did not exist when his father was his age. He wondered for a moment if it was also dangerous, but he was so in awe of the sensation and the speed that he soon forgot about these worries.

Chapter Sixteen

Even though he was almost a decade older, Edward Green suffered from arrested development and perceived that Frank Converse, at sixteen, was his ideal peer. He confided in him, although vaguely, about his financial troubles. The urgent requirements of others for income to acquire necessities and the perils of falling into debt were unfamiliar to Frank. His mother instilled a bit of a frugal nature in him, but the young man was never in need or want.

He told Edward one morning, "I'm earning my allowance and learning in great detail about my father's business. Maybe one day, Eddie, I'll be running the company all by myself. I know this is my father's plan, and Mr. Merrill's my own private tutor, giving me more and more responsibility all the time."

Edward assumed the allowance Frank earned from his father must be in excess of his own salary as postmaster. *This is so unfair. Frank has no need for additional funds and I am desperate for them,* he thought but said instead, "Great news, Frank. I look forward to the day when you, alone, are in charge of the bank."

"Thank you, my friend," said Frank as Edward walked back to the post office, and Frank considered how he felt about the postmaster.

Frank sat down at his reading desk, and Charles Merrill said to his new employee, "Did you have a good talk with Eddie?"

"I did, sir. When Eddie arrives to talk to me as he picks up or drops off the deposits of the post office, I listen with a caring, sympathetic ear."

"You are a kind young man," said Charles.

"You know something I just learned in a book about names I found in my father's study?"

"What is that, Frank?"

"It's kind of funny."

"Go on, you have my attention."

"The origin of my first name, Francis, is an English form of the Latin used for 'Frenchman,' whereas the origin of Edward is 'the guardian of fortune or prosperity.' I find this ironic since I'm a bank clerk, the guardian of money, and my friend, from what he tells me, possesses only debt and complains of it frequently on his visits. Eddie's an odd duck, easily wound up, and almost talking as in a fit when he gets excited."

"I would agree with that," said Charles.

The bell rang and Charles walked to the door to greet a customer. Frank returned to a book about currency and banking regulations Charles had asked him to study, but his thoughts remained on his friend. When the customer left, Frank continued to confide in his superior about his relationship with Edward.

"Mr. Merrill, I seek guidance from Eddie on women and romance, having noticed how easily he flirted with the ladies outside his office and then married a very lovely one. I'm aware that Eddie rarely speaks as honestly or as openly to others as he does to me, and so I feel comfortable to do the same. I can always rely on him. Having him right across the street from the bank gives me a sense of security."

"It is important to have those we trust nearby, Frank," said Charles, but he rolled his eyes in dismay when Frank wasn't looking.

Frank viewed his friend one way, and the postmaster regarded the bank teller another way entirely. Edward thought of Frank as outgoing and well-liked by all, yet Frank was also the kind of fit specimen Edward secretly envied, and not just for his youth. He had recently confided in Marshall about his mixed feelings toward the Converse boy. "Frank will never suffer the limp I've known for most of my life, or feel the judging eyes, intentional or not, which follow me as I walk down the street. Marshall, he also brags to me of the miraculous plumbing in his house, that he can take a hot bath whenever he wants without having to boil water and letting the tub sit until it has cooled enough to allow one to slip in. If you or I or most others need a bath, we must just take a dip in the Malden River, regardless of its temperature, whether we possess soap or not. What a luxury for Frank. All is at his fingertips."

"You know it, Eddie, indoor plumbing, oh my gosh, such a dream to possess."

"Very true, and the boy will have no trouble with the ladies either now that he is coming of age," stated Edward, jealous he had to perform what he viewed as a mighty effort of charm to make up for his own poor and feeble circumstances. Edward believed fate treated Frank kindly and him with little regard but wanted to assure his friend he was not uncaring.

"Marshall, I genuinely like Frank. He's brainy yet thoughtful and approachable. Frank easily could put on airs for someone of his family's means and standing, but he doesn't. I wish Frank well, but I know he'll easily make the most out of his life with all the gifts he's been given."

Edward thought to himself, *The boy is the mirror image I wish I spied in my own reflection and fortune. Instead, the image I behold in the glass as I leave the bank is always just my own pitiful likeness, one of disfigurement and incompetence. I've been bequeathed my father's meager post, as the bank and all Elisha's ample business interests will one day be given to young Frank.*

The baker stared at his friend, knowing he was deep in contemplation. Edward decided to speak his remaining thoughts out loud to Marshall. "Frank will certainly grow and prosper and make his father proud as he reaches adulthood. Frank can become anything he wants, I guess, bank president, mayor, or some other elected official. Perhaps, he could be one of the many generals in Lincoln's army, for all I know, depending on how long this war goes on. My own father, if he could see me now, would react exactly how to my current circumstances?"

"He would be proud of you, Eddie," said Marshall.

"No, Marshall, I believe he would most likely view me very poorly. I have piled debt upon debt and have nothing to show for it but lost sleep and anguish. I've reached the end of my rope. I have ambitions and I have desires. I want to enjoy life and have fine things for my wife and a proper upbringing for any children which could come. But there's always a worry about money, about providing for myself and my new wife. I have hopes, I have plans. Will they ever come to pass? How can they? I don't know. My life's goals are now seemingly farther away from my grasp instead of being any closer."

Edward gazed at Frank sitting at his reading desk across the street. The windowpane of the post office offered his scant reflection in reply, but Edward stepped forward closer to the glass so he could block out any version of himself, so all he could view was the bank and the boy within it.

"Eddie."

Edward had not heard his wife enter the post office. "Eddie," she said a second time, tugging at his shirtsleeve.

Dizzy, his head pounding, he turned to her.

"Clara," he said, his face expressionless. In contrast, she was absolutely beaming at him.

"I've such wonderful news. We're to have a child," she said.

"What? Really?" Edward fidgeted and then contoured his expression to one of pure delight and embraced her. He was overjoyed but also instantly terrified of the new expense of becoming a father. Tears ran down Clara's cheeks, and she pressed her body closer to his. Their faces were inches apart. Edward smiled at her, but then he spied his own terrified image in the mirror behind her head, and while holding her and saying how thrilled he was, his thoughts swirled. *A child on the way. Woe is me. How will I find the means to afford this new development? For I am truly at my wit's end to ease my enormous expenses and preposterous bills already.*

After Clara departed, her husband walked to the back of the office and banged his head three times on a support beam. Returning to his desk, he opened a drawer and, grasping the bottle it held, lifted it up and took a long swig and then another before returning it and closing the drawer with a thump.

Later that morning, George Bennett stood in front of the postmaster holding his infant son, Wiley. Edward shared how Clara was with child. "I never thought I'd be a father," George said. "Not at my age."

"I always hoped for a child but was not sure with my limp if I could marry," said Edward.

"You've got a fine woman."

"You as well," Edward said, but he was lying. His Clara was a true prize, and he knew he was lucky to have attained her. Bernadette Bennett, in his opinion, was a rather sizable woman, one known to throw her weight around and henpeck her husband. *George must be a smothered man, both literally* and *figuratively*, thought Edward. *How does he sleep at night? Probably curled up in a tight ball in whatever section of the bed his wife's girth and attitude allow.* The thought made Edward chuckle, but he held it in. The boy, Wiley, was quite handsome, he had to admit. At least that had come of the union of the older, meeker man and the domineering, larger woman.

And now Edward would be a father himself. What a grand thing but also what a financial commitment. Money was running tighter and tighter. Feeling some pity for himself, Edward focused on a recollection of seeing some of the young men of the town returning from battle with limbs lost. These men had gone off to war healthy and able-bodied and had come back from the battlefields in pieces and shattered physically and mentally. Now home, they were looking for whatever work they could find to support their families.

Edward had a limp, but at least he had both legs, a stable job, and no need to risk his life in a war that meant nothing to him. This gave him some solace. Maybe God did not hate him after all, although he was certain the Lord did not love him as well as he did some others. A few of the town's youth had avoided service in the war because of their fathers' positions. The obvious one to always come to mind was Frank Converse. *He's truly blessed. God's chosen him above all others,* Edward thought. *Frank's victim to neither disease nor the consequence of war. His life will always be one of wealth and ease. The contrast between us is so unfair.*

Edward sought leisure where he could, but mostly it was beyond his means. He loved his friend, but his envy for Frank was growing exponentially just as were Edward's debt and money concerns.

Frank confided to Edward about how he and his classmate spent their days up on the Mount in the warm weather, staring off into the distance, imagining faraway places and all the possibilities the future held.

"My father loves climbing the Mount for silent reflection. It's sacred to him. We all have our own hills or mountains to climb for different reasons.

It's a solitary place for him. The Mount's a place I like to be with others. Unless I have a book in front of me, I prefer not to be alone. I like company."

"You're good company. I've always enjoyed our chats. And I've some special news to share with you today. Frank, I'm to be a father!"

Frank's smile was immense. "God has truly blessed you."

"You think so?" said Edward, his own smile crooked on one side. *He's not blessed me anywhere near as much as he's blessed you,* he thought but instead said, "Thank you, my dear friend. You're one of the first people I wanted to share this news with."

Chapter Seventeen

As their baby began to grow and slowly cause Clara's belly to protrude, she rejected Edward's nocturnal advances more and more. The summer was hot, and Edward was overheated in body and spirit. A man always seeking pleasures and the release of his constant stresses, Edward became unfulfilled and agitated. He did not wish to cheat on his wife, but he soon found himself tying the carriage he had hired from Jackson's livery to the once familiar post near Mrs. Lake's establishment.

Edward was walking along the edge of the dirt road when he was struck frozen by a commotion before him. A policeman was struggling with a man who clearly wanted to escape his clutches.

"Get in the damn paddy wagon, you damn Paddy!" the officer shouted. "We named it just for you. We didn't want Papists like you in our country, but now Uncle Sam welcomes you into his army, nonetheless."

"Don't conscript me. I don't want to fight. I fled hunger and the British, and you lot ain't no bargain either," said the man in a brogue.

The officer placed him in a half nelson, and the man struggled to get free.

"You have three hundred dollars to hire a substitute, do you?"

"Are you mad? Who has such a sum?" said the Irishman, gasping for breath.

"A few do, and they don't have to fight, and the lame get a pass as well." He shot a look at Edward and then stared back at his captive. "But you seem able-bodied enough. So, get in!"

The officer released the man and gestured to the wagon. When the man hesitated, the officer removed the three-foot-long club attached at his hip and struck the man repeatedly, forcing him into the back of the wagon, and then slammed the door shut.

The officer glared in at his prisoner through a small opening. "You scoundrels had your little draft riot in July, not as bad as what happened in New York, but a few of my fellow patrolmen were still roughed up quite a bit." The officer banged on the door, and the prisoner stepped back, which caused the policeman to laugh menacingly. "But now you are all ours," he said. "You came over on your coffin ships, and now we will send you south on our trains to fight Lincoln's war. You will be in regulation blues by morning, Paddy! There is no escaping Uncle Sam for your kind!"

The Irish in Boston and New York had risen up when officers came to their doorsteps with conscription papers; the riot in Boston had lasted a day whereas the tumult in New York City raged for three days until quelled.

"This is unjust. I survived peril only to be forced into further jeopardy. I don't want to fight. I've just been in this country a few days after weeks at sea. The journey was a purgatory, and now you are condemning me to hell."

"You will fight and go to hell as well, for all I care," said the officer, thumping his club on the back of the wagon once again.

The man's face drew away from the opening, and he slumped in his cage.

"If I come back alive from this war, I will remember you and seek you out, you bastard!" yelled the voice from within the wagon.

The cop snickered. "If you do, which is unlikely, I have no fear toward you or the dozens of boyos like you I round up fresh from the boats and send off on trains all the time."

Edward, feeling apprehensive that the policeman's eyes were upon him, exerted no effort to mitigate his limp as he entered Mrs. Lake's establishment. Later that evening, he rode through Charlestown, west into Medford, and then north into the outskirts of Malden. While heading home, Edward passed many of the tenements in Edgeworth, where the workers of the Boston Rubber Shoe plant dwelled. He thought dozens of them, perhaps scores, lived upon a land mass equal to the Converse estate, where the wealthy man and his family resided in tranquility, their every need attended to dutifully by a handful of servants. However, the apartments of the factory workers were unquestionably not as cramped or dangerous as living among the streets of the Black Sea. The Irishman he had witnessed arrested earlier that evening strived to free himself from Victorian oppression and instead of a welcoming American shore, discovered first squalor and then ultimately conscription into a conflict of which he had been beforehand completely unaware. Three centuries before, the Spanish had transported the first potatoes east across the Atlantic; the crop's blight in recent years had hastened thousands of Irish to take the perilous journey to the Americas in return.

Though he had not traversed any treacherous seas, the waves of financial uncertainty and uncertainty in general pummeled daily against Edward Green. The world was cruel for most but not the lucky few. Edward admired the Converses, and Frank most of all, but he disliked them for their privileged life more and more just the same.

The debt was mounting; the salary from the post office was insufficient in providing for his wife and forthcoming child. Edward sweat even on the coldest of days as summer faded to autumn. His drinking and opium consumption increased. The skies appeared to be filled with so many clouds, dark storm clouds, that compelled Edward to stare up, holding his breath until some sun shined through. Only then would he allow himself to look away and exhale deeply.

Edward could not sleep for he bit his tongue inadvertently during the night. He banged his head against one of the exposed beams in his office more and more when he was alone. It was becoming a habit. Every day, there was a growing ringing in his ears and an even greater sense of imbalance than he was accustomed to feeling on his uneven feet.

His accounts were deeply in debt, and an order was sent from Washington directly to Mr. Gray in the head post office in Boston for Edward's removal. But once again, through the influence of some of the principal citizens of Malden, such as Elisha Converse, who still regarded him as a deserving young man, Edward retained his position. The postmaster gained some sympathy in this matter, due to his affliction and the fond memory of his father by the townsfolk. The amount in question was made good by these friends, but he was left in debt to them and he was already living beyond his income.

Additional funds were needed, and one day an unexpected visitor offered a helping hand. John walked into the post office but held no parcel. The two stood watching each other carefully, wondering when and if the other would speak first and what he would say.

"Eddie, Agnes tells me Clara is doing well in her condition."

"She is."

"It is expensive to raise a child."

"You would know, I suppose."

"Ah, yes," said John, rubbing his chin, "I certainly do." He paused and looked away and then back at Edward. "As you know, I am a member of the school committee."

"I am well aware you are a member of many outfits. You are a very important man. You've spent your time devoted to business and the town, and you believe that I've spent too much of my precious time on pleasure and frivolous matters. Marshall has told me you have stated this often. I don't like being looked down upon, especially by someone I held as a friend. These harsh opinions are the reason we are no longer close. No offense, but you've gotten too big for your britches."

John sighed. "Eddie, please don't make this difficult. We were once great friends, but now we are related by marriage. I have an offer that can help you and your family."

"You do?"

"Yes, we need someone to purchase schoolbooks for us. The town has allocated five hundred dollars for this appropriation, and I have arranged a ten-percent fee for you to work as our agent. That's fifty dollars in your pocket to go toward the baby."

Edward was surprised. John, Elisha, and others had stood by him when there were questions about his competency, but this offer was unexpectedly generous.

"I want to be clear, Eddie. It is not charity. This is something that the children need."

"Thank you, John. The money is helpful, and the task will be approached with great care." Edward offered his hand, and the two soon came to an arrangement.

On behalf of the town and with the surety of the United States Post Office, Edward ordered the books from Brown, Taggert and Company, a publishing house, and they were delivered and distributed to the schoolchildren.

For Edward, this infusion of cash was a temporary lifeline. However, instead of using it for its intended purpose, he allocated it for his own use, to pay the deficiency in his post office account. Thus, Edward became indebted to the publisher for the $500. This bill had been overdue for some time, and he also accrued additional debts to the Boston post office. His poor handling of the post office finances was little known, just to a handful of people, but John was made aware that Edward had not paid for the schoolbooks. He confronted him, but Edward was dismissive.

"Don't worry, John," he said. "It is my problem, not yours."

So, the two returned to staying out of each other's way.

These debts were soon compounded by other debts, individually small but collectively growing out of control. Edward attempted to keep these secret from the town for as long as he could. He sat at his stove and contemplated the flames. Crumpling up some paper and watching the fire grow, he added more fuel to it and became captivated by the dancing yellows and oranges. He smiled. Edward began to conceive of a way for the settling of all his accounts at once. He pondered over how to carry out this plan for several days, trying to weigh all the variables and the danger involved to others in the building, but the danger to himself if his endless debts were discovered concerned Edward most of all.

Clara's usual tender mood had turned to surliness, and Edward longed to please her.

"Eddie, we need so many things for the baby, who will be joining us ever so soon."

"We will have them," said Edward, but the heavy sweat on his brow contradicted this statement as well as his belief in its veracity.

"Agnes and Susie have spoken of the three of us going shopping for baby items, and we plan to ask Sophia to join us so she can carry anything we purchase. We need a lot of things, Eddie, clothes and toys, and—"

He cut her off. "Sure, my love."

However, this was an excursion Edward was well aware he could not afford without incurring further debt. His bad leg and head both ached at the idea of providing these items and the many other expenses to come.

On the night of November 1, nearly a year after his marriage to Clara, and perhaps two months or so before the expected birth of their first child, Edward stood leaning against a second-floor window, trying to balance his weight and weigh his intentions.

He gazed out at his place of employment, across the street and to the left, and wished the contents within it destroyed, his trail of debt forever hidden. During the previous half hour, Edward had sat on a nearby chair pulling the volunteer company's fire hose across his lap, section by section, and pushing several lumps haphazardly from one end to the other hoping they would cause blocks and tears. He was not concerned about anyone interrupting since the station was rarely busy.

As he squeezed and tugged on the objects, the words *toys, dresses, diapers* repeated in his head, again and again.

Soon, after gingerly spinning down the circular stairs and exiting the building, he found himself back in his office. Edward scattered kindling all around the floor but then, hearing footsteps above him, stopped and pondered a moment. He wished to burn the evidence of his mismanagement but allow time for those above to escape the flames. So, Edward started tearing away sections of lath and plaster in the wall that adjoined an apartment on the right side of the first floor. When the hole was sufficiently large, he quickly picked up all the paper and kindling and stuffed it deep into the wall.

This should obliterate the ledger and my misdeeds, burn them both to a crisp, obscuring my debt in smoke and in ashes, he thought.

Edward lit a match, staring as the flames danced and tempted him to join their chorus. Mesmerized, he walked out of the building and stood about five hundred feet away, where Pleasant Street met Main Street at the town's pump. Edward dipped his head under its faucet to quench the desires the fire had summoned within him.

Minutes later, the bell at the top of the volunteer fire department rang out. Soon, men gathered, staring at the smoke issuing from the upper part of the Dawes Block, adjacent to the post office.

More time passed and Edward became elated. Yet he started to feel nervous as the flames sought refuge on the building's roof. He sensed his own need for oxygen and took a deep breath. His throat, irritated by the smoke, forced him to cough and lose his breath for a few moments.

The horse team of the fire brigade arrived on the street, and a line was forming where he stood at the pump. A man he hardly knew placed a bucket below him and said, "Green, start pumping the water!" Edward did so and watched as a human chain spread out from where he stood to a terminus at the flames. No sooner had Edward filled this one bucket and handed it to the stranger, who passed it along in a sea of hands to quench the flames of Edward's desperation, then there stood another man handing him another bucket. Edward filled it and repeated the effort as more men and more buckets flooded his vision; full containers left his hand and empty ones were given in exchange. After several minutes, he was exhausted, both mentally and physically.

Why did I choose to stand in this very spot? I should have known better, but I was thirsty; I am always thirsty. Is this my purgatory, as the Papists believe, forever being trapped in the moment of my *crime, repeating it into eternity?* he wondered.

The horse brigade tied a hose to their stores of water and began pumping to extinguish the flames, but the line sputtered and the spray was uneven. So, more water was required from the town's pump, and Edward was obligated, by his proximity to the source, to do all the pumping. His arms grew numb, and soon his mind joined them. Collectively, his mind and soul were growing weary. After almost an hour, Edward collapsed and was carried a short distance away as another manned the pump and the buckets continued their back and forth between water and fire. Edward helplessly watched from a crouch as the noble men of his town smothered his bad intentions one pail at a time.

He slumped, his head falling into a puddle. But he was stirred as the men cheered; the fire had been contained, and only wet embers remained.

Most of the damage was to the room used as a wardrobe and library by the Bell Rock Lodge of Good Templars; they had endeavored to keep him sober and on the right path and had been repaid by Edward burning down their hall. The fire had reached the very top of the building, and the roof was destroyed. The firefighters had valiantly fought the flames and were able to douse them before they engulfed the entire building. The post office remained intact. Even Edward's ingenious plan—to sabotage the rescue by puncturing and blocking the hose with fine coals—had been thwarted. When the cause of the leaky hose was discovered, W. H. Cromack, the head of the local fire brigade, stated that it "could not have got in there by any accident."

Edward's debt remained, and now he feared they would also suspect him of starting the fire, even though he unintentionally had joined them in a false effort to smother the inferno of his treachery.

With his plan of burning the evidence having failed, Edward contemplated a bolder and more desperate solution to all his money troubles, one he could barely admit to himself and certainly would never confide to another soul. As two parts of him quarreled in the depths of his mind, Edward thrust their internal parley as far back as possible from his surface thoughts, but he knew he would have to make preparations just in case he was capable of the act they were debating. During the first week of December, he purchased a revolver and a quantity of ammunition from the store of Mr. Reed in Boston.

Chapter Eighteen

"MARSHALL, I PLAN to name the baby Reuben, after my father, if it's a boy. But whether it's a girl or a boy, I know I'll love my child with all my heart. My main responsibility is to be a provider, but I believe I'm unable to do so with my meager wages as postmaster."

"You'll be a fine father, I have no doubt," said Marshall.

"Thank you. You've witnessed as I have enjoyed grand fancies. However, I can't focus solely on myself anymore; my days of going to balls are over. I've married the girl of my dreams, and now I know my attention must be entirely focused on the tiny being which Clara and I are about to bring into the world."

Edward thought it was his duty and privilege to provide for his child. The dilemma was that he was unable to do so. There were many debts which preceded the birth, and he was well aware there were many more which would follow. And so, his mind was always searching for any quick fix, no matter how drastic the means. Now, he had begun contemplating what seemed like a surefire solution to all his problems, yet this dire action terrified him. Edward wanted to put it out of his mind completely but could not.

One way or another, Edward needed a drink to make his decision. To clear his mind, he often muddied it. It was the cycle of his day-to-day existence. With Clara's gentle goading, he strived to drink less, but Edward, convinced he was already drowning in debt, thought any additional liquid could not in fact hurt and could perhaps make the difficult choice which lay before him a little easier.

Edward lifted an ale to his mouth and let the foam linger on his mustache. *So now my problems have expanded,* he thought. He felt the urge to lick his lips and take in all the goodness, the beer, the sweet alcohol, but he let it remain there, knowing he could consume it when he wanted it, when he required it; there was no need to be impetuous. The trick was to wait. When the time was right, as in all other things, simple or even difficult, it would reveal itself.

A few moments passed, and Edward could wait no more. He took a deep swig and then he licked his tongue along the bristles below his nose. He held the satisfaction, both of the beer within him and also of the beer remaining on his person. Edward Green always desired more than the world dealt out to him and schemed all his life to gather everything that he could acquire by whatever means. *It's satisfying, but it's not the sensation I expected. It's fraught with nothing. Nothing.*

The thought made Edward smile for the way he had with words. *I'm clever. The ladies always have been impressed with my wit, just as Clara was on that first meeting in Cambridge, when John was courting her and I began scheming to win her heart. How could something be full of nothing? An action has a result and hopefully a reward. I'm clever indeed.*

Hill's Tavern was busy, as usual, crowded with men not pious enough to accept complete temperance, even if some of them espoused it. Edward took another sip, this one direct and satisfying, and scanned the room from his perch on a stool at the end of the long mahogany bar. George Jones, or as he liked to be called, the Count Joannes, was close by at a table on his left, talking to Constable John Abbott, who was listening but seemed more interested in the drink in his hand than the mutterings of a man who, while only a visitor in the town, acted as a know-it-all in its affairs. Soon Abbott got up to leave. Edward had seen the Count exiting the barbershop several times but had never encountered him in the tavern.

Edward breathed deep. He knew John Chapman was seated past the other end of the bar, at the corner table, in the very spot where the two once-close friends had shared many a drink and many a conversation. Edward had glimpsed him as he entered the establishment, but neither man made eye contact. John was gathered there with several gentlemen, including Thomas Dowling and George Bailey. Edward thought about how he had sacrificed his friendship with John to obtain Clara for himself. He supposed John was suspicious of him, curious about how things had played out far differently than he had anticipated. John was a planner, and a successful one, but Edward was a schemer, and successful as well. A good scheme could always sabotage a good plan; Edward knew that very well. *We're not the close confidants we once were, but we're bonded as brothers-in-law, nonetheless.*

Edward looked at John, but John was turned sideways; yet Edward was sure he could detect him on his periphery. As Edward continued staring at John, he thought about all the events of the past, all his acts of jealous deception, convinced that Clara's life would have been so much finer and less complicated if she had married John Chapman instead of Edward Green. A far kinder fate. Having recently added arson to his repertoire, Edward wondered what else he was capable of doing for his own gain. His thoughts veered to the new sins he had come to the tavern to contemplate. *I've got to stop dwelling on the past and decide whether to complete the bold action now before me, which could forever alter my future.* Edward thought an ale would distract him for a bit and maybe convince him against any of the schemes which inhabited his mind.

Edward conceived one couldn't attain everything in life, yet if one could recognize an opportunity, such as he had discovered when Clara unexpectedly crossed his path, one must not squander the rare chance presented. If another opportunity presented itself, Edward was prepared to act immediately as well, without considering the consequences.

Edward took a final deep swig and waved his arm to get the barkeep's attention and his mug filled again. While waiting for his drink, Edward glanced back over to the Count, who didn't pay him any heed. Instead, he was staring at the table at the end of the bar and listening as he sipped from a tumbler, which Edward suspected the man had brought with him, since Edward had never seen such fine glassware at the tavern.

Standing on a table, George Bailey began to declaim to a large group of people about President Lincoln's address at Gettysburg, which occurred within the last couple of weeks. Bailey was rather small in stature, with a bushy head of hair and short, crisp whiskers, keen eyes, and a sharp businesslike air. The crowd seemed to hang on his every word as Bailey recited from the newspaper and then offered his own opinion. "It's still staggering to think of all the dead. Brother slaughtering brother. The blood runs through the fields and renders our nation's crop of young men fallow for a generation. Eight thousand killed in three days of battle, and many more since that brutal day. And so, we're all Cains now."

The onlookers gazed at Bailey wide-eyed, taking in all his words. They all cheered; everyone except the Count. Edward noticed he appeared to be frowning as he sipped his whiskey, nimbly tilting his mustache so as not to wet it. Edward turned back to Bailey as the onlookers, including John, applauded once more at Bailey's words. "We're all disposable. Able-bodied men, vulnerable in a battle that widens in a blood-soaked garden. There is a beginning and an end for us in life, but it is truly only the middle that matters most. The question I pose to each of you is: Do we, individually or collectively, have any redeeming qualities? Do we stand for something? Do we contribute to a greater cause, or are we mere charlatans? Do we act, or do we scheme? Do we covet, or do we create? Do we destroy to build, or do we build to destroy? Our forefathers fought against the chains of an English king, some while sitting in this very tavern. Our nation, now split in two, must unite so our black brothers can free themselves from their bondage. Slavery is an abomination, and blood will spill until it is eliminated and our country is healed and reunited." Edward noticed the whole crowd, which was now even larger, was enthusiastically applauding, with the exception of himself and the Count.

Is anyone in town more beloved than Bailey? Perhaps only Elisha Converse and more and more his son, thought Edward. He was somewhat indifferent to Bailey. He found him charming enough, but Edward thought him as interchangeable as any man, including himself. Elisha Converse, on the other hand, Edward believed was a great man who earned and deserved the respect of all. He employed half the residents, if not more, with his massive rubber factory, and he was perceived as generous, kind, and forward-thinking.

The world was changing, and Elisha Converse, Edward had to admit, maintained a very good feel for the direction in which it was heading. If not for Elisha and the man who sat at the other end of the bar, a man whom he could no longer look square in the eye without a difficulty of effort, Edward knew he surely would have lost his position as postmaster, more than once. They had vouched for his character and bestowed upon him a wee bit of hope when his future looked dire. They had bet on him, and he had taken that chip, that trust and charity, and bet pell-mell on many things, large and frivolous both, and now the debt was tremendous and, frankly, overwhelming. Alcohol kept it at bay from his thoughts at times, but it seemed like an entity unto itself, unyielding and untamed.

The men of the town were socializing and lessening their various pains while their women, for those married, waited for them to arrive home. Some of the wives were fully prepared, through habit, for a rough night upon the return of their husbands. The tavern was heavy with smoke, as was normal. Edward picked up his cigar and took a long inhale. The sensation caused him to long for a whiskey, but he could not afford it anymore at the public house, so he would stick with beer, lots and lots of beer.

He noticed that the Count had a full bottle of the good stuff at his table and poured himself another glass. Edward stared at him with both envy and contempt, but the Count's attention was still focused on the end of the bar, where the men were conversing about the war. *An eccentric fellow,* thought Edward, who had spoken with him a couple times on the street. The bartender filled Edward's mug, and he took a long swig from it and then another and another. Beer would do for now. He knew a cheap bottle of the harder stuff was always in the drawer in his office for when he truly needed it.

When Edward had his fill of ale, he exited the tavern and turned right. He passed the stocks and whipping post without paying them any heed and stared reluctantly at the town pump near the square as a landmark to guide him home, biding his time as a horse and buggy passed. The horse snorted, and the bells around its neck chimed. Its rider's face was obscured, but Edward sought to make it out. Still, it was just a darkened blur and then it vanished, as did the beast and the carriage it pulled. He knew it was heading back to Jackson's livery.

"Sleep well, beast," he said and longed for slumber himself. The path the horse had taken was rutted and waterlogged, and Edward wished to pass it and not be mired down in the mud splattered on the ground. Noting the large divots of these fresh as well as older hoofprints, Edward felt as though he levitated above them nimbly without much effort or care. He bounded across the street in a way he imagined that he would have done as a boy, before his infirmity, before everything changed. He was floating in thought and spirit.

It was an illusion and it was an escape. He could, for a while, experience something outside the chains of his existence, far from who he was, had always been, the sickly teenager who had transformed into an unable man.

Not being able-bodied had prevented him from dying on the crimson hued fields of Lincoln's war, but the life he lived remained a battle for him, nevertheless.

Then Edward took another turn, this one a left, onto Pleasant Street, to return to his Clara and their tiny apartment. He gazed into the windows of Joslin's Big Store. There were so many items in there he coveted but could not afford, luxuries beyond his means. In the main display window, an ornate stroller taunted him. He desired the very best for himself, Clara, and the baby. He contemplated breaking the window and taking the item home, but reluctantly kept walking. In his current circumstances, he needed much more than a stroller.

Edward's mood turned dour again at the thought of having to be thrifty. *No more riding in carriages. I am stuck on my own two legs, one of which rarely cooperates. I know it's just an illusion, but when I'm drunk like this, I feel I can walk straighter than normal. There's no limp; I'm able-bodied, just like everyone else. It's a square deal. Things are even, and I can be the man I've imagined myself to be . . . but will never be.* Edward was fully aware that false hope had sullied his very existence from day one. But things were different this night. Edward could feel it in his gait, and the negative thoughts evaporated as he began to skip. He had not done so since being in his single digits. He leapt from step to step. His feet, now both equal in merit, ability, and possibility, barely touched the ground beneath him.

The moon above was full and vibrant, and yet Edward's thoughts were significantly dulled. He stared into his reflection at the window of the bank and paused a moment. This night he chose not to take notice of his own reflected image, but imagined he truly was Frank Converse instead. He smiled at the glass, and a visage of Frank smiled back at him. Edward was so joyful. If he were Frank, all his problems would vanish in an instance. Plus, beyond the glass, confined in these walls, was wealth beyond his imagination. *I am the son of a rich man, I am young, I am handsome, I am able,* he thought. "No, you are none of these things!" he shouted at Frank's image as it mutated back into his own. He winced and, being taken aback, found himself laughing and crying at the same time. Whether he should commit the sin about which he ruminated was as unclear as his own blurry image or the one he wished to project to himself. The internal argument was unbearable.

"I am not you," he whispered. "I was not bestowed any of those things, but I was given the will to take them if I must, and my need is great." His expression was reflected back to him in sadness, and he spoke in his normal voice: "But it is a hard choice for me to do to you what I am contemplating. Money could solve so many of my problems, but I'm also searching and hoping to find the wealth within myself as a person instead of the dark thoughts that consume me. I'm conflicted. Does any wealth exist within me?" Edward didn't know. He turned from the bank to the street and continued his journey home.

He thought of Frank. *As I skip across these streets tonight, my young friend is sound asleep, no worries upon his mind, and he will arise a bright boy in the morning, the town's eyes gleeful upon his warming glow. I love the boy, but I'm well aware that no matter how strongly I try to visualize myself as him, I am and will always remain just a poor reflection of young Converse. I can't fool my own mind. If only I could be Frank's equal—that's all I desire, to be like my friend and have all the opportunities he possesses. Is this so much to ask? Why have you denied me? Lord, where is my share?*

Edward attended a temperance meeting the next day. He strived to clear from his head the clutter of any bad thoughts which were building. Usually, he was spiteful about his limp, but today and on occasions like this, it conveniently disguised his intoxication. This was a mixed blessing. Without the limp and his circumstances, he would not need to drink as much, he thought. But the limp gave him an excuse, a cover. He could simply blend in by being who he was, the person people expected him to be, regardless of any ambitions he laid out for himself.

The grace experienced as he walked while inebriated was a facade, but he wondered if everything was merely a facade, a game in which his Maker enjoyed mocking him and raising his hopes up without any reward. Oftentimes, Edward believed the puppeteer cast the strings that pulled him along unevenly to occasionally give him the illusion that the wires were level, that he was similar and equal to all the other players upon the stage. But this was a cruel joke, one Edward would allow himself to play along with when very drunk, which was the usual way he ended each night.

God, why have you done this to me? I have sinful thoughts, and I know you are aware of them. But can you stop them or the dire actions that will grow from these intentions? You have all the power, but then why do I feel that you will allow me to do as I choose, no matter how terrible my decisions? I've made many horrible choices. You have not restrained me. Maybe I should take a drastic chance and become my own puppeteer, seize the opportunity if the moment presents itself clearly to me. I've arranged some strings out of sorts before without your approval, married and bedded the object of my desire when she was my friend's sweetheart. If only I can manipulate the strings to allow myself to escape this great debt that I inhabit, one that I know is not just monetary but also of spirit. Perhaps, to plunder the treasure I crave, I must ravage what remains of my once pure soul as part of the bargain.

Chapter Nineteen

THE EARLY TUESDAY morning began dreary, and William feared it would only worsen. He turned left. After crossing over the train tracks of the Boston and Maine Railroad, he paused. Turning south along Washington, directly down to Pleasant Street, would be the fastest route, but the barber decided to take a detour farther east. Eyeing the towering spire of the Methodist church, William walked along the Spot Pond Brook, the rising sun reflecting gently on the water. There were some ducks along the edge and herons as well.

The brook originated at Spot Pond a couple of miles north, and from the area where William walked, it winded along farther south, into the square of the town, then joined the Malden River and eventually spilled first into the larger Mystic River and finally into Boston Harbor. Following its boundaries, William passed the brook down the hill and then the dye works. The smell of chemicals was strong as it was on most mornings. Small snowflakes began to fall in the brisk air. After proceeding along Waverley for a short while, he arrived at his place of business.

He turned the key to unlock the modest entrance. He reached up with his walking stick and tapped the very base of the red-and-white-striped pole for luck, as he did each morning. With the fallen snow and Christmas just ten days away, it reminded him very much of a candy cane.

William began his morning ritual of preparing the shop. His goal was to make it tidy and presentable to the townsfolk, who expected him to be their waiting man. The day not having fully arrived, the barber lit a candle for illumination.

His shop faced north, away from the war. As he toiled in his trade, he often thought about how the South lay far behind him, but he also knew that it remained with him always, no matter how far he traveled from the place of his birth. It was distant in miles but always adhered to his thoughts. William prayed his family members and friends down there were safe. He had no way of knowing if they were, yet he was glad in his heart that at least he and his immediate family were out of danger, although feeling so caused him to experience a twinge of guilt.

The morning's light grew stronger, illuminating the square as the sun rose over the town hall, located on nearby Main Street to the east, but it appeared reluctant to shine as it mixed with ever-increasing snowflakes.

Pulling out his pocket watch sporadically, William swept away any remaining hair from the prior day's work. No matter how fastidious he was, remnants of the powerful men he served always remained. Preparing the tools of his trade, he turned the sign from "closed" to "open" at nine o'clock sharp. He would start the day alone, but Caleb would join him late morning to learn the trade, as he often did.

There were no immediate customers, and the barber had not expected one to appear. He knew the weather may have slowed down the progress of the beginning of the day for some. William prided himself on always opening on time regardless of any conditions. It would be bad business if a gentleman arrived first thing in the morning expecting service, only to find the barber absent or ill prepared. It was his deepest fear that these gentlemen would not return and word of William Shiloh's tardiness would play into some stereotype from which his business might never recover.

He peered out on the town patiently. George Bailey walked by and tried to clean the snow away from his scarf as he approached his tinware business just before the bank. William saw Mr. and Mrs. Bennett pushing their son, Wiley, in a baby carriage in the opposite direction, right in front of his premises. They had the wind at their backs and so seemed less put out from the storm than Bailey, who appeared very uncomfortable and in need of getting safely to his destination as quickly as possible before the storm captured him. It was just a short distance, but William could tell by his posture that Bailey's travel seemed intolerable as the Bennett family coasted by as if there were no snow at all. They were a nice family, but he was aware Bernadette, from prior interactions, was not one to trifle with on any occasion. She walked slightly ahead of her husband, who pushed Wiley's carriage carefully through the accumulating snow. George appeared more aware of the coming storm than his wife. William noted her frame was more suited to braving a storm than her smallish husband. However, from knowing George Bennett better than some and hearing about his early history of surveying in the West, as well as his time in Florida, William held respect for the man.

During a recent haircut, George Bennett had told him of a creature called an *alligator*, a swimming reptile with large, gnashing teeth. The barber found such a beast hard to fathom. The gentlemen of the town looked down on George Bennett, perhaps due to his small frame and reputation as a henpecked husband, yet William saw a hidden strength in Bennett that evaded any others' image of the man, including Bennett himself.

Charles Merrill exited the bank and turned west down the street. William knew he was headed to the train depot on Summer Street to travel into Boston on the ten o'clock train. Having been in for his haircut the day before, Charles had mentioned it to his superior, Elisha Converse, as the two men chatted away like the old friends they were. William knew it was Merrill's custom to go to Boston on bank business at least once a week or send young Frank Converse as a surrogate if he planned to remain at the bank.

Within ten minutes or so of turning his sign to "open," William had his first customer. The Count entered. He had arrived by the earliest morning train and planned to head back into Boston for a series of what he proclaimed would be sold-out performances as Hamlet. The Count was eager to tell the barber every brilliant detail about his preparation and acting method, and William prepared himself mentally to dutifully listen.

The shop's single chair faced away from the street, toward the inner wall with the carefully selected oval mirror. William positioned himself out of the way so his customer could see himself and the town behind him as the barber worked. William had another mirror higher up in the back of the shop, as well as a bell on the door, to allow him to notice if anyone entered the establishment. William would first look up at the mirror and then turn his head to see who had come in. The oval mirror in front of the customer gave a wider view of the street behind, but the edges were beveled, so images moving just to the right or just to the left were often blurred.

The Count sat down with his normal bit of flair after hanging his coat and scarf on the gold-tinted hooks by the door. "Barren winter with its wrathful, nipping cold."

"Excuse me, fine sir?"

The Count chuckled. "Just the words of the Bard himself. Sort of a messy morning, wouldn't you say, Shiloh?"

"I would indeed, sir."

William reached for the straight razor, picking it up from the fine linen on which it was placed on the countertop, left of the barber chair. He then walked back behind the Count.

"A shave, Your Excellency?"

"Yes. Bit of a hurry today. Make it quick, but be careful about it. You are skilled, Shiloh. It must truly be a great honor for you to shave a count like myself."

"It is indeed, sir!" said William, but he quickly bit his lip. Although a relative newcomer to the barbershop and the town as well, it was not the first time the man had stated this to William.

Everyone in the town obliged in calling him the Count, though they all thought such a moniker was of no true noble merit but merely to please the man's ego and delusions. Of course, the barber could not make this opinion clear to his customer, neither to his face nor in a more indirect way. Doing so would gain him nothing and perhaps would lose him all. The man could be a count if he wanted, even though he was mostly viewed by the townsfolk as a jackass. Elisha Converse had once stated to John Chapman, while the two were in the shop, that George Jones was often off chasing windmills.

William was not certain what this pertained to exactly but ascertained by its context that the man was an utter fool. But this was plain for all to see, he thought, windmills or not. "Shiloh, what do you call an itchy Indian, do you think?"

"I couldn't hazard a guess, Count."

"A scratchy Apache!"

"A fine observation, sir."

"It's not an observation, it's a joke. You're supposed to laugh." William laughed.

The Count rolled his eyes and said, "That's why I truly enjoy trying my material out on such as you, Shiloh. You and those of your kind are always an easy audience, and I always know what's in your heart. What you're thinking, every single thought. It's a simple thing, really. Albeit, you're not a paying audience, but I am compensating you for the fine work you do as a hairdresser."

"Thank you, Count."

Albeit, William thought. *I could give a cow's behind about your opinions or jokes.*

William believed the upside of the Count's particular delusion of royalty and importance was he always wanted to be presentable to his public. So, he was in for a shave on most mornings at William's barbershop and suddenly had become his most consistent customer because of this pining need for the adulation of others because of his fine grooming and appearance.

Mostly, the Count would take the train back to Boston to his home on Tremont Street, but oftentimes he stayed at the Evelyn Hotel, which lay not far from the depot. One thing William admired about him was, while he might be vain, he was not frugal, at least not in his business dealings with him. So, the barber would play to the Count's vanity and prejudice as a service which paid him handsomely in return.

The Count was very unusual in comparison to most white men, but he shared their most powerful attribute, the lightness of their pigmentation, which allowed him to be as eccentric as he desired.

That was the biggest contrast between the opposite shades the barber knew—one could act the fool freely without being on the end of a whip, while the other dared not. William bowed. "Indeed, a great honor, indeed, that you should grace such a humble shop as mine and allow a wretched soul such as myself to shave your handsome and royal face."

William knew that he had used "indeed" twice in one sentence, but Mr. Jones, the Count, mentioned to him once that "indeed" was a superb word, and so William sprinkled it into conversation as frequently as he could with this man. The customer was always right, even if he believed himself a man of royalty and renown, when clearly he was not.

As he had told Emily recently while they lay in bed together late one night, "The color of our skin gets us noticed right away, darling, so in the barbershop, it's not wise to bring any more attention to myself than necessary."

"You must understand your clients pretty well now that you've been cutting hair here for some years."

"I do. I'm aware who likes to be chatty and who I should remain quiet for as they read the papers. I know to treat the Count with even more reverence than I do other white men because the Count expects it, and he's pleased to always find it in my chair. I'm aware he may not find it anywhere else, even if the Count himself is oblivious to this fact. He is a fool, but I try to be a good Christian."

Emily said, "Yes, for a man like that, I would suggest you remember what the Scripture says: 'You shall love a stranger, for you were once strangers in the land of Egypt.'"

The Count was quite content with the barber's deferential attentiveness, which he provided on each and every encounter. He envisioned the barber's chair as his throne oftentimes as he sat there, surveying the town behind him in the long mirror. The Count thought of the queen in *Snow White* looking at her magic mirror and seeing all she wished to survey. He presumed he could see everything in the mirror, all his perceived subjects, and William was, indeed, his servant, his waiting man.

"Should I lower your chair back now, Your Excellency?" William held back a chuckle as he addressed him this way again, but he just smiled wider and tightened his lips so no sound could escape.

"Proceed!"

William gently lowered the lever and the chair reclined slowly, with the implied majesty he hoped the Count recognized. He did not lower him as far as most customers. He knew the Count would like to retain at least a small view of the town, his imagined fiefdom in the reflected surface. William noticed as he shaved the man that his eyes often darted to catch any image which interested him, often on the blurry edges of the mirror. William assumed the Count saw what he wanted to see. He himself would look at his smaller mirror and its clearer image from time to time, never staring as intently as the Count did at the images behind them but perhaps seeing more.

The barber was cognizant that the Count's view was backward and distorted, yet the Count was always confident that what he saw in reflection was accurate. William, on the other hand, who was of sound mind, never trusted any reflected image to be what it appeared, even if logic told him it must. Part of this reasoning was his position in society and this town. Caution was a way of life for him from dusk to dawn, and he thought he would sleep with one eye open if he could.

William rubbed a rich cream and some shaving oils onto the Count's face. He once had mentioned to the Count that he only applied the most exotic oils on him, since he was royalty, but in truth, he used the same products on all the gentlemen to whom he tended but placed some oil in a more ornate bottle for just this one customer. William allowed himself this lone deception to white men. Lying to them was dangerous, but it pleased the Count and it pleased William quite a bit as well. He knew he could get away with this one falsehood because the Count was so narcissistic that he wouldn't expect to be treated otherwise, especially by a Negro.

His mind focused again on his profession and the men he served. William had gained lots of insights into the workings of the rich, white world of politics and industry, but he never let on too much that he understood or allowed himself to seem overly curious about such issues. However, he was. William was intrigued; he strived to gain as much information as he could and learn how it could help him and his family in any possible way. His home was modest and sparsely furnished, but William Shiloh took pride in his ability to provide for himself and his family. He had traveled a long way, and the journey still had daily twists and turns, but William had no choice but to become skillful at navigating them, just as he had become skillful at using and maintaining his razor. With every motion, he held the customer's life, and, as a consequence, his very own, in his hands. He had heard mention of a Negro barber in the South who used his razor to slice the throat of a white man, killing him.

Of course, it was the Count who had disclosed this tale. William wondered if the man did so just to get a reaction out of him, and whether the story was fact or fiction. *The Count has a bit of a reputation as a blowhard, and other men who sit in my barbershop's chair have said so on many occasions. Although I'm considered a mulatto, I do not* have *the power and certainly never the intention of repeating such an insult out loud to the Count, or any other person of a fairer complexion. Black is black, even if some white has been mixed in somewhere along the line. And this fool thinks of himself not just as a white man, but as a white man of royal lineage. He can be a very precarious man indeed. Best to handle him with more care than any other. The Count is like a razor, dangerous and sharp, but I am practiced in how to handle such things and people better than most are,* thought William.

Sometimes, William was astounded he could hold a shaving razor right at the throat of a white man and let it linger there, just for a fraction of a second, as he pondered slicing it open. He would never actually do such a thing; he was a God-fearing man. And some of these men whose hair he cut had sons off fighting on the bloody battlefields of Pennsylvania and Virginia so that all his people might gain their freedom.

The Count had no heir apparent to his self-proclaimed title. No sons in either gray or blue. He had a daughter, whom he raved about—she was a famous actor of the stage like himself. William took the Count's word on this; he had never been to the theater, but he had learned quite a bit about the works of Shakespeare since the Count first sat in his chair. The man would often practice his lines as he was groomed on his mostly daily visits. However, William's favorite quote from the famous English playwright had not been spoken to him by the Count but by the deacon, in reference to the Count, on a day when Elisha was just coming into the barbershop as George Jones departed. "A fool doth think himself wise, but a wise man knows himself to be a fool."

"Who said that, Mr. Converse?"

"Are you familiar with William Shakespeare?"

"I'm a little more each and every day, sir."

That had made Elisha laugh. "I admire you, William, and I aspire to know my place in this life to prepare myself for the next, as I know you do as well. Some others may have other priorities or misconceptions about themselves."

The Count is chasing windmills, indeed, William thought. Peeking at his mirror, he studied the reflecting whiteness of the weather that blotted out his vision. Returning to the task at hand, he moved the razor sleekly and confidently across the Count's stubble, leaving smooth skin in its wake. It was automatic, the motion was fluid as if the razor were part of his anatomy.

He wished the rest of his life was as simple for him as giving a man a shave. But life was cruel, crueler to some, such as those in bondage. William always prayed that all men could be free and equal and wished that God would make it so. President Lincoln had promised in September of the previous year after the victory at the Battle of Antietam that the slaves in the South were to be freed within a hundred days.

William's hopes to hear about it in the papers by the end of that time had come true when the Emancipation Proclamation was issued on January 1, 1863. *Oh, what a fine day that was! And hopefully the boys of the Union can whip the Rebs so the country can be united again and our people can begin to eventually become a part of it. Each man is equal, as stated in Mr. Jefferson's Declaration of Independence. The war is vulgar,* William thought, *but necessary, even if there is such a terrible price to pay.* William had read reports of the huge numbers of dead and found it completely incomprehensible. Many were buried in mass graves. Others remained where they had fallen. The deacon had shown him some of Mr. Brady's battlefield photos.

William knew there was a colored regiment, the Fifty-Fourth, out of Boston, fighting and bringing pride to all colored folk. Several of the fine boys of Malden had been called to duty, and some came home wounded, missing an arm, a leg, or an eye. God had somehow spared their lives in this noble cause.

There had also been numerous bodies returned. William recalled one coffin in particular. Town officials, such as the treasurer and the postmaster, had met the coffin at the train depot. The victim's only kin, his sister, Bernadette Bennett, instead of being mournful, appeared deeply traumatized and uncomfortable. It was a closed casket, but there was quick gossip that surprisingly the corpse had not been mangled as many expected, as in the photos of Mr. Brady. Prescott Clampett was dead but retained no marked wounds upon his body.

The Count had much to say on the subject when it happened, as he always did, to anyone who would listen. William took it all in, since it was in his best interest to pay attention and to observe everything he could. Even if others did not notice his need to do so, he must safeguard his position by being diligent to the whims of his clients always. They considered the Count a fool, who believed things which may not have existed, like his noble birth, yet these same men also paid William Shiloh no heed. To them, he was just a simple, attentive barber who knew his place and minded his manners and business. William prayed that they could mildly respect him for that.

They could ridicule the Count as they wished, but he was still a white man, and though most likely not bestowed with the royal European prestige he proclaimed, he was still born with the birthright of being of European stock. The Count could make a spectacle of himself; the barber could not. Instead, his best bet, he knew, was to be barely seen. William told himself it was prudent to make them believe he unquestionably understood his place and always repeated this advice to himself. "Keep your mouth shut except to offer pleasantries to the gentlemen you serve. Also, trust them sparingly and with extreme caution only."

William shaved the Count and counted his blessings.

Chapter Twenty

LATER THAT MORNING, Edward slumped in his chair in the post office staring at the bank through the gathering snowflakes. He hadn't slept well, and his sight was still blurred from drinking the night before; the squall outside further impaired his vision, one layer of uncertainty piled upon another in his view of the world and his place within it.

He questioned his judgment and if he should have just stayed in bed this day and let Tenney tend to the office instead. Mindlessly, he shuffled the papers and letters on his desk but found this activity did not provide the needed distraction from his proposed evil intention. So, he started looking through the desk drawers, opening and then closing them repeatedly. Opening one, he beheld his enemy, the hated ledger. He shuddered and shut this drawer immediately, as if it surely portended a dire future for him in its altered figures. He would be found out! He would be fired; he would be destitute. Edward laughed uneasily, thinking that his own figure had been altered since childhood, and he had created scores more of uneven figures in his bookkeeping. Edward was rich in falsehoods but poor in actual funds.

There is no way to fix my bad leg; I will walk within its limitations and pains as long as I live. But there is a way to correct the false figures in my account book, and it is guarded by my young friend across the street. The manipulation of this book has been but a mere crutch for me whereas my solution is steps away, both my financial salvation and my moral ruin.

At seven minutes past ten, Edward ambled by the bank and then paused and examined every particular through the window in detail, going over each several times in the moments he stood there.

Most obvious was a large stack of money placed neatly on the counter. The pile was immense, each individual bill a plethora of solutions for his myriad financial woes. Edward had watched intently as Charles Merrill left the bank and headed toward the depot during the hour prior. He now observed the cashier's young protégé, Frank Converse, sitting at his desk, writing, apparently lost in thought. His eyes lingered for a moment upon Frank. *Studious and kind*—those were the words that came to mind as Edward viewed his friend.

He could turn around, or better yet, walk far away from this temptation. The boy was pure, but unfortunately, Edward Green was aware he himself was not. Merrill would not return anytime soon. Frank was all alone, and Edward was confident that he trusted his dear friend, the postmaster, implicitly. The boy would have no reason to suspect or fear him. The terrible act would be, should be, easy, Edward hoped; like snapping a chicken's neck, the result would be final for one of them . . . and perhaps, he worried, in time, for the other as well.

The inclement weather kept the streets mostly clear of other townsfolk. Edward had not spotted a single soul as he wandered out and about. With so many troubles and stresses revolving in his mind, Edward perceived there was finally a chance to silence them all for good. His bills were overwhelming; he had gained an extension on paying the $500 bill overdue for the schoolbooks. This was due in mere weeks, the first of the new year. Mr. Gray from the main post office in Boston had already visited him several times unexpectedly, including once in the week prior, and implied to Edward clearly that he would surrender his position as postmaster if he missed this deadline. The publisher also threatened legal ramifications if it was not paid promptly.

These debts were one end of the rope tugging at him; the knowledge that his baby would arrive in mere days was the other end, and together, as if a garrote, they suffocated him as each thread grew tighter and closer to their due dates.

Part of him knew that if he was successful in loosening one of their ends, he would only tighten the other and choke, nonetheless. Yet, Edward felt there was no other choice than to try.

His hands trembled. Three mouths to feed on scraps and overdue debts, coupled with a strong possibility of the loss of all his income, severely contrasted in his mind with the lavish lives of the Converse family, which appeared to Edward to be an infinite buffet of riches and opportunities without end.

God, you are unjust and unfair in your treatment of me. I'm impelled to do this horrible act. I don't want to, but you've given me no other choice!

Edward walked back to the post office with determination and, without hesitation, opened the drawer that contained the now-loaded revolver he had purchased in Boston. From his window, he surveyed the street and watched a couple of men enter the bank and exit while he nervously alternated the revolver from one hand to the other, trying to gather his courage and stifle his conscience.

Fifteen minutes later, Edward watched patiently as the horse-car conductor, Foster Lichfield, carried a pair of ice skates into the bank.

After Lichfield departed, the postmaster gasped a difficult, deep breath and walked across the street. Edward did his best to steel his nerves as he entered the bank, but he was disheartened to see that the conductor had placed the skates just inside the door. Edward patted the gun in his pocket repeatedly, reassuring himself that the revolver was still there, and adamantly convinced himself of what he needed to do with it. However, his eyes kept falling upon the skates. He resented them. He feared their owner could return at any minute to retrieve them, on the chance he had left them there by accident.

There was nothing Edward could do. The moment was too risky; the peril seemed to outweigh the reward.

"Can I have change for this bill, please?"

"Sure thing," said Frank as he grasped the bill and turned away toward the cash drawer. Edward took notice of this fact. *Perhaps I won't have to look directly in his eyes if I commit the act,* he thought.

Frank returned with the change. "Here you go," he said and paused as if he wished to say something further but was overcome by reluctance.

Edward said, "Okay, Frank, I got to get going, but I will be back."

"I look forward to it, my friend. Eddie, I um," he stammered.

"What is it?"

"I desire your counsel on a matter of great importance to me. There's something, um, I want to talk to you about. I truly need your advice, Eddie."

"I'll be damned, Frank. I told you I'd be back, and I will. We can settle matters then." He offered a half smile and departed.

Edward felt nervous and uncertain, impatient with his circumstances, and so returned to the post office head bent down. He chided himself for being rude to Frank. He placed the gun back in the drawer and covered it with papers, then hesitated a moment before closing the drawer. *Out of sight, out of mind,* he thought and hoped.

He remembered helping Frank when he was but a lad, spending so much cherished time with him. *That was when I was a good soul,* he thought. Now Frank had grown, was a man almost; he was certainly Edward's peer. And most importantly of all, he was his friend. *Maybe it's not meant to be, no need to go through with it, I'm in the clear now and can't do it. Or can I? But what if Lichfield came back for his skates at the wrong moment? Then it would have all been for naught. My debts wouldn't be paid, and my troubles would be exponential. Clara and our child-to-be would be castoffs inheriting nothing from me but shame. Frank would be dead for no reason, and I would be signing my own death warrant as well.* Edward opened the drawer next to the one he had shut. He removed a bottle and took a long swig. He wished he possessed as fine a whiskey as the Count had at the tavern, but this cheap, watered-down bottle would do just fine in the moment to calm his nerves.

His thoughts returned to the day he had buried his father. Frank had been greatly affected by Reuben's passing as he also, for the first time, contemplated the inevitable demise of his own father. Death was a scary thing, a terrible thing. And now Edward was about to suddenly and violently bring about his friend's death. *Murder? What am I doing?* Edward took another sip. He thought instead of the debt, the endless debt. He needed a way out, and now it lay right in front of him, a terrible solution but a solution, nonetheless. If he had a shovel, Edward was certain he would be halfway to China, but at this point, he may as well find hell on his way there since the size of the hole he was intending to dig for himself was indeed vast. *If I go through with this, will it lead directly to my fiery damnation, or am I damned already?*

Uncertain of the answer, at a few minutes to eleven Edward placed the bottle back in the drawer, closed it, and opened the other drawer and took the gun out once more, securing it in his coat pocket. Soon, Edward was back on the street, walking toward the bank, even more determined to plunder the money and secure a way to free himself of his debt.

The wind blew snowflakes directly at him. He opened his mouth and a large flake landed on his tongue. It was gone in just a moment but in that very second, just for a fraction of an instant, Edward felt alive.

He entered the bank again. Lichfield's skates remained in the same spot. He believed they were mocking him. Even worse, of all the people he could encounter, Mr. Gray entered the bank and engaged him in small talk, as if ambushing him. Edward was in no mood for talking, and the conversation quickly turned to a topic he didn't wish to address at all, a matter that he and Mr. Gray had already discussed ad nauseam. "I was planning to talk to you at the post office when I saw you crossing the street to the bank. You are running out of time, Mr. Green. When will you have the payment owed for the schoolbooks?"

"Soon," said Edward as his mind whirled. Two men stood before him: one to whom he owed a great debt; the other possessed of the means to pay that debt many times over, though only with unavoidable violence on Edward's part.

He sensed that either God was taunting him or the devil was now seizing the strongest opportunity to finally poach his soul. Each stood upon his shoulders, but the balance, like that of Edward's legs, was greatly uneven. Being confronted by Mr. Gray and his demand for payment reminded him directly of all his financial troubles, his need to take care of his wife and the baby to come, his desire to live as others could, as the Converses easily did with their big mansion and none of the worries or concerns that Edward dwelt in every day—from the moment his eyes opened to the moment they closed.

Mr. Gray eyed him warily. "I will see you in a couple of weeks to collect the schoolbook money. You have until then. Good day."

"Good day," murmured Edward.

Edward heard Mr. Gray greet Frank, and the two began to chat about the success of the Rubber Shoe Company.

As the bank's clock stuck eleven, Henry Stone entered to deposit a check. At the threshold, he stood aside for the postmaster. "Hello, Mr. Green," said Stone.

Edward made no reply as he passed him and exited the bank. Stone nodded at Frank and took a seat to peruse a newspaper until the clerk was through talking to his current customer.

Edward wanted to get far away from Mr. Gray immediately and all his financial concerns as soon as possible.

"Your father's a very prosperous man; he knows how to manage money properly, unlike some in this town," were the words Edward heard as he was mere steps from the bank. His face reddened in rage. The mocking tone of Mr. Gray's voice remained echoing in his head as he entered back into his office.

Edward put his gun back in the drawer. Feeling overheated from his thoughts and from sweating more than he was accustomed to, he took off his wet coat, placed it by the stove to dry it, and shivered. Edward remembered there were a couple of warmer, dry coats in the lost-and-found box in the back room. He was about to walk back to retrieve one when he noticed a strangely clothed man gazing into the post office window. Edward walked toward the door to see if the man needed assistance.

"Hello, sir, excuse me, please. My name is Alessandro Santilli. It is my first time in your town. I was visiting here with my brother, Gianni, and our friend Pietro Caso when the weather turned. They departed before I did. I'm unable to find them or my way back to the depot, where I expect them. I don't want to miss the next train or keep them waiting. Can you direct me, please?"

This man's tongue's as foreign as his attire, thought Edward, looking at the man's clothing carefully and calculating a bold idea. "Please come out of the cold and warm yourself in my establishment," he said, putting on the most gracious smile he could muster.

"Mr. Postmaster, I also had a letter I wished to post for my brother, but I have misplaced it. I suppose I will just tell him he will have to write another as soon as we begin our journey home. Thank you so very much for your hospitality." The man entered the post office, and Edward sealed the door against the outside world once more. He eyed the stranger from head to toe and considered him fully. There was no question, he was someone who clearly stood out in this town, and Edward continued to ponder how he could use this fact to his advantage.

"You're welcome. It's a cold day . . . Oh, I see you've an awful big tear in your coat," he said.

The stranger glanced down, frowning. "Yes, it was once a fine coat, but it has traveled with me a long way and so it has its wear and tear."

"Besides the tear, it appears to me to be an excellent coat. I have never glimpsed another like it."

"In my country, it is very common. My brother, Gianni, has the exact same one, as does our friend. When we leave Boston and before we sail from New York, I plan to purchase one in the American style if time permits."

"Oh, would you be interested in trading it for one of mine?"

"You have more than one? This is a rich country indeed!"

At this, Edward went to the back storeroom, and in a few moments, he returned and set down two coats upon his desk. The stranger looked shocked but then after taking off his own, tried on one coat and then the other. The two were very similar, one being a slightly lighter shade of brown and having more buttons. After a couple minutes, Edward said, "Which one do you choose?"

"I'm not sure. I can't decide."

Edward scratched one of his thick side-whiskers. *I need to get this over with quickly,* he thought but said instead, "Then you can take both of them, if you also throw your fur cap into the bargain."

"The hat is very old and worn. You sure you want it?"

Edward scratched his other side-whisker. "I very much do." The coats he was trading away had been abandoned by other visitors who hadn't returned for them, so they were of little consequence to Edward, but these new items of clothing could have a value their current owner would not recognize in them at all. But the postmaster did. Once the trade was completed, Edward became curious. Knowing he would never see this stranger again, he asked, "Where are you from?"

"I live in Brussels, but I am from Bologna," said the man. Edward was unaware of both of these places, but he suddenly felt a hunger in his belly, so he did not pose any further questions. He decided he would eat some bread after the man left; perhaps that would help him think more clearly since he had not consumed anything since breakfast. Thanking Edward, the man left with directions to the depot, wearing a newly acquired coat and carrying another on his arm.

Edward put on the stranger's coat. *It doesn't quite fit, but I am not planning on wearing it more than once.* Next, he placed the fur cap upon his head and agreed that the stranger was correct—the cap was worn and flimsy. Yet Edward was still enamored of these items. While the fit was not perfect, they were quite warm, much more so than his own winter attire. Edward looked in the mirror at his image and didn't recognize the man before him at all. He sipped from a milk bottle and then bit into the loaf his friend Marshall had delivered to him the day before.

Maybe I can change who I am on the outside to fool myself about who I am on the inside and forget, at least for a few crucial minutes, how very much I love the boy.

Before leaving, Edward looked out the window to survey the street. He was annoyed to see that the snow had not deterred activity as much as he had hoped. He noted George Bailey entering the bank and exiting a couple of minutes later. John Rich left the barbershop and was walking east on Pleasant Street, just across from the post office, where he nodded at Bailey talking to a man outside Edward's view beside the bank.

Edward looked up at the clock, which stood at 11:24. Seeing Rich move farther up the street and out of eyeshot, and then Bailey and the other gentleman travel farther down Middlesex Street, Edward exited the post office. His pace was slow, more so than usual, but with a new, more defined purpose. He projected his image outwardly as well as inwardly as someone else entirely. Edward entered the bank and, seeing it empty besides Frank, took a deep breath.

"Good to see you, Eddie. You look different. When you approached, I almost didn't recognize you. It's been busy this morning. You didn't say anything on your last visit. I thought maybe you were mad at me."

"I wasn't. I'm not mad . . . at you," Edward said, and he meant it. "I would like some change for my twenty-dollar bill, please. Are you able—"

"I am," Frank answered before Edward finished his sentence. Frank got up from his desk and turned his back to reach for the change and the loose bills he kept close by.

Edward scampered forward. He entered through the small gate behind the counter. His own footsteps almost caused him to stumble. He didn't want to hesitate. He had been hesitating too long. Setting the fire hadn't worked; his debts remained, and his desperation had only grown.

Do it, he thought. There would be no witnesses. He had tried his best to make sure of that. *Do it,* his thoughts demanded again. He was directly behind the boy.

At that moment, Frank turned his head over his right shoulder. Edward raised his revolver and pulled the trigger instinctively, as if he had been threatened, as if he were responding to an attack instead of perpetrating one. He was in shock as the pistol exploded. Edward recoiled both in body and in spirit. The right side of Frank's head shattered, and the noise of the impact somehow seemed louder to Edward than the firing of the pistol. The boy fell.

"Eddie!" Frank cried.

The terrible deed being started, and knowing there was no going back, no undoing it, Edward stepped closer, with the boy now on the ground, his head angled to one side but still looking up at him, and fired once more as Frank wore an expression mixed with confusion and pain.

Edward would never know what Frank wanted to discuss with him. He wondered about what it could be for an instant, maybe it was about a girl, but all he could see was Frank's agony and all he could hear was his friend calling his name. Edward did not want to see that look or hear that cry anymore, but he was aware that neither would ever depart him.

Chapter Twenty-One

THE LARGE CLOCK on the wall was at 11:31. Knowing the children would be exiting the nearby schoolhouse soon, Edward seized all the money he had spied through the window earlier and the larger sum he discovered in the drawer, stuffing it in one of his substantial pockets while placing the gun in the other.

Lightheaded, he stumbled in his haste to flee and fell upon Frank's reading desk. He heard the wood of the chair creak and break. There was a gash on his elbow, seeping blood through the coat. Edward dabbed it with his other sleeve until matching maroon circles spiraled on each. He steadied himself and stood, taking a labored breath.

Time to move, to get away from these actions and their possible consequences to my life and the definite consequences of them on my soul, he thought. Not sure he could escape either forever, Edward dragged his bad leg behind his good one and walked outside.

Since he was attired in these unusual clothes, he decided not to immediately return to the post office so as to continue his ruse of being a stranger. As Edward trudged away in the snow, his head was thumping, his mind racing. He believed the snow ridiculed him. *A million flakes falling to the ground and not a sound from any,* he thought. The silence crashed around in his eardrums. Edward's tracks were disguised as if he had never walked the earth, although he worried now that this sin of the murder of a man who was the closest thing he ever had to a brother, more so than his own flesh and blood, would doom him to walk the world forever.

He was Abel, and I've become Cain. This nation is divided, brother versus brother in Lincoln's great war. Sadly, Frank was collateral damage to the woes placed before me. His obstacles were scarce. His path clear, until I pointed my pistol at him, and his earthly journey ended while I have now condemned myself to being a hapless nomad, according to Scripture.

"And so, cursed shall you be by the soil that gaped with its mouth to take your brother's blood from your hand. If you till the soil, it will no longer give you strength. A restless wanderer you will be on the earth."

Your words, your judgment—but I have a will of my own. I'm a sinner, but, God, you've indeed played your part in my sin by stacking the sides unevenly. I was doomed from the meagerness of my birth. Certainly, from my youth, my injured leg, shorter than the other, always holding me back, keeping me a step behind. Your chosen son of Malden walked carefree with nothing ever restraining him—the world was Frank's for the taking.

I killed him. I'm sorry. I miss him, and it has only been a minute or so since I shot my pistol those two times. My ears are still ringing a bit, my conscience a lot more. You can condemn me to hell now, but you have condemned me long before this sin or any other blemished my soul. You loved him more than you loved me. He is dead. I'm alive, and for the moment, I'm quite rich.

The snowy imprints that trailed the man who had just spoken to his God were uneven and placed hither and yon in an odd pattern, as if the walker, unsure in his steps, were trying to travel in opposite directions at the same time. It was dark for midday; the gaslights that could have illuminated Edward's path away from his crime would not be lit for several hours more.

He crossed the street toward the church. A black dog with white markings approached him and stood in his path. "Get out of here, you mutt!" shouted Edward.

The dog considered the man before him, then raised his leg and urinated in Edward's direction before trotting to the other side of the street.

In the distance, Edward could hear the steam engines of the Boston and Maine train entering the depot and the faint sound of the hoofs of the horse railroad trailing almost outside his hearing range. He believed the stranger he exchanged coats with would soon be departing on the arriving train, never to return to Malden.

A strong gust caused one end of his scarf to fly backward; the remainder was wrapped tightly, holding on as best as it could to his bare neck. He glanced over his shoulder at the fleeing fabric. There was no visible tether in the storm, but Edward sensed something pulling him. Was he being drawn to the barber pole, which angled out several feet toward Pleasant Street into the snowstorm like a fishing rod? Edward visualized himself being flung backward by the wind and his scarf wrapping around William Shiloh's pole like the red-on-white stripes which twirled around it. There was a symmetry of red on white. Blood and snow, stain and purity. The pole transfixed him like a siren, but Edward struggled to deny its call. Coughing, he secured the scarf as well as he could in the circumstances. He needed to get off the street. Away. Edward thought he glimpsed in the corner of his eye, the dark face of the barber in the window beneath the pole.

No, it can't be. Just a shadow. I can't make out his face in this storm; it's only the back of the barber's head I glimpse. If this is so, the nappy hair can neither see me nor ascertain the hideous sin I have just committed.

Shiloh, Edward convinced himself, surely had not taken notice of him, had no reason to do so. Edward traveled back and forth on this street several times a day, every day. His limp rendered him distinctive but after a while one got accustomed to it. Edward blended in with all the other townsfolk, and now he was dressed in disguise. Confident, he kept moving. He considered himself as unremarkable as any snowflake.

The snow drifted to the ground in great purpose and abundance. But the innocent blanket created on that morning when he awoke and throughout the forenoon, as he thrice walked toward the bank, registered his opportunity, and then seized upon it, would eventually melt, evaporate into the sky, and be gone as suddenly as it had appeared on the earth—as if it never existed.

Oblivious to the passage of time, sadness and guilt fell upon Edward in equal measure, just as the snow continued to do. *I stole Chapman's sweetheart, his love, the wife promised to him, and now I have stolen Converse's life as well. I've left only heartbreak, deception, theft, and death in my wake. A blizzard could not cover my many sins, in God's eyes or my own, for that matter. It appears likely that I am damned—utterly, entirely damned.*

There were too many thoughts in Edward's head, ramblings, mixing him up. But one thought stood out more than any others. The world was white, but his vision was hued crimson.

I pray there is no afterlife. It would only include more misery for a wretch like me, and you, dear Frank, would exist forever with the knowledge of what I've done to you. Even though my footprints betray me, at least for a few moments, until they are discreetly layered over by this snowstorm, there's only forward for me and no backward, and yet in a way, I now feel truly rudderless.

He kept moving, slow and steady, one foot dragging behind the other reluctantly, as it had for most of his life, and then repeating. Edward strode directly into the wind. He wanted to wrap his scarf tighter, cover his face from the gusts that confronted him, but he was afraid the two precious lumps in his pockets might escape. His hands, like sentinels, stayed on guard, pressing tightly against his coat pockets even as his scarlet scarf flung freely, carelessly, in the wind. A gust from the side wrapped it tightly for a moment around his neck, causing him to cough, to search for his breath.

After a few moments, the scarf fell limp until the next gust. Clara had knitted the tartan pattern so lovingly. She told him it was to keep him comfortable during his various errands around the town until he could return home and be safe and cozy with her and their child growing within her.

Would either of them love him if they knew what kind of man he was, especially the man he was now in this very moment, a robber and a murderer? Every one of his actions was for Clara and the baby to come, to create for them and himself the sort of lives he thought they deserved. Edward sought out any solution he could find to pay his debt, retain his position, and provide for his family. He was not a man able to travel far, and a pile of money, just across the street, in plain view before his young, close, trusting friend was a temptation too strong to resist. It was his for the taking if he was able to also steal Frank's life, and under the dire circumstances, he was.

The money currently in one pocket had been the result, the Smith & Wesson revolver, which had destroyed the smiling face of his dear friend, had been his terrible means to do so.

Looking askance at both sides of the street, Edward thought of himself as both puppet and puppet master, interchangeable and intertwined. He was in control of his actions—and yet pulled strongly by a secondary means of which he was sure he did not hold a single string. What had he done? Why had he done it? The why was easier to understand. Necessity or desperation, or a mixture of the two, like rain and snow, one a part of the other but the second different altogether.

Edward crossed the street once more and approached the town's grammar school and thought of all those inside, so small, so free of sin. Wasn't that how Frank had been? How he himself had once been as well? If he tarried much longer, these hungry children would gather among the storm of flakes and guilt that surrounded him. This worried him. Spying a single figure emerge from the school, Edward fled into the alley between the structure and Swain's photography studio for cover.

He will see me. I'll have to kill a second boy in mere minutes.

Young Robert Merrill passed within feet of him. Close, too close. Edward relaxed the grip on his pistol. Robert was the son of the cashier of the bank he had just robbed. The boy was certainly heading there to see his father. This had all been for naught. Edward was certain now he would be caught. He was doomed. There would be a search, and they would find on his person the money stolen as well as the gun that had stolen the life of Frank Converse. He would be arrested. He would be hanged.

Perhaps it was best to go east, leave the town, enter North Chelsea and go to the long beach there, leave the shore and wander into the ocean until he was no more, search for the land of Nod. He took a deep breath and decided against this course of action. He could return to the thought if he chose, but he desired to get out of the storm and settle the storm of his mind; the external and internal were mixing and causing him confusion and deep anxiety. Edward could not escape from the latter, but he could find refuge from the former until it passed. He was lost in a sea of snowflakes, regret, and wandering.

But the crime was about to be discovered. He must hide the money immediately, and Edward knew exactly where to do so. But it would involve even greater risk of his capture, for he must go directly by the scene of the crime once more.

He followed the Merrill boy east on Pleasant Street. Edward stayed at a safe distance, but he was not capable of keeping up with the fourteen-year-old, even if he desired to do so. Ahead of him, he watched young Merrill enter the bank. Edward peered into the windows as he strode by, observing the boy go behind the counter. Thankfully, Edward did not have to behold his victim, his close friend, once more, but he knew this child was now doing so.

Edward quickened his pace. Thinking only befuddled him; better to just walk, but his thoughts spun around like the weather that surrounded and smothered him, snowflake upon snowflake. Edward imagined these as God's frozen tears, punishment for smiting his favored son. His legs were sore from the increased tempo of his stride, the bad leg that was always ginger, and the good one that had to pull along its burden and begrudged it for their shared responsibility.

Normally, he hated, loathed, his limp but now thought he deserved it for he had killed his friend. "I've lived my punishment before the crime. I was born with original sin, and now it has come to its fruition," he muttered under his breath. "I didn't think; I reacted to seeing young Frank alone in the bank. I had played with him when he was but a child, thought well of him. I needed a way out and, Frank, you became my sacrificial lamb."

There were too many debts to pay. The noose was closing in on him quicker than he could think, compelling him to act. But killing Frank? "There was no choice, stop your groveling! The deed is done," he told himself. The boy was no more, but his murder, his loss of life could be, would be, the gain, the result Edward needed, or so he hoped.

Edward arrived at the volunteer fire department. He climbed the stairs to the top floor and immediately noticed the old fire hose with the holes pierced into it, the failed instrument of his earlier plan to rid himself of his debt. He finally possessed the funds to solve his problems, but he must stash them away for now. Leaving a scant few bills in his pocket, he placed the remainder of the money in an old boot, securing it under a floorboard.

When he exited back onto Pleasant Street, Edward detected a man inside the bank moving so frantically as to be oblivious to his nearby presence. Shivering, he wondered if he should go home. They had no evidence he was the criminal, no one had seen him as far as he knew, and even if the money he had just concealed was eventually found, it could not be connected to him as all the town's men had access to the volunteer fire department. Clara would be surprised to see him home at this time of day, and he could not look her in the eye so soon after what he had done, even if it had been done for her. No, he could not, he would not. Had he left tracks? Had the barber spotted him? Had the Merrill boy seen him? Exhausted, Edward crossed the street, went into the post office, and, his odyssey over, crouched on the floor behind his desk.

Robert Merrill, excused early from school due to illness, entered the bank, expecting his father to be there. Not seeing anyone outside the counter, he wandered inside and found Frank Converse lying upon his back on the floor, groaning as if in great pain. He noticed some blood running down his head and supposed Frank had fallen in a fit. Robert ran out in search of medical aid and, not finding any of the three physicians who resided near the bank, he called on the assistance of several local storekeepers.

He first rushed into the grocery store of Charles Shepard, near the bank. "Help, please go to the bank! Frank has got a fit, and there's a horrid, great hole in the side of his head." A minute after Robert exited the bank, James Buckley arrived to make a deposit. When he discovered Frank on the floor, he attempted to tend to the wound, and then also left for help. Moments later, the grocer arrived. He was shocked that Frank was still breathing, due to his stricken condition and the pallor of his skin. He presumed Frank was in a fit due to the blood on his face, which, as Robert Merrill had exclaimed, looked as if were "bursting to a boil."

When Shepard carefully lifted Frank's head and shoulders, his head was bleeding, but not profusely. There was a small amount of blood on the floor, and all in one place.

"Frank?"

The grocer could tell he was recognized, but Frank remained silent.

"Frank, what happened? Did you fall?"

Frank, with great effort, twisted his head an inch to the right and then several seconds later, twisted it to the left. Having no more strength in him, it remained there.

Shepard scanned the room for any evidence as to what could have oc-curred. He first noted there appeared to be no sign of a struggle, but then his eyes fell upon Frank's broken chair. He wondered if the boy had fallen out of it and crawled behind the counter. He thought this odd and discounted the possibility.

"Frank," he said again, but the boy remained motionless, with the exception of his left pupil, which darted up toward the grocer. The boy groaned, a word attempting to form on his twitching lips. "Ehhhhhh . . ." But no second syllable followed to complete the name of the friend who had attacked him.

Chapter Twenty-Two

*G*OD'S HAND HAS *afflicted me with this limp,* Edward thought, still hunkering down behind his counter, *but I've stained myself by my own hand with the blood of my brother. The money I sought is now mine. Some of it will be spent in short order to settle my many debts. Clara will not know or suspect. And hopefully, nobody else in town will either. I should keep the gun on my person for a little while, just in case. Better to have a means to defend myself if I am suspected, or even worse, captured.*

Edward willed himself to peek a couple of times over his desk at the bank and the crowd of men gathering there, which grew as the time passed. He crouched closer to the floor. He had left the door unlocked. Part of him did not care if someone entered or if he was caught. Maybe that was for the best; he was already guilty in God's eyes, and there was no hiding in that, not even if a single man, woman, or child of Malden gazed upon him and did not recognize his sin.

Edward knew it was true, and that was all that mattered. He reached into his pocket and removed the instrument of his folly, the revolver. He held it for a moment, wanted to caress it, but was afraid to do so, and instead placed it on the floor beside him. It was still warm, cooling with the temperature of the cold world, but its barrel still produced some heat. It was subsiding, but the warmth remained. Maybe Frank was the same way, subsiding, cooling slowly and then his life fading away entirely.

There was still some snow melting on Edward's face; he had only been inside for a minute or so. He curled up as tight as he could, as if in a cocoon, to warm himself. Edward believed the second volley had ended it, but there was no way to be sure. He practiced target shooting in the woods near Melrose before the murder, but this was a living, breathing thing, this was a person, this was his friend, this was his brother. He hoped Frank died right away, when the second shot entered him, with more precision than the first.

But how was he to know if he had not? Edward needed to grab the money and flee as quickly as he could. After firing two rounds; he could not risk a third. The first seemed so noisy, he was shocked that the entire town did not greet him at the door as he set his mismatched feet outside in the snowy abyss after he fired the second. But if Frank was still alive, by cruel fate, suffering in the blur of time—had it been minutes? It felt like it had taken hours for Edward to get to this fallen position on the floor.

"Eddie!"

The last word Frank would ever utter, Edward's nickname, reserved for only those dearest to him, echoed in the postmaster's eardrums, causing him to weep as he lay on the floor. His beloved friend was shocked, unsuspecting of Edward's motives, his needs, and his jealousy. Edward had shrouded them all so well from Frank, but now they had exploded in such utter, pure violence upon him.

If only, he thought over and over, he had been born a Converse instead of a Green. If Frank and he were blood brothers, he would have protected him always, doted on him as he once did, as he always intended to do. But the two were not blood, and Edward would never be his equal in any way. He only by chance had been Frank's peer. Edward stirred and tried to warm his body by contracting further into himself. *If I'd have been born Frank's equal, I wouldn't have done this terrible deed. Even if I were still a cripple, at least I would be a Converse cripple, and any animosity I held toward my younger brother would never lead to murder since I would hold no financial concerns,* thought Edward, feeling his life had always been about monetary matters from the moment he exited the womb.

Frank's face was floating in his head; first the fresh-faced, happy youth he knew so well and then the very epitome of anguish as Edward's rage and desperation transformed the kind expression of Frank Eugene Converse into one of pure terror—his friend's eyes shocked and afraid as Edward Green's gun shot him and then pointed at him again, preparing for a second shot.

Confusion, sadness, pain. These were the feelings Edward sensed inside himself. He never before could have imagined the depths of misery he viewed in those last, terrible moments, his friend's pain, a life he assumed was a vessel of tranquility now torn asunder by the brutality committed by one the victim held as a confidant.

Edward took the Smith & Wesson in his hand without a thought. Time had warped for him; to his mind, he hadn't been sure he could kill his friend, though he was certain he would do so once he saw the large stack of cash and Frank alone in the bank. Now to kill himself, there was no thought at all. His life held no merit. Edward pressed the pistol to his temple and squeezed the trigger without the hesitation he had shown Frank when he perceived the circumstances were more dire. There was an awful feeling of finality and then an unexpected sound. The chamber was empty. Edward was still alive, although he did not want to be.

Most likely, Frank was dead. If there was a kind God, Frank was dead. Even if he, Edward Green, was an instrument of the devil, a kind and just God surely would have taken Frank and made him a special angel in heaven immediately, without causing further suffering. A just God would deem it so, and Edward hoped a just God would continue to treat Frank as kindly in the afterlife as he had done until Edward caused the utter end of his mortal one. Edward held no idea where his own soul began or ended. It was lost, but he hoped the Lord would reward Frank in death, as he had chosen to do so for him in life.

No matter if the gun still has bullets in its chambers; it is useless to me now. It worked fine to get me into this mess, but when I needed it most to get me out of it, to mercifully relieve me from the pressures upon myself, it chose not to do so.

The door from the street swung open, startling Edward, but he lay perfectly still. There was silence, but even on the floor, sheltered by the counter, he could feel the cold winter air entering the space, enveloping him.

"Mr. Green, are you there?"

How had they come so soon? Had he been caught so quickly? His act was so brazen—a daylight robbery done haphazardly. No, the voice was that of a boy. He recognized it as the one he had come close to muting by the school—Mr. Merrill's son, though it could have easily been Frank's from just a couple of years ago, before his voice changed to its lower tone. The boy had become a man, at least for a short period. Frank had blossomed like a butterfly, whereas, no matter his own efforts, Edward believed he always remained just an unfulfilled caterpillar.

"Mr. Green, are you there? We need you! Frank needs you! Please help him!" Another moment passed in silence and dread. Edward's muscles grew rigid.

I can't help him. I can't even help myself, he thought.

Then the bell rang, and the cold air withdrew, and whomever it was, young Merrill, or a phantom of Edward's own conscience, was gone.

After the door closed, Edward could still hear the voice back on the street, seeking help from others. Edward was alone. But more doors would now surely open for him—that is why he had committed the terrible deed in the first place. He put the gun down. Its service rendered, its task done, he reached in his other pocket and pulled out the wad of cash, several Malden Bank notes, a partial amount of the blood money stolen, yet more than he ever possessed before this day. He spread the bills across his chest in a small pile. *God be damned.* The moment Edward thought this, he was terrified and wanted to take it back, but part of him felt a small joy in finally allowing himself to express it.

Edward paused a moment, confirming there was no cold breeze entering again from the outside. The door was secure and the wind ceased. "God be damned," he said in a volume just above a breath and then once more in his normal speaking voice as he gained more confidence. He had not been given what he wanted, but he had taken it. The Lord had not helped him, so he had helped himself.

There were many debts for Edward to pay, both in this world and the next, but at long last, he had now secured the means to live well in this life. Clara and the baby could receive nice things from him, maybe even that fancy baby carriage in the window of Joslin's Big Store he pondered stealing. The cash, Edward thought, could at last allow him to be the husband and father he yearned to become.

At close to a quarter of twelve, Foster Lichfield, the conductor, returned to the bank to thank Frank for letting him borrow his ice skates. Shocked to see his friend prone on the floor in such a dire state, Foster said, "He needs fresh air."

"You may be right; let's lift him toward the door."

The conductor clutched the boy's legs just under the knees, and Charles Shepard grasped under the arms. The two awkwardly lifted the boy. Frank's head banged against the grocer's chest, and he moaned fearfully as they started carrying him toward the street. Bleeding profusely from the temple, Frank's hands intermittently scraped against the floor.

Robert had run into every storefront nearby for help. When he returned, all those whom he pled with directly were present. William would have answered his plea for assistance, but the barber and his son were behind his shop scaring a dog off that was rummaging through the garbage. Only one person had heard and directly ignored the call, but the boy was unaware of this fact.

"I'll go for the doctor," shouted Shepard, and he left right away.

Robert turned to Foster. "What do you think is wrong with him?"

"I'm afraid I couldn't fathom a guess."

"What can we do? I wish my father was here." Robert began to weep. Falling down on the floor next to his friend, his trousers were soon steeped in Frank's blood. He sat there and, like Frank, he felt unable to move.

He stared up at the conductor, pleading, "Why won't his head stop bleeding?"

Foster was unable to respond.

A young lady named Dorothy Sprague walked toward the bank to visit Frank. After playful flirtations in school, the two had discussed the possibility of a courtship. Frank had promised to talk over the matter with his father and then seek the approval of her father.

Surprised by all the commotion and the group gathering in front of the bank, Dorothy fought through the crowd to see what was going on inside the door.

"Oh, Frank!" she screamed, and the scarf on her head flew away as she ran in hysterics.

William had just returned from the back of his shop after shooing away the stray dog, and the young woman's cry drew him and Caleb to the scene. William couldn't believe what he was seeing—the boy, the blood, the palpable fear of all those around him. William noticed all the locals who worked or lived close by were gathering, with the glaring exception of the postmaster. He casually turned his head toward the post office and saw no activity whatsoever.

Shepard returned with Dr. John Burpee. The doctor knelt beside Frank and placed his medical bag on the floor, where Frank's blood was now mingling with his brains. He held a small mirror above Frank's mouth for a few moments and then lifted it to his own eye. "I can't be sure if he is breathing," Burpee said and then frantically grabbed Frank's left wrist. "But I feel a faint pulse."

Burpee withdrew a probe from his bag. Pushing the matted hair soaked in blood to the side with his left hand, he ran the probe gently with his right to see if he could find the source of the wound.

He looked up at all the anxious faces surrounding him. "The boy has been shot. There is nothing to be done."

There was a collective gasp, and Robert, sitting opposite the doctor, fainted and fell to the floor next to his friend.

It was too late for medical aid, and within minutes death came. No further trace could be found of the bullet or bullets, although a close search was made of the premises.

The surprise and consternation of that group of neighbors and friends when the announcement was uttered that a murder had been committed, as it were, under their very eyes, can hardly be imagined. That a young man whom all loved and esteemed was sent into eternity by the foul hand of the murderer when a single cry of alarm would have called a hundred strong arms to his defense, might well strike dismay into the hearts of all. In such a moment of mutual distrust, what wonder that each should look upon his neighbor with suspicion.

Was there one in the heart of the village who had just imbrued his hands in the blood of his brother? So paralyzing was the effect of this sudden revelation of crime that no effort was made to seek or detain the murderer, who must still have been nearby, since not more than ten minutes could have elapsed from the commission of the deed until its discovery.

But there was, in this quiet town, no one on whom they could rely in an emergency so sudden and peculiar, so detectives had to be sent for from Boston. And so, the assassin escaped.

When Charles Merrill returned to the bank, he concluded that all the funds he had left had been carried off; the check cashed for George Bailey alone remained in the drawer. No attempt had been made to enter the safe, which was situated in the corner of the room, close to where the deceased was discovered, and most likely, the murderer had immediately left the bank by the front door, after securing all the money found on the counter and in the drawer. Merrill, as soon as he could leave the bank, went back to Boston to stop the payment of the stolen bills, all of which were issued by the Malden Bank.

Elisha was at his office in the city at the time of the murder, and Mary was therefore first informed, at their residence on Main Street, that her son had been shot. She was not able, however, to reach Frank in time to see him alive. Of course, her feelings on finding him a corpse cannot be described. She was terribly affected, and fears were expressed that her reason would leave her.

A messenger was sent at once for Elisha at his office at 67 Congress Street in Boston, and he returned home by two o'clock. Elisha had been notified that his son had been shot but was not aware of his death. As he entered, he made inquiry if Frank was dead and was informed of the fact. Leaning upon the arm of a friend, the grieving father turned away, overwhelmed after looking upon the lifeless form. The agony of the parents was heartbreaking and elicited the profoundest sympathy.

Immediately after Frank's death, Benjamin G. Hill, who acted as both the town's justice and coroner, was notified. He took charge of the remains and the premises and summoned a jury of inquest to look into the circumstances. They viewed the body, examined the building, and then decided to adjourn for two days, until two o'clock on Thursday afternoon.

Edward remained at the post office until after dark. He glanced over the counter sporadically for a couple of hours, watching as groups of men went in and out of the bank. To his relief, no one else entered the post office after the visit of young Merrill. Edward gazed in horror as three men carried Frank's body outside. He committed the crime, brought Frank to this end, yet Edward still felt shocked at the sight of Frank, lifeless, bloody, and limp, as the men gently placed his corpse in the back of the coroner's wagon.

Edward slouched down on the floor once more, his head teeming with so many thoughts, but without any focus. His hands were shaking. He was dizzy and developed a headache. Yet one moment of clarity rose to the surface of his mind. He had to dispose of the foreigner's clothing he was currently wearing. Edward needed to completely vanish the homicidal avatar he had created, to feel safe once again after the crime. The townsfolk would naturally suspect a stranger for a brutal act so unfamiliar to their Christian hearts and thoughts. Edward knew they thought this sort of heinous violence was for battlefields or faraway foreign places, not the town of Malden. Edward had also believed the same until earlier that morning, when he first gazed thirstily upon that pile of money, an oasis in his desert of debt.

Edward no longer desired to be the person he transformed himself into, a facade to fool all of them and himself about who he truly was—an impetuous, depraved opportunist. He would shed his disguise. Once the activity across the street ceased and the world outside grew quiet once more, Edward lit his stove. Several minutes later, after the wood was burning hot, he took off the coat he had gained in trade from the foreigner.

For some reason, he thought to rummage through the inside pockets and was surprised to discover a letter at the bottom of one, the envelope written with words he didn't comprehend. He opened it in the same manner he had opened previous letters not meant for his eyes and scanned the page, not understanding anything written except the name Gianni Santilli at the bottom, with the phrase "Greetings from Malden" written in English. Edward tossed it in the fire and watched it burn. Next, he laid the coat upon the glowing wood, and the fire grew high, the fabric mostly disappearing into a yellow flame before his eyes. The material was worn and, except for the metal buttons, it burned well. Lastly, he placed the fur hat in the stove. The flames fought but failed to engulf the hat as if it were fireproof; it was still soaked from the snowstorm. Edward's anger burned in response.

Edward was growing impatient and utterly exhausted. Clara would wonder why he was so late. He determined he could incinerate the remaining wisps of the coat and the stubborn hat in the morning and then properly dispose of them for good. He tamped out the fire until the embers faded entirely. Edward put on his bowler and slipped into his black coat, the one he had worn in the beginning of the day, as he did every day, before he had replaced it to wear what he now thought of as his temporary murder coat.

Edward exited his office, the street just as empty as the third and final time he crossed over to visit Frank. The postmaster locked his door and proceeded home, keeping his eyes directly forward, not wanting to gaze toward the bank. He attempted to block out the terrifying images of his friend's confused agony and the visual certainty of the townsfolk carrying Frank's corpse out of the bank, which proved to Edward's hazy mind, without a single doubt, the definite consequence of his sinful, irretrievable actions.

Chapter Twenty-Three

December 15, 1863
Boston Evening Transcript
The tragic result of the desperate crime committed in Malden
this forenoon has shocked the community to an intense degree.
Both murder and robbery were committed. Elisha Converse
is a wealthy citizen of Malden and president of the bank and
his son, Frank, is the victim. No clue has yet been discovered
to the persons committing this double crime. The Chief of
Police in Boston was at once notified, and every effort will be
made to detect and arrest the parties.

Frank's body was conveyed to the Converse residence on Belmont Hill at
about three o'clock. A messenger was sent to request Dr. John L. Sullivan, a
close friend of the deacon, to come examine Frank's wounds.

Mary kept the children upstairs as Elisha awaited the physician's arrival
next to his son's corpse. Robert stood outside dutifully and escorted Dr.
Sullivan in when he arrived by buggy. The doctor had rushed when he heard
the news, and his coat and shirt had a disheveled appearance.

Elisha stood up to greet him and shook his hand. "Thank you for coming, John."

"Certainly, Elisha."

The doctor placed his medical bag on a nearby table, opened it, and removed a probe. Frank's body lay on a long plank. The undertaker had folded his hands across his stomach as if he were in prayer. The suit Frank wore to work looked crisp and had been laundered just the day before, yet blood and dirt were caked around its collar and down the arms of the suit. Two towels were under Frank's head to prop it up slightly. Both were stained maroon.

The doctor leaned in close to the head, inches away, and scrutinized first the left temple and then twirled around the plank to get a closer look at the ear on the right side. He smoothed away the hair matted with blood by the ear and carefully pushed his probe in to see if he could find an impediment such as a bullet.

Elisha took a step back at this action and shifted his eyes toward the fire, allowing himself to be mesmerized by the dancing flames as a distraction.

A minute later, Dr. Sullivan wiped off the probe with a rag and placed it back into his bag. "Frank was shot at close range under the right ear, and the bullet exited from the left temple. I searched with my probe to find fragments of the bullet, but it is not long enough to push through. I am very sorry, my friend. He was a sweet boy."

"He was."

"Please give my condolences to Mary and the children."

"I will. Did you find anything else in the examination?"

"No, there will be no need for a postmortem. You can bury your son without any further meddling into his wound. Again, I'm sorry, Elisha."

Elisha offered his hand and bowed his head. Dr. Sullivan shook it. Robert was waiting by the door to escort him out.

Later that afternoon and well into the evening, many sympathizing friends called to volunteer any assistance in their power, and to gaze upon the features of one who but so shortly a time before was full of life and vigor, and who from but a child had been a favorite in the village.

After the last of the townsfolk offering consolation to the Converses had departed, the breath of David Roy, the groundskeeper, hung in the air. He looked around past the portico to see if any more would appear. Roy presumed everyone would allow the grieving family the privacy they sought for the next few days, knowing the wake on Friday and the funeral on Saturday would bring scores more mourners and sympathizers from the town and beyond.

To his relief, he spied no further shadows stirring along Main Street as the last horse car of the day headed back to the square. All of the passengers, he thought, were gawking at him and the enormous mansion behind him. Their inquiring eyes were carried off by the plodding footsteps of the horses who, with blinders on, could only stare ahead and not upon the somber house. Roy turned back to the home and strolled to the front door. He paused as he saw the two motionless figures hovering over a motionless box in the main window. He considered his next action and then decided that he would remain out in the cold a bit longer.

The chill emanating from the outside world caused Elisha and Mary to shiver as they stood in the drawing room of their mansion. Even with all three of the home's fireplaces fully engaged, Elisha tightened his coat and Mary drew closer to him for any available heat. *As husband and wife we cling to each other while the one person we both wish desperately to hold on to in this moment has slipped forever from the mortal coil.* The deacon corrected his thought: *My son has not slipped but has been flung from this life by an evil into his heavenly place, far too violently and far too soon.*

Rueful, Elisha and Mary increased their embrace; they needed each other more on this sad night than in any night before. But their spirits and the vessels that carried them could not keep warm. In their despair, both perceived their souls, their very essence, their warmth fleeing from them suddenly, just as it had done so impossibly and irreversibly from their boy.

The next day, two detectives from Boston, Benjamin Heath and William K. Jones (no relation to George Jones, aka the Count), exited the depot and were met by the town's elected constable, John Abbott.

Law enforcement in Boston and several other cities and towns across the nation, until the decade before, had been only a patchwork of small groups of watchmen who also held other occupations. In 1854, the Boston Police Department had been established with 250 officers and an elite group of five detectives, the very first of their kind in the entire country. Jones had joined later, but Heath, now aged forty-two, with a receding hairline, a bushy mustache, and large, jutting ears, had been chosen as one of their original number.

It was easy to see why he was selected. On his first night of duty in 1850 as a watchman, Heath had arrested two men caught in the act of larceny. Soon after, as an excellent swimmer, he came to prominence for saving two people from drowning. That same year, he had also pointed his finger before anyone else at the correct suspect in what had been one of the most sensational murder investigations the country had ever seen. Harvard professor John Webster was convicted of murdering George Parkman after his burned remains were discovered in Webster's lab. Webster had been the last man to hang in the commonwealth for murder, in August of 1850. The Converse murder being so ghastly, Heath suspected that the man they were pursuing, once captured, might be the next.

Interviewing the townsfolk, the detectives soon discovered speculation was rife regarding who the murderer was, with the citizens holding various theories about the crime, but two accounts caught their interest most.

Visiting the bakery of Marshall Shedd on Ferry Street, corner of Holyoke, they presented their badges to him.

"You're here about the murder and robbery," he said, placing a tray of buns into his oven and then closing the door tight. Marshall wiped the sweat from his face with his forearm.

"We are. We and Constable Abbott are going about the square and surrounding neighborhoods asking if anyone noticed something suspicious," said Heath.

"Out of the ordinary," chimed in Jones.

"Has anyone mentioned the strangely dressed man?" said Marshall.

"What strangely dressed man?" said Heath.

"Where did you see him?" asked Jones.

"Hold on a moment," said Marshall, turning toward the oven. He carefully opened the door with a thick towel. "I had these in earlier, before the last batch." He placed the white-hot baking tin on the long table before them. "Fresh out of the oven. I can provide some butter if you are here for food as well as answers."

"Thank you. We have an appetite to solve this crime," said Heath.

"But we also have an appetite in general," said Jones, looking at his partner with a mischievous smile.

Heath laughed. He, like Jones, was hungry; they had been canvassing all morning, and this was the first person to offer them some sustenance.

They sat down and Marshall placed one ample bun in front of each of them and then a small metal tin with a smattering of butter between the two plates.

Jones immediately started eating. Heath held the hot bun covered in butter before his mouth, but before taking a bite, he said, "Tell us about the stranger, please."

"Yes," said Marshall, stripping off his apron and taking a seat across from the detectives, "I saw a man in clothes of an unfamiliar style."

"Like that of a foreigner?" asked Jones in between bites.

"Yes, his coat and hat."

"Describe them, please," said Heath, putting down the half-eaten bun for a moment.

"He had this fur hat that was quite unusual, and his coat was like one I had never seen before. He was at the depot," said Marshall, picking up one of the buns and slathering a heaping amount of butter onto it. "A half hour later, I saw him or someone just like him go into the bank, apparently about the time the murder was committed." Marshall took a big bite out of the bun, but the detectives across from him stopped chewing and stared at him, mouths agape, full of half-eaten bread.

Heath swallowed hard and said, "You saw this stranger go into the bank?"

Jones continued eating and said between chews, "Around the time of the robbery and murder?"

Heath took the pencil from behind his ear and moved the plate aside so he could write in his notepad.

"Yes," said Marshall, polishing off his bun. "Do you think this man was the perpetrator?"

"Perhaps; it could be an important clue," said Jones.

"Thank you for your time, Mr. Shedd," said Heath.

"And the bread," said Jones.

They paid him and promised to call again.

Later, as the detectives were finishing up for the day, they walked around the bank and saw a woman entering a house just behind it. "Excuse me, ma'am," said Jones. He and Heath flashed their badges.

She held a bag of groceries and introduced herself as Mrs. Caroline Vinton. "I have been waiting to talk to the law," she said. "Come up to my apartment, please. I have something to share."

Heath offered to carry her bag and Jones opened the door for them. They ascended two flights of stairs. A girl of around fourteen sat in the kitchen shyly, and Mrs. Vinton nodded toward the table for the detectives to have a seat. "Do you want some tea?"

"Yes, ma'am," said Heath.

"That would be fine, thank you," said Jones.

She poured some water from a bucket into a kettle and hung it over the fireplace. "Should be ready in a few minutes. Anyway, I saw an odd-dressed man pass by the street along Middlesex and up to Pleasant along the side of the bank the morning of the murder."

"Was he, this man, wearing a fur hat?" asked Heath.

Startled by the question, she said, "Oh, yes he was. The clothes were far from any fashion I am familiar with."

"When was this, please?" said Jones.

"A few minutes before I heard what I guess was the sound of a gunshot."

There was no warm bread in their mouths this time, but the detectives' mouths were, once more, wide in surprise. No one else had heard a gunshot, and they had talked to dozens of citizens up and down the street, not thinking of the home that lay directly behind the bank.

"To be honest, I was not sure what the sound was at the time, but my husband engages in target practice quite often, so the sound is familiar to me."

The kettle started screeching, so she paused, picked it up, and poured the hot liquid into two cups with loose tea leaves.

Heath blew on the cup, but Jones took a quick sip and regretted it, placing the cup back on the table.

"Should have warned you, might need to cool a bit. I apologize, I have no cream. The milkman comes tomorrow and we ran out two days ago."

"That's fine, ma'am," said Heath as Jones pursed his lips, scrunching his face. "Continue, please."

"Well, after the news of the Converse boy's murder, the time it occurred, I became more certain of the fact that the bang I heard must have been a report of a gun."

Heath asked for some more general information from her as he sipped a little of his tea. Jones, reluctant to drink any more of it, instead wrote down her answers to Heath's inquiries.

After the interview, the detectives walked back into the street and soon stood in front of the bank.

"This has been a long but good day, pal," said Jones.

"Yes, we have made some progress," said Heath.

"More than some, Benjamin. We have two witnesses who saw a stranger around the bank at the time of the murder, and the baker also noted him at the depot. It is clear. The murderer came into town by train, killed Converse, robbed the bank, and then left again by train."

"Perhaps," said Heath.

"We may wrap this up in a week!" With the roof of his mouth burnt, Jones contorted his face into a smile.

"Let's not get ahead of ourselves, William. There is a lot more shoe leather for us to wear out. Here's what I have deduced at this point. The boldness and audacity of the crime seems to indicate that it was the work of one deep in guilt, and many circumstances support that idea. But if the person who came into the bank was a complete stranger, it is somewhat remarkable that the deceased should have allowed him to go behind the counter, as he must have done before firing the shot."

"You may be right, but I have a feeling about this. Let's hope the solution to finding this criminal is the simple one I propose."

Heath shrugged.

The two walked away from the bank and toward the depot to head back into the city. They were unaware the postmaster was eyeing them intently, and the postmaster was oblivious to the fact that the barber was scrutinizing him as he watched the detectives.

While the detectives were sleuthing, others in Malden were doing their part to solve the mystery of Frank's murder. The selectmen of the town offered a reward of $2,500 for information that would lead to the arrest and conviction of the perpetrator. Elisha and Mary added another $5,000, for a total of $7,500, and the directors of the Malden Bank made the following statement to the public:

> Mr. Merrill, the cashier of the bank, on leaving the rooms, placed in the hands of the assistant cashier, Mr. Frank E. Converse, $5000 in the bills of the Malden Bank, and this sum comprised the whole amount obtained by the robbers. All the other valuables and coinage of the bank were locked within the vault, and the cashier had the key in his own possession. Of the money stolen, $3000 was in one hundred dollar bills of the Malden Bank, near $2000 in bills of smaller denominations of the same bank, two twenties and a ten of the Exchange Bank of Boston. The bills of the bank will continue to be redeemed as usual at the Bank of Mutual Redemption. But few one hundred dollar bills are in circulation and no more will be issued at present. The public are informed that a sum equal to twice the amount stolen has been reserved by the bank from its earnings, after paying all dividends, so the stability of the bank is in no way impaired by the robbery. To the afflicted parents and relatives of the estimable young man whose life has been inhumanely sacrificed, while in the faithful discharge of the duties and trust committed to his care, the directors of the bank offer our heartfelt sympathies.
>
> Ezra D. Lamson

The next day, at two o'clock, six jurors and Coroner Hill assembled at the town hall to hear testimony for the inquest of Frank's mysterious murder.

Robert Merrill was first to testify. He described how the outside door was ajar when he arrived at the bank, the gate leading behind the counter was partly open, and the chair that Frank used was not in its usual place.

"When I first saw him, he was trying to move and was shaking all over. I didn't see any bills upon the counter. I did not speak to him, but only went in and looked at him and went out again." The boy stated he then went to search for a doctor or help from any nearby business.

Robert's father, Charles Merrill, testified next, explaining that he had traveled to Boston and then arrived back in Malden at 12:20. "I was told by the switch tender that there was trouble at the bank and a man shot. I jumped into a carriage, and upon arriving at the bank, saw Converse's mother and other ladies there and young Converse lying dead on the floor."

Charles testified about the missing money and that the pistols in the bank were accounted for and had not been discharged. Straining not to cry, Charles kept his head low as he spoke of the slain clerk. "Frank had been in the bank as my assistant for seven or eight months. I always cautioned Frank about keeping money on the front counter. There is a little desk where he liked to write, and he always kept the money there and nowhere else." Charles paused to compose himself before continuing. "Frank was a very modest, sweet-tempered boy, without an enemy in the world. The boy changed the check which Mr. Bailey drew and must have been shot directly after. I think he must have been wounded some twenty minutes. The armchair was broken some time ago, but repaired. There is blood on the chair now and it is damaged. I think there might have been some kind of struggle.

"My first impression was that it was an accident, but that seems impossible from the nature of the wound, and my conclusion is that someone came into the bank and wanted to make change of a five- or ten-dollar bill, and when Frank turned around to the desk at some distance, where he kept that money, the person who wanted it must have entered through the small door and fired the pistol at him from directly behind."

Charles Shepard testified how he had discovered Frank. "It was dark behind the counter. His eyes were partially closed. Lichfield, a conductor on the horse cars, helped me carry him to the door. Frank moaned a great deal. The air of the room was very hot. I wanted a cloth to wipe off the blood, and went in the back room and took a pillow slip from the bed. The blood ran out quite fast as I was holding Frank, so I went to fetch Dr. Burpee."

George Bailey testified next, explaining that he had departed his place of business that morning around twenty minutes past eleven with the intention of going to his storehouse behind the bank. "As I approached the bank, it occurred to me that I had a check in my pocket that had been there for some time, and I thought I would go into the bank and have it cashed. I found Converse sitting on a chair outside the counter, reading a newspaper. I told him that I had a check that I wished to have cashed, and he immediately got up and went behind the counter, taking his paper with him. I went to the desk and endorsed the check, and then handed it to him. He took some money out of the desk and gave me the amount I was to receive and put the rest back. He paid me $171.86, a one-hundred-dollar bill and bills of smaller denominations. I left the bank immediately after transacting my business. It was about ten minutes past twelve when I heard of the murder. When I left the bank, Converse was sitting at the desk behind the counter reading or writing. I do not think he charged the check while I was there. There was about two hundred dollars lying on the counter at that time. Converse had his cap on when I saw him."

The last witness to provide testimony was Dr. John Burpee. "I found the boy lying on his back in the front room near the middle of the floor with a wound upon the left temple from which blood mingled with his brains and was somewhat slowly flowing. There were no signs of breath, but the pulse was beating. In perhaps a minute or so Converse drew a labored breath, accompanied by a convulsive movement of his arms. There was no other breath drawn. He lived perhaps four or five minutes more."

He explained that his first thought was that it was a gunshot wound; and upon close examination, he found a greasy, blackened mark immediately forward of where the blood was issuing that could not be wiped off with his finger, concluding it was burned powder.

"I then found that just back of the ear, there was a swollen thickness of an inch or inch and a half in diameter. Seeing no money, I thought that the boy had been shot and the bank robbed. I told one of those present that Converse had been shot. He soon repeated this to others. A murmur gathered into a crescendo among the townspeople, who were in utter shock.

None of them had ever come directly across a murder scene before. Honestly, neither have I; this is my first, but I have studied many cadavers who died from various ways and have some scant familiarity with gunshot wounds, far more than the general public. I came to the conclusion that the pistol ball entered the left temple and passed out behind the right ear. I do not think Converse lived more than ten or fifteen minutes after the injury was inflicted.

"The blood where the young man was lying was bright red and apparently formed from two sources, and by the look of the wounds on both sides of his head, I believe it's possible he was shot twice. I understood that on examination it was found that powder was burned in at the wound at the back of the ear. I have not seen the body since the first time. There was not more than four tablespoonfuls of blood behind the counter, and twice that quantity had flowed while he was in front; the blood on the floor had not coagulated at all. The wound in the temple was ragged, but a pistol ball would make a smooth hole where it entered. It is my strong suggestion, and I am prepared to argue most adamantly, that an autopsy of the body should occur to make certain of the number, if any, of the bullets remaining in his head."

The court said they would rule on that at the end of the inquest, which would be adjourned until the following Tuesday at two o'clock, to allow time for the town to prepare for Frank's memorial and burial, where they could grieve and offer condolences to the Converse family.

Chapter Twenty-Four

CLARA GREEN, PREPARING to travel to the Converse home to pay her respects, felt an ache in her back and in her feet. She wished for her baby to come soon. She longed for the new shoes Edward had promised to buy her. She was wearing a falling-apart pair loaned to her by Susie to use in the meantime. This was better than being barefoot but still not comfortable.

With the brutal murder of Edward's dear friend, now was not the proper time to ask, so she would suffer through her situation, as she often did. She regarded her husband. *Oh, the horror, the poor boy!* she thought. *This has affected Eddie so very much.* Edward did not make eye contact but sat in his chair as if almost lulled to sleep and unaware that his wife was leaving the apartment.

She smelled that familiar scent on him which often caused her concern, but under the circumstances, it was not surprising. *He is upset. Sad. Working directly across the street from one another, Frank and Eddie crossed paths often, but their relationship had been more than that,* she thought. *They truly enjoyed each other's company.*

Fate had thrown them together, but Edward had told her on more than one occasion that Frank was truly like a younger sibling. He stated he considered Frank "a mirror image of myself, but slightly skewed to be younger and more handsome." Edward often repeated this joke and laughed. This morning, after saying it once more, Edward did not laugh but instead pretended to tend to the doll he was whittling for their coming child, occasionally glancing up at Clara while shaking his good leg and then eyeing his bad one with contempt.

She did not think it altogether out of the ordinary when Edward begged off from going to Frank's services. Then she smelled his breath and stared in his glassy eyes. If her husband was staying home, Clara would represent the family and offer her condolences to the Converses. The whole town was collectively in deep mourning and shock, and she supposed perhaps besides the family of the deceased, her Eddie was certainly the most affected by Frank's murder. Their baby was due soon, but Clara deemed it still safe to travel the mile or so to visit Frank's grieving parents. Having spent so many hours at home, Clara felt like she never ventured out of their cramped room. She said goodbye to Edward. He gave a limp smile as she departed.

Agnes helped raise her up onto John's new carriage. John nodded at her but didn't say a word. They rode in silence, and Clara paused to ponder about the last carriage ride she had shared with John. *That was so long ago. A truly joyous time,* Clara recalled and felt she would perhaps cry, yet held the tears back. *But this current ride is one of solemnity. I worry that the whole town will be at the Converse mansion with the exception of my husband, and I'm concerned as to how that will be perceived.*

Malden was draped in sadness. All of the town's businesses were closed, out of respect for the deceased. The flag at the bank where Frank was killed was at half-staff, and would remain so for weeks to come, and so, too, were the flags at all government buildings, including the town hall. Edward had consented that Amos Tenney could do the same at the post office when the boy had come around asking if he should lower the flag since all the other businesses nearby had already done so.

The throng of mourners gathered was immense. It seemed to Clara as if just about every honest soul in Malden had assembled to offer their respects to a son of the town. It was as if they all had lost a child and certainly a bit of the innocence of childhood with this brutal crime. Frank's life was gone forever, and so a segment of each member of the town felt empty as well. How could this happen? Who would commit such an evil deed? These thoughts were on everyone's mind, repeated as scant whispers and myriad concerned speculations throughout the day.

Many scanned the crowd, wondering if the sinner was hiding plainly in their very midst. More than one mentioned to Clara that the killer may be so sadistic that he might enjoy seeing the suffering of the bereft parents and the palpable fear of the entire town up close.

Elisha's menservants, noticing Clara was with child and unsteady on her feet, kindly ushered her and her party inside the doors and out of the bitter cold.

The Converses appeared to her to be quite stoic in the receiving line as Clara's eyes adjusted to the illumination inside the home. There was an abundance of natural light, but a gloom hung over the occasion, darkening the spacious room. Clara assumed the hearts of the boy's parents must be beating uncontrollably, wanting to burst from their chests in agony, but the Converses did not show it; they did not even imply it.

Their son was dead, murdered in broad daylight, and yet they stood there nobly with their daughter, Mary Ida, while a servant held their infant son, Harry, nearby. Elisha and Mary shook the hands of those lining up to offer condolences, and the line was very long, indeed. It stretched well down Main Street, far from the Converse home, and included all Frank's classmates from the high school, and perhaps a hundred or more of the employees of the Boston Rubber Shoe Company who owed their livelihoods to Mr. Converse and were acquainted with Frank from a young age as he often accompanied his father to the factory.

Approaching the receiving line, Clara detected clearly the strain on Elisha's face, and how Mary's eyes seemed glazed over from the stress of not releasing any stored-up tears publicly, yet Frank's mother strained a slight smile for each person nonetheless. Mary Ida mostly stared downward and raised her head a little as another person advanced. Off to the side stood Detectives Heath and Jones and a well-dressed man with a whimsical mustache and a cape, whom Clara had never seen before. She noticed that every once in a while, this man would whisper in Detective Heath's ear, and the detective would shake his head.

Soon, it was Clara's turn to offer her condolences to the grieving family. She thought to mention how upset Edward was, but decided it was best not to bring attention to the fact that her husband was too saddened, too drunk really, to attend while this family stood there with such aplomb as the whole town came to visit their home all at once, a home in which Frank had once filled their lives with such pride and possibility. Now, he was lying there lifeless in a closed casket. Clara was standing directly in front of the family, with Agnes and John behind her. Elisha held Clara's hand in one palm while patting it with the other. She had seen him do this with the other mourners before her in the receiving line, and the act appeared repetitive. But once she felt his grip and gazed into his eyes, she could see that he was genuinely touched by her being present, as he was for each and every person that had come to pay their respects. He gently released his grasp and nodded, glancing down at her midriff.

"I wish you the best with your child, Mrs. Green."

"And I with yours, Deacon Converse."

The deacon looked flummoxed for a moment. He took a step back. Clara saw him hesitate. Had she unwittingly rattled the man from his austere dignity? She sensed he wanted to turn to the wooden box that contained Frank's remains and fall upon it. She felt cruel, to no fault of her own. She was adding a life as he was just losing one.

The deacon raised his eyes to hers. Clara held her breath.

"You mean, Harry. Yes, of course, you do. He is a fine boy." He gave her a soft smile and she exhaled sharply. Agnes stepped forward and Elisha clasped her hand the same way he had Clara's. She saw John place a palm on the deacon's shoulder as a condolence, and the two spoke.

In a daze, she did not understand the words exchanged between them. Clara next stepped forward and met the sad orbs of Mary Converse; they seemed to look through her and beyond, perhaps intently searching for her perished son to walk forward and embrace her as he had done since his boyhood. Clara, perceiving how earnest Mary was, attempted to offer the appropriate measure of sadness for the situation. She sensed it was much more difficult to do so to the mother of the murdered child than it was to the father, since Clara was almost a mother herself and also because Mary seemed to inadvertently cast her sadness over the proceedings much more so than Elisha would ever permit himself to do.

The women's palms met and clasped, but each may as well have been clasping air since Mary's grip was so light and fragile. Clara was afraid of gripping too tightly, frightened Mary's hand would wilt within her own.

With the life inside her ready to emerge, Clara could only imagine the pain of losing a child so young, as Mary had suffered, after bearing him, raising him, a child with such purpose and future, ended by a horrific bullet. Clara crumbled inside at the thought and almost burst into tears. She released the grip that was barely there anyway and stepped humbly back. There was sadness for this woman, but Clara was determined that she would not lose her own baby! Never this way.

Then, to distract herself from this dire thought, Clara shook the hand of the Converse daughter, who appeared to be in a dream state, one in which she seemed to project herself so very far away from her family's pain. Clara was certain that Mary Ida was succeeding in this, since the girl looked like an apparition, covered in black from head to toe.

They were all alive, these remaining Converses; Clara could verify this, but she knew that each had died a little along with Frank. Whatever lives each was fated to live would never be the same; their loved one was barely a butterfly released from his cocoon when he met his brutal demise, and the absence of him clearly permeated them each to their very cores. Suffocating in the melancholy that hung in the air, Clara walked as briskly as was proper, away from the morose estate, away from the sadness and death.

The barber, his wife, and their children were patiently waiting on the road, just outside the line entering the home. Staring at them, Clara sympathized with the mother and the children, who were shoeless, with just rags wrapped around their feet on such a cold day and with only William wearing a tattered pair of shoes. To her eyes, it was as if the Shilohs were but a mere rock in a river, the current of people flowing around them, the barber politely nodding at each wave that skirted along their boundary. He received no response as the townsfolk moved past the family as if it were not there at all, instead following the queue and moving closer to the house. The Shilohs idled outside the stream of mourners, patiently waiting for its end, so they could eventually join the ebb of the current and enter the home to pay their respects when it was appropriate.

Clara sensed the barber's gaze upon her as she approached John's horse and buggy. She thought it queer. She knew of the man and his shop but had never seen him properly before and had been unaware to this very moment that he possessed such a large family. Clara had always observed him in her periphery but was certain he never regarded her before as he appeared to be doing in this very instance. Surely he was staring at her, but why? As she looked back at him, he quickly averted his head from her and longingly looked toward the mansion from which she had just exited.

The barber must have known the Converse boy well and given him many haircuts over the years since his fancy barbershop is where the rich gentlemen and their sons go to have their hair trimmed. My Eddie visits the man occasionally, sometimes for a shave, since his whiskers are unwieldy, but he often cuts his hair at home with scissors since it is more practical. Shiloh's shop is mainly for rich men. I wish that Eddie was as frugal with the bottle as he is with his bristles, she thought and then, sighing, had one more thought, *Most of all I wish Eddie had joined us on this journey today.*

Clara's attention turned from William Shiloh to John and Agnes as they exited the mansion and joined her. John assisted her up into the carriage, and then Agnes sat beside her. Clara wanted to get home to her husband. She wished she could hold her baby to her breast immediately, for she couldn't wait any longer for its birth. Clara's dearest desire was to cling to her little family and never lose them. The Greens were a meager family, a humble family, but she sensed each of them was utterly alive, immune to the trials and tribulations of those wealthy beyond their means. Frank's demise was sad, but Clara was aware death came for the affluent as well as the meager. It was God's way.

John's carriage plodded down Main Street, then along Pleasant Street, leading Clara to her boardinghouse, back to the man she loved and depended on more than anything. *Eddie has given me so much tender affection and helped to create the child in my belly. The Converse boy is dead, but my child, Eddie's child, is aching to enter the world. My family will be a happy one,* Clara thought, assuring herself earnestly that it would certainly be.

Mary Converse sat in the den, talking to Detectives Heath and Jones on the morning of her son's funeral. The wake the night before had been difficult for her. Elisha was in his study, pretending to be working on company matters. He had spent an hour conversing with the detectives about the investigation and the possible suspects in the crimes. He judged it wise for the pair to also inform Mary of these updates, though Elisha stipulated strongly to them that they use the greatest of caution in doing so, so as not to upset his wife.

In the meantime, Elisha sought some sort of peace and went to the parlor. Everything appeared so topsy-turvy. One day, his son was training as a clerk in the first of many steps to rise up the company ladder and eventually be bequeathed all his father had to give him, and the next moment, Elisha was staring at his lifeless child. The shock was still so vivid to him. He asked Reverend Faunae, pastor of the Baptist church, who was there preparing for the service, to pray with him by the casket.

"Lord," Elisha prayed, "I should have kept Frank safe. I failed him." He started to weep.

"Seeing the bloody, sprawling remains, the expressionless stare of what was once my son prone on the bank floor split my very being in two. If only I had been there while Frank was still breathing, before you called him to heaven. Or better yet, I wish Frank had never been left alone at the bank, vulnerable to such unseen treachery."

"It is a difficult time, Elisha. I am so sorry you and your family must suffer this way, but God has a plan, and now Frank is bathed in the Almighty's love for eternity, just as he was by you and Mary during his life. One day your family will be together again, I assure you. You can't blame yourself."

"But I do blame myself and question my decisions. Frank loved numbers, so the bank had been the logical place to begin his business education. Should Frank have instead been given a position at the rubber factory, the business which is truly prospering? I believe no one would have harmed Frank at the factory. Yet, there hadn't been a thought in my head before that anyone would harm Frank at the bank either."

"Elisha, I agree. Who would do such a thing? It's so completely incomprehensible that a person could walk into a bank in the late morning with the intention of stealing and killing."

Elisha bent his head and covered his eyes with his hands for a few moments, wiping his tears. "That was two commandments broken in mere seconds," said Elisha, taking a long breath and leaning back in his chair.

"The evil and folly of man is growing more pervasive. The country's split in half; perhaps it might heal if the war ever were to end. However, the current fissure in your family, I know, is so much, too much, too sudden, so unexpected."

"Yes, now all my hopes for the legacy of my various businesses lay in our infant, Harry. One day, it will be all his, and Mary and I will do whatever is in our means to protect him so Harry can attain it. It should've been Frank's. I'd always planned it for Frank. Now we will have to start over. I wish Harry were older so he could take Frank's place immediately." Elisha was stung by his own words. No one could ever take Frank's place.

Elisha stood up and collapsed his face and arms across the casket.

"Reverend, I am lost, so utterly, consumingly lost," he muttered through his tears. "The grief is overwhelming." The deacon stood up, attempting to compose himself. He did not make eye contact with the reverend. He sat down in a thump in his chair, beside his friend.

"It is not proper to show it in public. It is difficult enough for me, and I have asked Mary to be strong as well, to keep the stiff upper lip of a New Englander. God has been kind to our family, guiding me in business and success after success."

"The Almighty has blessed you first with a son, a daughter, and then a baby boy. Now for reasons we cannot explain, God has seen fit to take Frank away from you at an early age."

"Oh, what great promise Frank's future held! I was building everything for him. Every decision, every long day, every hard-earned investment was for Frank and the children Frank would one day bring into the world. Alas, you are right. God has willed it, and those children are never meant to be."

"For the rest of your life, there'll be overwhelming sadness for Frank, but when those times seem too much, you must ask for God's grace to help you through them."

"I will love my family, and I must purse my lips tight and throw myself completely into my work for relief, for the distraction from the severe pain of losing my son." Elisha's tears fell now as he no longer had the power to hold them back.

"You must try your best, my friend, and God will bring you some solace and peace if you pray for it. Trust in him." The reverend offered him his handkerchief and the deacon accepted it and wiped his face.

"I am devout, you know that. Yet this is my greatest test. The bullet or bullets of that greedy, violent robber have taken more than money, they have plundered a part of my soul and perhaps a greater part of Mary's. She is, was, Frank's mother, after all, and is still so young herself, just thirty-eight. I often look at her and see the young maiden she once was. Mary's retained much of her beauty and charms since we first met."

The reverend nodded.

"The legacy I've built will be Harry's to carry on. But, Reverend, what if something were to befall Harry as well?"

"One cannot dwell on such fears."

"How can I not? The idea would have seemed so far-fetched about a mere infant just days ago, but now the world is upside down and anything, any terrible thing is possible."

"Pray, think positively as the man I know you are."

"If God will see fit to provide me, I may need another son to take over my business and carry on the family name, just in case. I'm not sure if Mary is up to the task after the loss of Frank." Elisha stood up again and looked out the window. The buggies, including the one that would carry his firstborn son on his last earthly journey, were lined up outside. "The thought of pregnancy and childbirth may only remind her further of Frank and cause her more pain. It's quite delicate at the moment for both of us."

If we have a son, Elisha thought to himself, forcing himself to look away from the funeral carriage, *he will also be named Frank. Just as my father replaced one Elisha with another, Mary and I will produce another Frank to fill the void of the first one, if God wills it.*

Chapter Twenty-Five

THE SUN WAS dim in the sky, and the mood of the town, dimmer still. Mary had permitted her daughter to sleep late on such a morose morning. Yet, it still required considerable effort to convince Mary Ida to release her grip upon her doll and vacate the sanctuary of her bed. While a servant readied Mary Ida, Mary joined Elisha downstairs to spend some quiet moments alone with the closed casket. They were forced to conceal Frank's ghastly image from the world and to block out the horror of his final expression of pain and shock from their own eyes. This is not how Mary and Elisha wished to remember the boy, but it would remain with both parents for the rest of their lives; no matter how they attempted to affix other more pleasant images of their firstborn in their thoughts, the horror of his murder would endure nonetheless.

Frank must have suffered greatly and so unexpectedly, they believed. He was their boy, a part of each of them, created by their marriage, their love for each other and their hope for the family's future. God had provided them so much, and now he had snatched away his most special gift to them, Frank, so cruelly. They were at a loss, neither one knowing how to proceed. Even in the depths of their grief, each had thoughts of having another son. There was Harry, but his life and their own all seemed to be made so uncertain by the brutality of Frank's demise. Any calamity could strike at any time. Frank had been spared from the nation's battlefields, which continued to ravage so many of his peers, but violence had sought him out nonetheless.

The Converses were growing older. They had invested so much in Frank as their firstborn. They wanted more offspring than just their daughter and remaining son but knew it was solely up to their Creator. Neither had spoken this wish to the other. Frank was gone; he could not be replaced, no matter what.

When Reverend Faunae returned to the parlor, Elisha requested he read from the book of Job to prepare them for the throngs of visitors that were about to arrive to mourn their son. The parents clasped hands over the body of their child as the reverend stood a few feet away, speaking in a soft voice.

The pastor, like many in the town, knew Frank well and held him in great esteem. However, he was not sure to what end his violent murder could be justified in God's eyes. What sinner, that perhaps lived among them, had committed so heinous a deed? It was equally disturbing to him that conceivably one of his own flock could stray and sin so greatly against one of their town. The man of God prayed daily for the many young men losing their lives in the war, a vicious affliction he perceived as spreading throughout the nation, threatening to tear it apart. Now violence had come to dwell among the townsfolk so intimately, so close to home. This murder was not based on war but on simple greed; a single act and a single victim, but it had shocked the town as no other deed had done before or would again for many years to come.

At one o'clock, the funeral began with a prayer by Reverend Faunae. The body was encased in a beautiful rosewood casket and dressed in a black suit, although none of the visitors could see Frank with the casket closed. Three young girls stayed far away from the coffin, deeply fearful of it, but one of their young brothers let his curiosity get the best of him, and when no adults were paying attention, he ran up to it and gave a light knock on the wood and ran away.

A plate upon the coffin lid bore the inscription "Frank E. Converse. Died Dec. 15, 1863, aged 17 years, 2 months, 15 days." Across his coffin lay a beautiful wreath of flowers donated by the Hayward Guards, a military company of boys numbering close to thirty, of which Frank had been a member. When it was time to transport the coffin, at two o'clock, the Hayward Guards acted as his honor guards, while Frank's closest friends acted as pallbearers, and the remainder of the young men formed a path from the front steps of the house directly to the hearse.

The horses whinnied as Frank's casket was placed in the buggy. Elisha, Mary, and Mary Ida, who carried her baby brother, Harry, walked past the company, who continued their salute on either side of them. Robert assisted the family up into the next buggy. The honor guards assembled on either side of the hearse, fifteen to each side, and led the procession of thirty carriages up Main Street to the Congregational church, as the Baptist church where Elisha acted as deacon was under repairs. Many lined the street as the cavalcade passed by. Both Mary and Elisha were struck by the image of a young boy, who looked to be about eight, saluting as they passed.

Before the arrival of the procession, the part of the church not reserved for those closest to Frank was filled with sympathetic friends. Business in the town was entirely suspended during the services, and many gentlemen doing business in Boston left the city earlier than usual to join in this unanimous tribute of affection and esteem. Among them were the directors of the bank and the president of the clearinghouse of Boston, and many leading gentlemen of the rubber trade. The number present was estimated at over six hundred. The services began at about half past two with the singing of a hymn by the choir of the Baptist church.

Reverend Faunae stood to address the congregation. "All of us are mourners, and all have been afflicted and smitten in heart by the circumstances which have transpired in our midst during the present week. The shaft of death has wounded us all. We have been powerfully impressed with the brevity of life and the uncertainty of any plan for happy mortality. This is not the time nor place to speak of that indignation against deeds of wrong which is in every righteous heart; that indignation that demands for the security of life that those who have brought such a terrible affliction upon the whole community should be brought to punishment.

"We come here today to administer some word of consolation to these friends, and to learn what special lessons of God's Providence are to be gained from a contemplation of this sad event. This deep affliction was a dispensation of Providence which no human power could avert, and the great lesson to be learned from it is the uncertainty of human life. The example of the deceased—the praying child of pious parents—was also worthy of imitation in the kindness of his heart, and in the manner of his death: yielding up his life in the fulfillment of duty and the protection of property with which he was entrusted. The promises and assurances of the Gospel dwell within us as the only substantial grounds for hope and consolation."

Reverend Faunae spoke feelingly of Frank's character, which gave much comfort to Mary and Elisha, though their hearts were filled with unimaginable grief. The service then closed with the singing of the hymn "Thy Will Be Done."

Elisha had commissioned a local poet to produce an elegy to his son. The poet knew the boy well and had composed his work and presented it to Elisha within two days of the murder. At great expense, Elisha had printed out hundreds of copies on placards, which were distributed to the mourners as they departed the church and then followed the hearse to Woodlawn Cemetery, Frank's final resting place.

A TRIBUTE

TO THE MEMORY OF

FRANK EUGENE CONVERSE

AGED 17 YEARS

WHO WAS ASSASSINATED IN THE BANK OF MALDEN

DECEMBER 15th, 1863

> The youth went forth at early morn
> All healthy, bright and gay:
> Before the sun the zenith reach'd
> A mangled corpse he lay.
> Pity and fear stalk'd through the town,
> And thrilled was every breast:
> Commotion dire filled the day,
> And darkness brought no rest.
> To hunt the murder'r from his den
> Each lent a willing hand,

Nor sought they long before they found
And mark'd him with Cain's brand.
Had the wretch died on battlefield
A lustrous name he'd won,
In death dishonor'd now he lies,
That killed the well lov'd son.
The boy's true heart would never yield
From virtue's path to stray:
True to his trust, his life he gave,
The cruel robber's prey.
A life so young, so well begun,
He bravely might aspire
To win the civic crown of worth
With honor to his sire.
What anguish tore the parents' breast
When death untimely came,
And treachery with bloody hands,
Put out his life's young flame.
Tears avail not, nor loud laments,
To ease the throbbing heart:
Remembrance of his virtuous life
Alone can peace impart.
Where Woodlawn spreads its stately boughs
With winding walks around,
Beside a snow white monument
His bed of rest is found.
There flowers are strewn—there wreaths
are hung—
There woodbine marks the grave
Of all that was mortal was of him
Whom Jesus died to save.
Midst that Sacred Sepulchral Scene,
Near by a shady bower,
Where water sparkling from the fount
Within a rustic tower

Upon the mount the stone is rais'd,
There should you ever coy
In marble you will see impressed
The image of the boy.

— John Davidson

Later that afternoon, rumors circulated throughout the town that the perpetrator of Frank's murder had been arrested. It was even announced on the front page of one of the local papers. The story was that Constable Johnson of Winchester had apprehended a suspicious-looking man in odd-looking attire in the vicinity of the Stoneham woods, with the stolen money from the Malden Bank found on his person.

Clara, informed of this by a neighbor, rushed to tell Edward.

"Eddie, they have caught the villain!"

"What did you say?" He was unsure he was properly hearing the words she was speaking.

"Frank's murderer—word is he has been captured."

Edward was elated. It seemed like the best possible outcome for him. Someone else, for whatever reason, was arrested, and he could remain free and spend the purloined money without any fear of punishment. This feeling of bliss lasted just until the next day, when another paper, The *Malden Messenger*, with a direct quote from Detective Heath, discounted the story entirely:

> Such a report was current in Malden yesterday forenoon
> and we took prompt measures to verify the truth of it, when
> it proved entirely false. It is enough to say that no man had
> been arrested either in Malden or Winchester, and none of
> the money has been found. The circumstances of the murder
> are already widely known and discussed all over New England,
> and the numerous rumors afloat in regard to arrests made
> show that the whole community is on alert. We are continuing
> our investigations and we again say that the public should be
> on their guard against sensational reports, as the publication

of these only tends to defeat the ends of justice. It is our goal that the final scene of conviction and punishment of the murderer may not be far distant.

The following Monday, William Shiloh considered himself in the mirror as he gripped his razor above yet another lily-white neck. This was his third customer of the day, and he was having difficulty concentrating on the task at hand. The current occupant in his chair was the man who owned the building next door and one of the nicer gentlemen in town, a man who, like Elisha, treated William with respect.

"Are you okay, William?" asked George Bailey.

"Yes, sir."

"I suppose all our minds are clouded since Frank's murder."

"Yes. It was a shock to see the boy that way."

William toiled, mostly silently, in his trade through the rest of the day, his thoughts vacillating between the image of Frank's bloody body and his own reflection behind the white men he served. There was a duality in his image before him—how he viewed himself and in contrast, how most of his customers beheld him. He was not sure how secure his place in the town was, and if his tentative comfort and safety could be jeopardized if he chose to reveal what he witnessed the day of the murder.

There was a commotion behind his shop, and William spotted the dog he had last seen when he shooed it away in the minutes before he came upon a crowd gathered around Frank dying on the ground. The dog stopped rooting through the scattered refuse and stared up at the barber, his muscles tensing to flee at any slight movement from the man before him.

"Easy, boy. I know you're hungry. It's okay. I won't hurt you."

The dog backed away, his eyes steady upon William. William contemplated whether those eyes were considering him, judging if he was trustworthy.

"I promise you, I am a good man! Oh, you look so very thin, dog," said William, noticing the protruding ribs.

William reached into his pocket. "I have some dried meat." William knelt holding his palm out with the salted jerky. The dog was stone still, but his nose twitched, and William smiled. Over the course of a few minutes the dog edged warily forward. William strained not to move a muscle. The dog eventually stood within inches and paused and considered. He moved cautiously, his eyes concentrating on William's. In a quick lunge forward and a quicker one away, he snatched away the meat and retreated several feet while maintaining eye contact.

William remained on his knees, penitent. The dog continued to chew.

"I am a good man," William repeated, releasing his eyes from the dog and raising them skyward. He placed his hands on his bent knee open palmed and spoke in a whisper, not minding if the dog overheard but concerned that others could.

"Lord, it's not fair that I must provide an excuse for my very eyesight! Green complicates my existence. All white men certainly do, but this postmaster now vexes me to no end. No matter how darkened a white man's soul is, he is considered pious compared to one with skin the color of mine. Birth determines whether he is right and I am wrong. The choice is not mine, but the consequences always are, and always will be.

"When a slave picks cotton poorly, or his master reckons he did, or if the master is just in an ill mood, the consequence is the whip. Green has been marked with his poor leg by your Almighty hand, but now, out of greed, he has stained his own soul with the blood of an innocent.

"Why should Edward Green not have to answer to God and man for what he did to Frank? Why should he be spared the whip?

"I have seen both sides of this man, mirror images. He has robbed the bank, he has robbed the town, he has robbed the glorious future of the Converse family. But I cannot permit him to rob my soul.

"I must think this over carefully. There are many considerations. Do I have to be the one to accuse him? I will if I must, but my prayer for my sake and my family's is that instead, another white man will do so first. Being righteous should not contain such folly as this consequence does for me. Why should he not suffer for his sin just because the finger that aches to point at him is of a darker color?"

William sensed a wetness on his still-open palm. The dog was sitting wagging his tail as his long tongue sought in every crevice of William's hand for any remnants of the meat.

Slowly, William, his hand proceeding with great care, patted the animal. Its tail wagged. William smiled.

"Seems I made a friend in this town, boy. You're a good boy. You must have been someone's pet, but now you are alone. Come to me when you are in need, and I will have some food for you and maybe you can listen to me. That is my trade; does that sound fair, since I have no other counsel in this matter? We can help each other, boy. I don't want to call you 'boy,' anymore, that's not right. I don't care for it when some of the townsfolk refer to me as so. But what should I call you?" William caressed his cheek and then pulled his hand down. The answer came to him and he smiled and reached into his pocket for his remaining wad of dried meat. He extended his hand, and the dog ate right out of it. William rubbed the dog's head gently. "I have been seeking guidance and peace, and these moments with you have offered me some respite. I will call you Douglass, after Frederick Douglass. If I could but speak to such a great man as him, he would understand my quandary and he would offer a solution. But I now have you, Douglass, and that will be a small bit of a solace for me." He stroked the fur beneath the dog's chin and received a lick across his face in return.

Yes, a new friend indeed, thought William.

"I can't bring you home with me, it is not permitted, but I will build a shelter here behind my shop for you and feed you, Douglass. And if you choose to stay, if you decide it is safe for you to do so, I will bear witness to you as I determine whether it is wise for me to trust the men of this town with my safety and divulge to them what I have seen."

William wearily returned home to Emily and the children.

Later that night as the husband and wife lay close together with all the children asleep, William confided in his wife.

"When I look at myself as I work behind these men, I am unsure which vantage is more genuine or, more importantly, vital for my survival in this world, theirs or my own."

"William, just a few years ago, before we traveled north, there was no competing image of yourself to project, only what the white man and your own possible servitude mirrored back at you. You have told me this many times."

"True, yet I'm still a servant in a way, or at least have to act like one as I'm allowed to ply my trade and earn a living."

"You have your own place of business, and we have a home—meager as it is, we fill it with love, my dear." Emily kissed his forehead and lay her face against his.

"You're right. This isn't perfect, but it's better. If the threat of chains remains, and I often fear it does, they're figurative and not the ones that could chafe my ankles and wrists, although I ponder if invisible steel links now continue to cause injury to my soul."

Emily wished to comfort her husband.

"We are confined by this society from the moment we arrive in it, William, but there's now at least some breathing space, or so I hope. The war rages on far from us, yet everyday battles surround our people. Still, there's more opportunity than before, and we've reached for it, worked hard for both the freedom of our bodies and of our minds."

William hugged her tight, with one arm under her and the other above her. "Emily, my constant worry is that either can easily be conscripted by *them*, so I pray the Lord will provide for us."

"You put in long hours in your shop so I can remain home and tend to the children unencumbered by much outside toil, though, of course, I wash clothes for some coins when I can."

"I appreciate that, and I am so grateful for what you do for the children."

"I am grateful for what you do for all of us."

"Thank you." He kissed her and they gazed at each other for several tender moments, and then a thought caused him to frown.

"What is it?" Emily said.

"Others of our people here in the North mightn't think well of me, as they may be technically free but still carry out backbreaking work while I tend to the follicles of rich men and enjoy what I view as more of a craft than a toil. I know they resent me not just for my loftier position but also since they aren't welcome in my shop merely because of the pigment of their skin."

"A Negro turning Negroes away, this is a delicate path that you tread, one not of your own choosing but for our family's well-being in a society that we're forced to inhabit."

"This always causes a tinge of regret for me. But I don't make the rules; I'm privileged to be allowed to prosper a bit while others of our kind are locked out of this world which I can float in and out of without really belonging. I'm not one of the townsfolk but am tolerated since I'm skilled at a service thought below a white man to perform."

"William, you've told me many times, my love. It's an art, learned and practiced, the mastery of the straight razor, yet an affluent white man, or most white men, besides some immigrants, won't lower themselves to do what they perceive as such a menial task. But you attend to them well, and they frequent your shop. You should be proud of providing for your family."

William stared at the wall. "I'm still a servant to white men and perhaps seen as a traitor to other black men. It's a conundrum, yet one of which I must take advantage of to increase, or at least maintain, my position and a sliver of wealth. Envy, jealousy from one side and apathy and disdain from the other—both of these surround and smother me. Yet, those in the South have it worst of all. Since their chains, like the hardness of their lives, are real, harsh, and always tightening their grip."

William looked at his wife again. "These men, women, and children have little hope. We've some. I've got to hang on, persevere. As long as I cater to my clients' hair, beards, and especially to their egos, things can improve . . . or in the very least, not worsen for us.

"The trick for me is to not allow *them* to believe that any of their words cause me to have similar feelings of my own," said William. "This is a somewhat easy task. The customers think little of me; to *them*, I'm not a human being but rather another simple inanimate object to be used as needed. I may as well be but a piece of furniture in my very own shop."

Emily clasped his hands. "You are a person, a man, always remember that."

"I try, but it is hard. These men, they're aware I can hear what they say, but they speculate I can't understand their meanings and so possess no desire to do so. But I certainly do; I just don't reveal to *them* that I can. Emily, they sometimes have great disagreements with one another. I make it my business to never disagree with any of *them* or take sides in their arguments. If, on the odd chance, a patron solicits my opinion to contradict another customer, I just smile and make a compliment of each man's intelligence and make a vague reference like, 'I ain't capable of understanding the matters y'all are discussing,' and that I couldn't possibly solicit an opinion of my own, although I always certainly silently hold one, no matter which topic is being parlayed.

"It's a skill to play dumb. It's easier to do so, unfortunately, when you're thought of as a simple inferior by those of paler complexions. For our benefit, I must play the part they lay out. Our lots in life are a little better than our parents', and I hope our children will see some improvement in their lives as well.

"The future's hard to grasp, and the past is best forgotten." William rubbed a section of his cheek. "As you know, my uncle was a fine barber. Luckily, he passed those skills to me, and I took them north to a new land and a new life."

"Thank God for that," said Emily as she yawned, forcing her eyes to stay open. William gazed at Emily as she started to drift off in slumber. She had listened patiently and lovingly to him, but he saw now that she was completely exhausted. He knew she had a long day of toil behind her, and she would be up before he was the next morning to tend to their children for yet another one.

William shared everything with Emily and felt guilty about not divulging to her what was now his greatest concern. *It is best that I figure this out on my own,* he thought. *Informing her of it would only cause her undue stress. I've a great decision to ponder, and I worry about the consequences, first for the life and position I've struggled to attain for myself and my family but also for my everlasting soul if I choose to retain my silence on this important issue.*

A boy is dead. A family and a town are grieving. Standing outside for hours, I watched the whole town of Malden, including Edward Green's wife, visit the Converse mansion to offer their respects and the same the next day at the funeral. But Green and his guilt stayed far away.

He is the killer, but will they listen to a black man if I speak up? I attempt to obscure myself and not interject myself in the townsfolk's affairs, many of them small things really, perceived or petty disagreements—but murder, this is a wholly different matter. Since the very day the terrible act occurred, it's been difficult for me to not immediately come forward and state that the postmaster was the last to enter the bank before young Converse was found fatally injured.

If only I could be like most of the people here, the same color, the same status in society, the same freedom to speak openly on such matters, the decision would be easy. But will they *listen to* me? *And by assigning blame to one of their own, am I, indeed, in their eyes, just casting aspersions upon myself? After all, I'm just a Negro barber; that's how they see me. It's not an easy matter. I'll pray as to how I should proceed, and I know the Almighty will eventually guide me to the right conclusion.*

Chapter Twenty-Six

THE NEWS OF the first murder during a bank robbery was quickly disseminated all across New England. The *New York Times* reported on it the day after it occurred. Soon the story was told in newspapers across the country from coast to coast and even as far as London. Many were fascinated by it, but one reader was seeking out and devouring every sentence written about it he could find.

In the week since the murder, Edward attempted to keep a low profile, but each morning, he visited the news agent on Pearl Street to flip through the pages of several of the Boston newspapers. He far from stood out in doing this. The murder was splashed across the front pages of all the numerous Boston papers, and the newsstand was overwhelmed with patrons searching for any tidbit of news about it. Edward was not seeking information about the crime but only wished to ascertain what the police suspected. He handed the newsboy a few pennies and brought the broadsheets back to his office.

If there was clearly no one around on the street, Edward reveled in reading these fresh reports aloud in his office. "The whole affair seems to be shrouded in mystery, and altogether the murder was one of the most cool and daring that has ever come to our knowledge." Edward experienced an unexpected sense of pride at this line and then continued reading. The next sentence caused Edward to pause, and he scanned it a second time. "The murderer has gained little by his crime. The hundred-dollar bills will be impossible for him to pass; and the two thousand dollars which may remain to him seems but a poor recompense for the commission of such an atrocious deed."

Edward sat back, picked up a loaf of white bread, and ripped a section off. Using his butter knife, he spread a generous dollop of strawberry jam across it. *They really don't have any idea it was me. There seem to be no witnesses,* he thought, *and as for the money, no matter what they say, I now have more than I ever dreamed of possessing.*

Edward munched on his midmorning snack and found his fingers covered with jam; he had scooped up too much from the jar. He eyed the color of the jam winding around his fingers and, without thinking, stared over at the barbershop, then back at his hand.

He stuck his fingers deep into his mouth and licked off the sweetness, probing in between each of his digits with his tongue, and then rubbed any remnants on his pant leg.

Edward folded the newspaper back up and placed it with all the others he had been collecting in his drawers in the days since the terrible deed. The ledger, which had besieged him for so long, was now forgotten under the news of his crime. He was covering over his financial concerns literally, figuratively, and mentally as well. Edward took another satisfying bite of the bread and reached for his glass of milk to wash it down, then opened the next paper in his stack.

"The Springfield *Republican* calls it 'The cruel, cruel murder,'" Edward said to himself in his raspy baritone, then continued reading the article aloud. "No clue has yet been obtained of the perpetrator of the murder and robbery at the Malden Bank on Tuesday. All that can be learned is that a stranger was seen in the vicinity of the bank shortly before the murder, and that a man answering the same description was seen to leave the depot on a train for Boston."

Edward set the paper down and smiled. "It was a stroke of luck, perhaps of genius, to trade coats with that foreigner. Surely, this proves it!" And yet Edward became disheartened when the next article questioned the patsy he had created.

"The belief that a foreign man in a strange brown coat who asked for a sheet of paper and wrote a letter in the depot was the murderer seems absurd, since no man anxious to leave the scene of his recent crime would direct attention to himself by an act so noticeable as that. The first train coming to Boston after the murder passed Malden at fifteen minutes past twelve. At that time the fact of the murder was known, and Mr. Plaisted, the conductor, suspecting the murderer might be on board the train, scrutinized the passengers very closely. Although railroad conductors are known to be good judges of human nature, he saw no one whose appearance caused him suspicions. A train for Lawrence, Manchester, and Concord passed the Malden station about the same time, and it is possible that the murderer went in that direction instead of coming to Boston."

An earlier train left Malden as I walked from the bank and my foreign friend was aboard as it departed, thought Edward.

Edward gasped a deep breath and tried to calm himself as he read the next one out loud as well.

"A queer report comes to us from New London, Connecticut, that they had under arrest in that city the other day, a man suspected of being the perpetrator of the bank robbery and terrible murder in Malden, but they let him go! The story is that a man took the Boston and Providence cars at Malden, bound for Providence, on the day the tragedy occurred, who insisted on riding all the way in the private apartment of the passenger car, but gave no satisfactory reason for the unusual demand.

"Arriving at Providence, he did not leave the car, but kept on toward New London. At Providence, the conductor of the train heard of the Malden affair and at once thought of his queer passenger, whose singular behavior and remarkable taste in choosing his seat in the car excited some suspicions. He telegraphed to New London for the police to have an eye on him. Accordingly, when the train reached that city, the stranger was taken into custody. He was carried to Bacon's Hotel and there searched, and as we are informed, blood was found on his clothing. So much has leaked out to the public, but beyond this, nothing is clearly understood about the matter except that the prisoner was not detained. We give the report as we get it, vouching for nothing, however, beyond the fact that such a story is extensively circulated and has made considerable talk at New London."

Edward was elated that they were looking for suspects, both far and wide, looking everywhere but right at him. He had even avoided talking to the detectives and would attempt to continue to do so. He looked down at the bottle on the floor, picked it up, opened it, and took a long swig, then picked up the next newspaper.

"There was a report the other day that a man had been arrested near Malden with some of the stolen money on his person, but there was no truth in it."

Edward looked up from the paper and scratched his chin. "I wonder who they arrested? I suppose, it is of no import if they let him go."

Edward continued reading. "The fact that the murder was committed and the robbery consummated during an interval of fifteen minutes, which elapsed between the calling of one person at the bank on a business errand and of another who came and found the young clerk in the agonies of death, forms the strangest portion of the mystery and has led several persons to suspect that the crime must have been committed by someone who resides near the bank. But suspicion does not dare to point its finger at any particular party. The fact, too, that a pistol could have been fired off at noonday in the heart of the village, without the report being heard by neighbors, except one who was not sure of the sound at the time, and by passersby is also commented on as a strange occurrence."

Edward paused. "Who heard the gunshot? I would really like to know who heard the gunshot!" As Edward became agitated, he attempted to take another pull on the bottle but spilled the last remnants of whiskey across the paper. Now, even more perturbed, he threw the empty bottle on the floor, and shattered glass went everywhere. He snatched the soaked newspaper off the table and used it to pick up as many of the jagged pieces as he could.

Edward hoped that no one would ever deduce he was the murderer of Frank Converse, but right across the street, seated in William Shiloh's barber chair, was another highly interested reader of the daily newspaper reports. One who had decided that the capture of the elusive perpetrator of this terrible deed had now become his one and only focus.

"I am about to engage in what may be the greatest role I'm ever meant to play in my prestigious career, Shiloh. As you are aware, I'm a renowned, beloved actor, but my true gift is my ability to not just act on the stage with a playwright's words, often those of the great Bard himself, to thunderous ovations, but to act on injustice where I see fit, with my own bravado and a devout sense of right and wrong."

The barber moved his scissors across the man's head as if his hand had a mind of its own. "What role is this, Your Excellency?" William asked.

"I am going to solve the dual atrocious crimes of the murder of the bank teller and the robbery."

"The murder of Frank Converse?"

"Yes, I believe that is his name. I read in the papers how it happened here last week. Is the bank nearby?"

"Sir, it is right next door." William's mind was numb, but his hand continued the scissors' work.

The Count said, "That is good to know. It will be my next stop after we are done here." The Count reached for the glass he had brought with him, which William had already filled for the second time with whiskey. "As I was saying, it's my duty and honor to harness this prestigious ability that I possess to settle the score on the side of the righteous. I am the Count. I am a man of nobility, godly talent, and intellect. I hold the very power to deduce what others are sadly not able to perceive. The answer to someone as brilliant as myself is always in plain sight just as is the refined mustache on my face in a mirror when a mirror is so lucky to behold it."

William wondered if the Count would ask him any questions about his knowledge or thoughts about the murder since his shop was so close to the crime, but the Count, to his surprise, made no direct inquiries of him. It seemed no one wanted to ask him anything about the murder.

Each customer was content to carry on about their opinions and offer conjecture about the crimes, but William felt as if he was invisible to them. The constable had visited the shop briefly and asked William to mention anyone he had seen near the bank on the morning of the murder. Without any further questions, he then departed. No one had requested he testify during the inquest, as if they did not value his intellect, as if the murder of Frank did not concern him. And yet, their obstinance kept him safe.

The morning after the murder, William noticed a copper object on the street that he assumed was evidence, perhaps connected to the murder weapon. Because they paid him little heed, William knew he would have to lead another man to discover this evidence, but subtly, to retain his camouflage. To do so, he had lingered near the piece of metal, pretending to be oblivious to it, but stood there long enough to draw someone's attention. George Bennett spotted the object when he saw where William directed his eyes.

"That could be a clue, William," said Bennett, who picked it up and handed it to the barber. William carried it into the bank and presented it to the cashier.

"Mr. Merrill, Mr. Bennett discovered this outside your entrance and asked me to bring it to your attention."

The man held it in his palm, eyed it, and said, "Please thank Mr. Bennett for me, Shiloh."

William did not know what had happened to the object since but was happy he had played his part in finding it and hoped it turned out to be important.

"Shiloh, the moment I read about this evil crime in the various broad-sheets delivered to my luxurious Boston apartment, I made up my mind to take bold action. I did attend the wake and introduced myself to the detectives. I was very impressed by the turnout of mourners and the fact that the family of the murdered boy indeed possess a magnificent home. That piqued my interest in the case. Of course, regrettably, for a man of my numerous talents and obligations to my adoring public, a few days have passed with other pursuits, but I will begin my righteous quest today, since I am in town and there is no play scheduled for later this evening in the city."

"It is truly generous of you to devote even a fraction of your precious time, a sliver, a small amount of your great intellect to solving the horrific murder of a young man when you could be socializing, studying your lines, or enjoying your boundless existence."

"Yes, I am a very generous man," said the Count, pleased at what he viewed as a compliment. A man such as the Count was steadfast in the belief that he must always be presentable to the theater of the stage as well as the theater of life itself. William Shiloh was a skilled professional, but what the Count most admired about the barber was the respect befitting his royal pedigree that he perceived the man showed him. "My task, Shiloh, for the greater good and any unsolicited praise it will surely entail, is to seek out the murderer and cause the townspeople to no longer tremble in fear."

His next question shocked the barber: "Are you afraid of the murderer, Shiloh?"

William paused to consider his answer, then blurted out, "I certainly am."

The Count beamed a radiant smile. "Do not be concerned, poor fellow, I will save the day and then reluctantly accept any accolades that will indeed be lavished upon my royal self by you and the rest of the grateful populace of this town and its surrounding communities. The thievery and malice of such ugly deeds rendered onto such a dear boy would even have inspired William Shakespeare to put ink to parchment."

"In the real world in which we live, Your Excellency, there is certainly no greater actor than you!"

Misunderstanding the intention of William's words, the Count said, "You are correct in your assessment. For in my noble opinion, there is an unidentifiable villain and a desperate need for a hero. One such as a great detective with an agile mind to root out the felon and bring him into the light, whatever the danger to one's own person. With great risks, there are great rewards, most likely money, fine liquor, and finer women. Also, I will be the plebeians' hero and humbly accept their praise and any minor gifts they will doubtlessly be compelled to bestow upon my royal self.

"Shiloh, have you read about the monetary reward offered by the bank's board of directors for the arrest and conviction of the killer?"

"I have, sir," William replied and wondered what would happen if he came forward with what he suspected.

The Count continued his self-aggrandizing proclamation. "While I am positive the town will view the man who solves this crime and catches the criminal as a hero to be greatly admired, it is but my modest intention to humbly accept both the financial reward and their pure admiration with a modicum of reluctance, but to also do so while not disrespecting the grateful and celebrating masses. As a thespian renowned on stages throughout the world, it is always my utmost duty to never disappoint an adoring crowd. I am the center, the star of any theater production that is blessed by my presence, and now the town of Malden will be my stage to solve this mystery and bring the perpetrator to justice! I shall proclaim to the villain on the very moment I hold him in my grasp, 'Thou are unfit for any place but hell.'"

By this point, William possessed far more knowledge about the Count than any other man in town. This was mainly because he was forced to listen without complaint, on a daily basis, as the man rambled on about his accomplishments.

He knew all about the Count's acting across theaters in Europe and New York; for example, he just recently learned how he had performed *Richard III* with Junius Brutus Booth, an esteemed actor and father of fellow famed actor John Wilkes Booth.

Since his first visit, the barber had constantly been schooled by the Count on a series of books that he had written, which he assured William were of the most interesting of subjects. But one of the man's favorite topics to mention was the many libel cases he had pressed and won against newspapers that questioned his royal pedigree.

William reasoned the Count felt quite comfortable to express all his accomplishments and high opinions of himself in his shop since criticism or questions of his title were taboo to a black barber and so nonexistent in the ornate parlor where William worked.

He was a perfect customer for a black barber in a way—a white man equally vain in appearance and spirit. And William was perfect for the Count—a diligent, appreciative audience—although the Count was ignorant of the fact that if William held a lighter complexion he could openly treat George Jones as any other white man would, but he could not, and it was not in William's interest to ever contemplate such actions.

The Count could be assured that the man attending to his whiskers and hair had skill in his trade and a duty to listen and show interest. Of course, he earnestly believed the interest was authentic. In the Count's mind, William was in awe of him, thought highly of the actor certainly, and would never utter a libelous remark, as some were prone to do, either to the Count's face or, certainly and frequently as others did, behind his back.

Yet as long as he showed up for a shave and a trim of his delicate whiskers below his nose four or five times a week, William could care less if he was a count or perhaps the title was as counterfeit as many of his customers and other town residents speculated with such surety. More than one referred to the Count as a pompous ass. Whatever he was, the man was a steady customer for William. So this particular man's assumed title and the self-importance of white men of as a whole were not William's concern as long as their currency was genuine and the tips were generous—and the Count's always were.

As the Count was planning his self-appointed investigation into the murder of Frank Converse, just two days before Christmas, the adjusted session of the jury of inquest summoned by Coroner Hill was held at the town hall. Additional testimony was provided by the town physicians, Dr. Sullivan and, again, Dr. Burpee.

Dr. Sullivan was examined first and testified that he went to the house of Deacon Converse on the day of the death of his son, in the late afternoon and, by the deacon's request, examined Frank's head. "I concluded that the ball entered at the back of the right ear and the exit was near the left temple. In all bullet wounds the place of entrance is always smaller than that of exit. In this case, the entrance was undoubtedly smaller than the missile, in consequence of the elasticity of the skin."

He stated there was a good deal of diffusion of the blood around the place where the ball entered so as to make it look black and blue. He passed a probe in at the wound of exit, and found the bone somewhat shattered. "The probe passed easily along until it reached the opposite wound, but as it was not long enough, it did not come out on the other side. But it would undoubtedly have done so had it been long enough. My object was to ascertain the state of the bone. It was impossible that precisely such a wound could be made by anything other than a bullet. I think there was no reasonable probability of two balls having been fired, as they must have taken precisely the same course. The pistol ball must have been fired by some person near and behind the deceased, and the theory I have is the deceased turned partially round prior to the shot being fired. The wound I examined I think was the cause of the young man's death, and there were no indications a postmortem examination would have revealed any other cause."

Dr. Burpee was then recalled and testified he believed the death was caused by a bullet entering the left temple and injuring the brain. But he was adamant that another ball had entered behind the right ear as well.

"What made you come to this conclusion?" asked the coroner.

"I wished to elaborate on this at the original inquest before it was adjourned. My opinion was formed purely from external examination, with the use of the probe. The hair on the boy's left temple appeared to be singed or scorched, showing that the pistol must have been within a few inches of the young man's head when discharged, and near the wound at the back of the ear, powder was unmistakably burned into the flesh."

"To be clear, are you saying you think two shots were fired into the head instead of just one?"

"Yes."

Dr. Sullivan frowned.

"Elaborate, please," said the coroner.

"When I examined the wound on the forehead, I found a black, greasy appearance on the flesh, which could not be rubbed off with a finger, and which I supposed then to have been burnt powder. If there was but one shot fired, it would be a singular fact if the appearance of the powder should be noticeable where the pistol ball came out as well as on the other side of the head where it entered."

"No bullets have been found on the premises, only a small piece of copper outside, close to the entrance," stated the coroner.

"I believe both bullets remain in Converse's head."

The court gasped.

"Furthermore, under these circumstances, I strongly urge that a post-mortem examination be performed."

Dr. Sullivan stood up. "I wholeheartedly disagree. This suggestion is not just wrong but profane. I am acting as much as a family friend as I am a medical doctor. Sir, again," he said, turning to his peer, "I find the idea of a postmortem as outrageous. I've known the deacon for twenty years. The family has suffered enough. The boy is in the ground, the parents are grieving, the murderer is still on the loose. So it is pointless whether there are one or two bullets lodged in his head. He is six feet under!" Sullivan shouted this last part.

"Of course, I understand, the natural feeling of the parents would be against it. But for science and to know what happened precisely to the boy, that is what I am attempting to argue," said Dr. Burpee.

"Even if we were sure there were two shots fired instead of one, it will not bring Frank back to life or find his killer. Only an eyewitness or a confession will lead to an arrest. We all know that," stated Dr. Sullivan.

"Agreed," said the coroner.

Dr. Burpee raised his hands, paused, and said, "Agreed."

Dr. Sullivan continued, his voice rising: "I was present when Frank was born. I saw the joy in the Converses holding their firstborn. Over the years, I observed the profound pride they held in raising him."

Dr. Burpee became red in the face and pointed his finger at Dr. Sullivan. "Sir, I knelt there, helpless, inches away as Frank died. I witnessed the anguish of the parents arriving individually, each discovering their son slaughtered. It was like two maelstroms of melancholy, one and then the other washing over the gathering. The utter shock of one subsiding only to have the next swell up. The deep sadness permeated all assembled; we were not onlookers, but participants in their sorrow."

Dr. Sullivan's jaw dropped in surprise. Being so close to the Converses for so long, this description of their grief upon finding their boy in such a ruined state, a boy he had watched grow up, overwhelmed him.

Dr. Burpee went on. "First, the mother was in hysterics at the bloody mess of her child. In the throes of grief, I perceived she blamed me, as if I had not done enough to save the boy."

"There was nothing you could do," said Dr. Sullivan softly.

Dr. Burpee did not acknowledge the comment and continued, "Then the father arrived and, upon seeing Frank, would have collapsed immediately if not caught by those close by. He was taken outside for air. I would say, Dr. Sullivan, that I, too, am outraged by your questioning of my intentions."

"Gentlemen," said the coroner, "this discussion is over. I will proceed in a minute and ask my brother, the undertaker, to present his testimony and close the proceedings. For civility, I urge you both to shake hands and put this disagreement behind you."

The two men shook hands without saying a word.

Charles Hill was then sworn in and examined. He testified, "I am an undertaker in Malden, and was called by Mr. Turner to accompany the body of Converse to the house of his father, and I assisted in laying the body out. Mr. Turner and Mr. Richards were with me. We commenced to examine what was the face, and found marks of what appeared to be powder about the wound in the skin, near the right ear. The hole made by the pistol ball was very small. But on the left temple, where the ball appeared to have come out, the hole was larger and ragged, and around it, extending to about the size of a quarter, the skin was blemished, as though from blood, and this mark remained after the skin was washed.

"Around the right ear, where the marks of powder were, it was rather of a reddish cast. The blood ran much more freely from the wound at the ear than from that at the temple. There were no marks of bruises or scratches on the body. I saw no mark of the hair being singed on the forehead, although my attention was called to it."

This closed the testimony, and after a brief consultation the jury returned the following verdict: "Frank E. Converse came to his death on the fifteenth day of December, 1863, between the morning hours of eleven and twelve o'clock, in the building of the Malden Bank, by being shot through the head by some person or persons to the jury unknown."

Chapter Twenty-Seven

O N CHRISTMAS DAY, the weather was fine, with a crisp and bracing air, and even the most gloomy mind could find no excuse, out of doors, at least, for not being cheerful. Services were held in many churches in the morning and were well attended. Christmas was strictly a religious holiday, not one of celebration. The Puritans had actually passed a law in the seventeenth century that fined anyone five shillings who made merry on the day. The statute was repealed after a couple of decades, but attitudes toward the holiday remained rigid. It would not be named a federal holiday for several more years, and so both schools and businesses were open.

The good ice on the ponds around town offered an opportunity for invigorating and healthful sport, and skating was the most popular amusement of the day. Everywhere, in the city and out, where a square of ice was to be found, were gathered skaters of all sorts, shapes, and sizes.

But in a small Malden apartment, Clara Green moaned, "Eddie, fetch the midwife!"

Half-asleep, Edward stumbled out of bed and fell on the floor.

"Are you having the baby?"

"Yes!"

"What should I do?"

"*Fettttttccch* the midwife!"

Edward searched frantically for his britches on the floor and his shirt from the day before. Running as best as he could, out the door and down the stairs, he tripped a few steps from the bottom. Lifting himself up, he exited out into the street.

Knocking at the home of Mrs. Christenson on Mountain Avenue frantically until she appeared, Edward said, "Clara has reached her time of trial, the child is coming."

The midwife, always prepared to leave on a moment's notice, had her bag packed by the door. Following Edward to the entrance of his boardinghouse, she turned to him and said, "Thank you, Mr. Green. I will send the boy from your office as a messenger to locate you. Where will you be?"

"I will be at Hill's."

"Okay, thank you. And don't worry, I have been doing this a long time. All will be fine, with God's grace."

She closed the door and walked up the stairs. Edward headed toward the bakery to collect Marshall. Soon, the two friends were sitting on their normal stools, with ales in their hands.

"I'm a bit nervous," said Edward. "Clara has suffered with severe pain for a few days."

"Have positive thoughts, Eddie."

Edward took such a large sip, he almost drained his glass.

Marshall ordered two shots of whiskey and raised his for a toast. "To you, Clara, and the baby, may God bless you all!"

They snapped their heads back and downed the shots. *I hope he at least blesses Clara and the child. Most likely he will not bless me, for he is aware of all my sins,* thought Edward.

He ordered another round.

Soon, he could no longer keep track of the time or the glasses of ale that changed from full to empty before his blurry eyes.

At some point, he blinked, and Amos Tenney stood before him. "Mr. Green, Mrs. Green has given birth to your daughter."

Edward attempted to stand, but to him, it seemed like the floor moved away from him the closer his feet got to it.

Amos led the way, and Marshall and Edward followed him out of the tavern, the postmaster careful in each one of his footfalls.

The day had grown dark earlier than expected as clouds rolled in, but the gaslights were being lit one by one as they arrived on Pleasant Street, and the artificial world was growing brighter for Edward as he approached his home.

Walking back to his apartment to meet his child for the first time, Edward stumbled. Marshall helped him up. "Do you need assistance up the stairs?"

"No, somehow I'll manage. Good night, Marshall."

Marshall started to say, "Congratulations, again," but the door had already closed, banging into Edward's backside and propelling him toward the stairs. Somehow, he regained his balance, and his palm clutched the railing. Soon, having no memory of the ascent, he stood outside his apartment door.

When Edward entered the apartment, he found both Clara and their newborn asleep on the bed. Edward lay down on the floor beside them and promptly fell asleep himself.

That night, many a family was gathered in cozy reunion at the dinner table, while still others crowded into theaters and places of amusement. Behind the scenes, managers chuckled, and stars put on the sweetest smiles before advancing to the footlights. As the famed Count Joannes was exulting in a standing ovation, his second of the day for his lead performance in *Hamlet*, Edward was waking from his deep slumber on the floor to the sound of Clara's voice.

"Eddie, would you like to meet your daughter?"

Drowsy, he put an arm on the bed and pulled himself up onto it and lay beside his wife and new daughter, feeling equal parts anxious about what he had done and what he would do.

"I know you wanted a son and to name him after your father, but we have a girl. Here, hold her and we can think of a name for her." She passed the baby to Edward. He was disoriented and yet soothed by the strange, warm creature he held. He couldn't focus on her in the way he wanted to. He was dizzy. Edward was unsure whether the child was spinning or the world around her was.

"Clara, what do you want to name her?"

"I like the name Alice."

Having assumed he would have a boy, Edward had not pondered any female names and said, "And so, that will be her name. Edward looked skyward, and said, "Lord, on this day of celebration of your son, we're blessed with the birth of our daughter, Alice."

"Thanks, Eddie, and please remember to have the crib ready tomorrow." Clara yawned. "I suppose one night in bed with us will do her no harm, but she should have her own safe place from now on."

Clara smiled at him, and exhausted, she soon fell back into a deep slumber.

Edward said a silent prayer as he held this new life for the first time, just ten days after he had taken the life of another. *Yes, I will keep you safe, Alice. Lord, help me in this.*

Jesus was born to save all our souls, and I feel and hope that the birth of my daughter on this holy day is a sign that I've some redemption left. I've fallen so greatly. Part of me tells myself to flee, to walk the world. I'm a scoundrel, a cad. I've sinned immensely, each sin outdoing the last in its dastardly nature until the ultimate one of murder. At this point, it's safe to say that I've broken each of your Ten Commandments.

But I can't flee; I'm grounded like the roots in the earth of this garden. However, I, at this moment, hold in my arms a seed, a seed of redemption, a seed of promise. Her life, so new and untainted, like the fallen snow, gives me hope for my soul in this life and the eternal one that lies after. Father, protect us! I'll not cry, though I may choke up mightily.

After saying this prayer and looking upon the little face and body that was a mixture of himself and Clara, Edward sensed pure awe and love for his daughter. He knew about a mile away, another set of parents were continuing their mourning.

I miss Frank. There's sadness for the Converses at their loss. Yet, I'm utterly relieved I've purloined the money necessary to maintain my position. I can pay off my debts and still be able to support my family. This is most important. Little else matters. There's guilt, but it's mixed with relief. Yet, I'm also aware that by my attempt of solving one problem, I've perhaps created a larger one for myself.

As the new year of 1864 began, the circumstances of the Malden tragedy, so far as was known, continued to be laid out by various newspapers throughout the country daily. Even though the Civil War was raging into its third year and the death toll was mounting to the hundreds of thousands, each new detail of this singular unsolved murder in a town a few miles north of Boston drew great curiosity, reaching as far as major newspapers in Europe.

Like Christmas, New Year's Day was not yet celebrated as a federal holiday at this time. As Edward sat in his office reading about the murder he had committed, Marshall entered.

"I looked at all the newspapers earlier today myself," said Marshall. "I suppose they will continue to write about this until they arrest someone."

"I suppose so," said Edward as he finished reading the article while Marshall sat quietly.

Edward folded the broadsheet back up and placed it in a drawer in his desk. "I am going to visit Shiloh for a trim and shave. Then I have an appointment with a Mr. Chute in Boston. Amos will be tending to the office for the rest of the day. I see him approaching. Forgive me, Marshall, I have to step out now."

Marshall watched Edward amble out of the office and cross the street toward the barbershop, thinking his friend had grown more and more distant since Frank's murder. Looking at Edward's gait from this angle, it reminded him of the stranger walking a similar path on that terrible day. Nodding as Amos entered the post office, Marshall did his best to convince himself that this and his other recent concerns that Edward could be the murderer simply could not be true.

After informing William Shiloh that he intended to singlehandedly solve the murder, Count Joannes had made several more trips to Malden, investigating and interviewing its townsfolk. He was now certain of who the suspect was and prepared to reap the glory as the man who saved the town from such wretched villainy. That morning, from his spacious Boston apartment, which lay in close proximity to the several venues in which he performed, he composed a letter:

> *To the Selectmen of the Town of Malden, Mass. The Messrs.*
> *Hubbard Russell, Charles Sanderson and Samuel Shute:*

*Gentlemen: As a citizen and deeply interested with you
and all who are friends of public justice, in discovering the
demonic author of the atrocious and mercenary murder in
the Malden Bank, on the 15th of December last, I instantly,
upon the announcement of the terrible deed resolved to use
my time, intellect and every honorable means in my power
to trace and find the murderer.*

*Apart from my natural impulse in this matter, I was
further incited from my personal acquaintance with a
member of the bereaved family; and tenfold have my
feelings been aroused since my interviews with the most
broken-hearted mother and father of the murdered son—
Frank Converse—whose excellence and purity of character
daily prepared him—even suddenly—to meet the presence
of God. I conscientiously believe my endeavors to trace
out the assassin to the very "door of proof," by inductive
reasoning and aided by undeniable and admitted facts
gathered by me day by day, hour by hour, have not been
without success.*

*Therefore, in good faith, I write this letter to you,
gentlemen, upon a subject in which you and I, and all
citizens have a deep and abiding public, private and
mutual interest. A paramount duty and obligation are
cast upon me and every man in the community to discover
the cruel and cowardly murderer. In fulfillment of this
duty on my part and considering that I should morally
and legally be a participant in the guilt—ex post facto
—should I conceal what I honestly believe will tend to
discover the assassin, I thus announce to you—ex officio
as the selectmen of the town of Malden—the name of
that person, who upon reasonable and probable cause, I
conscientiously believe is the murderer. I hereby enclose the
name in Arabic cyphers with a key to translate the same
into English for your special knowledge, and I hereby claim*

all rights under this communication, and the arrest of the
accused, as well as all danger from whatever quarter.

On Christmas day, I told you (Mr. Russell) verbally,
that I believed I had traced the assassin. The feeling of
intense passion for justice and the right sways my heart,
mind and resolution in this matter; resolved however,
to protect the innocent while denouncing the alleged
murderer, and it would give me far greater pleasure to
prove a man's innocence than to establish any man's guilt.

You will acknowledge the receipt of this privileged
communication, which you will receive without prejudice
to me; and that my motives may not be perverted by
malignant enemies, I reserve my right to publish this letter
in self vindication of my public duty. I have the honor,
gentlemen, to remain Your fellow citizen, respectfully and
faithfully,

GEORGE, THE COUNT JOHANNES

P. S.—I have transmitted a duplicate of this letter directed
to the President and Directors of the Malden Bank.

Even though the city's main post office was a short walk away from his apartment, the Count elected to take the train to Malden to mail the letter. He arrived in Malden just minutes after Edward had departed on the train into Boston.

Upon entering the post office, he was annoyed that the town's postmaster was not present to receive the letter directly. "Where is the man in charge, boy?"

"He's off to get his picture taken, sir. Gone for the day, I'm afraid."

"Oh, will he be in tomorrow?"

"Yes."

"Fine then, you may assist me, and I will visit the postmaster tomorrow on other business."

Reluctantly, the Count allowed the boy, Amos Tenney, to take his letter. The Count paid for the postage and exited the office.

When Clara returned home to their apartment later that day with some vegetables she had purchased at Shepard's grocery, Edward was holding Alice on his knee, playing with her. Clara lifted up her daughter, held her tight, and gave her a kiss on each cheek. She then placed Alice back down on Edward's lap and gave him a peck on the lips. He returned the kiss but did not make eye contact with her.

"How did the picture go?"

"It's a long time sitting still and making this face," said Edward, his features dull and flat.

Clara thought that this would be of no difficulty since her husband had held that expression since Frank had been killed. *I wish Eddie would tell me how he feels,* she thought. *He's not spoken of Frank since the murder; didn't attend the services, which was embarrassing to me since the whole town was there. But maybe I should hold more kindness in my heart for my husband. He's clearly suffering at the loss of his friend. A shroud of sadness and uncertainty envelops him. It appears that Eddie's as equally upset about Frank's death as the Converses are; or even more so, if that's at all possible. Perhaps this makes sense in a way—the two were so close and Eddie feels the loss heavy on his soul.*

Clara prepared their dinner and gazed with affection as her husband continued to play with Alice. *He loves me and our daughter so much,* she thought, and her heart warmed for the first time this day. *Truly, he'd do anything for us, absolutely anything in his power, to provide for our happiness and comfort. I feel so blessed that he cherishes and cares for our little family so well. Thank you, Lord, for leading Eddie to my heart after it was left barren by two suitors. Eddie committed himself to me, and so I am committed to him. I'll stand by him through any storm that comes.*

Chapter Twenty-Eight

THE NEXT DAY, Edward Green, unaware of its contents and how it could affect his fate, delivered the Count's letter to the nearby town hall. He stopped by the news agent and purchased the latest edition of the *American Traveller*. And as was his custom, he laid it out across his desk and read aloud of his crime.

"The hellacious murder of young Frank Converse, in the bank in Malden, is one of those events which startle the community, especially those who live in a town or its vicinity, more than the news of a great disaster at sea, or a great battle in which thousands of men have been slaughtered. Those who have never lived in a town which has been visited by murder, cannot know the terrible sensation. This youngster was a bright-eyed, ruddy complexioned, fair-haired boy, whom I often used to see in the horse cars on his way to and from school. He would ride up front being friendly with the conductor, Lichfield, a young man himself who was only a handful of years older than Converse."

"Who has written this?" wondered Edward.

"The innocent and faithful guardian over other men's money, he was in one instant of overwhelming terror sent out of this world by the hand of a man whose only motive was plunder. All the elements of an atrocious and cold-blooded murder combine in this one. No provocation whatsoever; no motive except the worst; the utmost deliberation, and the coldest and clearest calculation of chances—these define the character of the perpetrator, and the household wreck which the catastrophe has made creates a chapter of horrors rarely equaled in the history of crime.

"The most frequent comment is that the success of such a plot in a populous town is a very strange thing. But Malden, though a big town, empties a large portion of all its inhabitants into Boston by the morning trains. The street where the bank is situated is like the main street of most country towns. Opposite the bank there is a large stable, the post office, and a tailor's shop. Nearby to the left stands a tinware business, a barber's shop, a photography studio and then a schoolhouse. On the other side of the bank, a block of stores runs farther along, opening into the square where the town hall is located. I have frequently been up and down this street without meeting in the whole distance, more than half a dozen people. The assassin must have watched the street closely and then committed the murder and robbery almost instantly. The people in the middle of the town, old settlers mostly, were startled out of their presence of mind. Though the alarm spread rapidly, little well-directed effort seemed to have been made to bar the escape of the murderer. Of course, the usual rumors and suspicions were shared, but I do not think any certain clue has yet been obtained."

Edward closed the paper and filed it away. "I am still a mystery to them. Let's hope it stays that way." He shut the drawer, which jammed due to all its contents. He opened it again, bore down hard on all the newspapers, and pushed the drawer shut.

The Count stayed overnight at the Evelyn Hotel. After a light breakfast, knowing a very busy morning lay ahead of him, he breathed deep to achieve the proper mood and mindset. He bent down to touch his toes several times. Then stared in the mirror practicing voice exercises. This was his tried and true ritual for many years each time before a big performance upon the stage. Feeling both exhilarated and a bit nervous, the Count attended to a very important errand, aware he had much more to accomplish this day to gain the accolades he justly deserved.

The tough bit is always the performance; it is the adulation afterward that I strive to achieve. But it is now within my very grasp. I have solved the murder. I will be held in the utmost regard just as I've always known I should be. I am a good man with the potential of being a great man. A very great man! That's how they should all view me, and they will indeed do so! Young Converse was the wrong man at the wrong time. The Count, my royal self, is the right man at the right time. Converse's murder won't go unpunished nor uncompensated. I am sure of it. My reward is so close at hand, thought the Count as he entered the post office.

"Mr. Postmaster, I am very pleased to see that you are in. Would you be so kind as to look at this?" Before Edward could answer, the Count shoved a folded piece of paper into his hand, which had reached up instinctively, if a bit reluctantly, to receive it.

Edward had not been looking at the door, nor had he heard the bell; his attention had been drawn skyward, as it often seemed to be this late in the morning. He was pondering over which book he would be discussing with his friend Frank, if the boy were still alive.

After the handoff, the Count twirled away hastily, his cape a blur, and seemed to scan the entire room before looking toward the door from which he had just entered and then intently back at Edward. A moment or two passed, but Edward sensed even more time had elapsed. Wiping some sweat from his brow and hoping the impromptu visitor would not notice, he gazed down at the paper in his hand. The texture of the parchment was harsh, like sandpaper, as if there were a danger that it would scrape against his skin and cause the postmaster to bleed. Edward could not see the Count looking at him but assumed the man's gaze.

"Please recite it aloud, sir," said the Count.

Edward unfolded the paper and scrutinized the Count's words once and then read them a second time aloud, with a quiver in his voice. "As the Great Bard wrote, truth will come to light, murder cannot be hid long. I, the Count Joannes, am the purveyor of that truth. I deduced who the murderer of young Converse was through thorough facts and gleaned testimony, and soon the whole town will also be aware of it. It will be on the front page of tomorrow's newspaper."

Edward found it hard to continue but feared he would reveal his sin if he stopped.

"Be not afraid of greatness. Some are born great, some achieve greatness, and others have greatness thrust upon them. For a man like myself, a renowned Count, all three have indeed been proven true. This is how excellent I am. It has been my duty, my calling to solve this crime and bring the criminal to justice, and so I have accomplished this!

"Townspeople of Malden, you have no further need to cower in fear and are most welcome that I acted on your behalf and valiantly captured the criminal before he gained any notion of my brilliant deduction of his heinous guilt."

Edward gazed at the Count as if he were caught in a snare.

"Not a horrible reading," said the Count," but it is perhaps best that a man such as you just stick to mere clerical work going forward." He bellowed with laughter at his observation.

The timing of the Count's arrival to his office a day after his visit to the barber concerned the postmaster. Was there a chance the barber expressed suspicions about him as being the elusive culprit to this dandy of a fellow? This actor, whom he attended to several times a week.

William could not have witnessed him on the street in the storm after the murder; Edward willed himself confident of this fact. He thought, *Even if the barber guessed I was the criminal, the man would be too terrified to come forward, and who in the town would believe a Negro barber anyway?* However, the Count's unexpected presence in his office was like a tide of veiled accusation crashing in upon his assumed safe shores, knocking Edward off his unstable feet.

Edward's hands went limp. He urged the coarse paper to dissolve to sand so its grains would slip through his fingers to vanish forever, yet the words and their meaning remained. He studied the Count. The man's attention was not on him. Surely, he must have averted his gaze before Edward glanced up from reading about his guilt. Perhaps the man was toying with him. It seemed like the Count cared more about the outside world than the postmaster before him since his focus was mostly on the street. He was clearly a vain, distracted man by his dress and manner. In fact, Edward had thought this the very first time he observed the Count entering Shiloh's shop. Maybe, the postmaster considered, he could use this against his accuser and flee unexpectedly.

Where could I go? I could slip out the back door while the Count stares out at Pleasant Street, thought Edward, *but perhaps this is what the Count is attempting to coax me into doing in the first place. Walk right into the arms of a pair of detectives, and my very flight would secure my guilt for them.*

Edward deduced he held one other option. He took a couple of paces to his right. They may have been the straightest steps Edward Green ever accomplished since his leg first went bad. Edward focused his thoughts intently, placing his body in the proper position for if and when it became necessary to attempt his daring move. What Edward sought was in the back of the room, and he crept toward it as the Count resumed talking. Edward reached tentatively for the drawer where he often kept his pistol after the murder, all the while keeping his eyes locked on the Count.

"The guilty should hang. The guilty will hang," the Count proclaimed with confidence.

Edward took a step back, both from the Count and the imaginary gallows that floated in his vision. He had trouble swallowing; his throat tightened. He reached up to loosen his collar a bit.

"I shall get the reward, and they will remember me as the one who brought the killer to justice," shouted the Count as if speaking to a crowded theater instead of just an anxious audience of a single person. The Count gazed out at the street, pondering how the town would soon embrace him, celebrating both his bravery and high intelligence. He thought himself a genius, and they would soon all view him that way as well. His actions would provide them stability and safety.

Do it now, kill him, shoot him, flee! thought Edward, seeing that the Count was distracted in his own mind. This man, with all his put-upon airs, was the most dangerous man around town, he thought, well aware that he, himself, had killed his own close friend. Edward was convinced that ideas could be as dangerous as actions and this man before him, with his cape and his elaborate mustache, was one that any prudent man should avoid in any and all situations. The Count turned to him with the biggest smile Edward had ever seen in his life.

Pompous bastard! I should shoot you! And I might if it comes to it! the postmaster wanted to scream, but he held his tongue.

The Count was again deep in the theater of his own mind and unaware of the look of contempt on the postmaster's face. *Solving this crime, allowing the citizens of the town to feel safe by my master detective work, will place me on a very deserved pedestal. Mr. Converse and his family, with their immense wealth, will owe me. Favors will not be asked for, but merely given.*

The Count stared out at the town once again as Edward's expression changed from fear to annoyance and finally to disdain. The Count noticed very few people were walking around on the street, going about their daily business. *Once the news of the arrest of the murderer pointed out plainly by my fine detective work is proclaimed, the whole town will gather in the square and perhaps carry me on their shoulders in immense gratitude. Mr. Converse will shake my hand firmly. The local constable and detectives will thank and praise me for solving the crime when they were all incapable of doing so, and I will gain my reward. As a rich, honored, deserving man of royalty, I will have the wife of my choosing. There will be so many, countless, exquisite ladies for the Count to choose from—all will want to marry such a calculating, brilliant man as myself and become my Countess.*

With my fame and new wealth, the undivided attention of the town and the undying gratitude of the Converse family, my life will forever be transformed for the better. It will occur as wonderfully as I have imagined it would, in fact, how I have always truly known it would be for me one day.

Edward forcibly restrained himself from shouting the question directly at the Count, asking whom he ascertained the murderer to be. Was the man merely taunting Edward before he accused him directly? *Can I kill him with the very same pistol I shot Frank with?*

Even though, in contrast, this day is clear and the streets are slightly busier, a customer could come in at any second. Someone could hear the shot. And I can't simply walk away like I did from the bank; this is my place of business. Plus, what would I do with the body and all the blood? Frank's blood has stained my memory and vision, first when I shot him and then, even more, watching as they took his bloody corpse out of the bank. I don't want to experience the sight of either event again. But can I kill this man if I must? Edward blinked several times and looked at the Count, realizing the man was now speaking directly to him.

"Are you all right?"

"Fine."

"Good, well, as I was saying . . ." The Count took a long pause and stared intently at Edward, who took another step backward.

Continue. Get to it. I'm most interested in what you have to say, thought Edward.

Edward could see that the Count's face grew more serious as the man approached and got closer as well to revealing the name of the murderer. A man the Count indicated was not only certainly guilty of the deed but should also suffer greatly for it.

The Count was all about delivering a performance and considered how to continue. *Why keep the postmaster guessing besides the fun of it? I know the key with any audience, no matter how small, even this audience of one, is to build tension until the room is thick with it, the air heavy and the audience uncertain. I want him to know that I have a superior mind to him and everyone else. Oh, his reaction in the end will be, indeed, satisfying!*

The craft is the most important thing; theater is perhaps more vital than anything else, and so it is my very passion in all my experiences. The mundane is not something I am interested in practicing, ever, in any situation. There would be no joy at his expense in doing that. Looking at this slight, uneven man, I consume the suspense fraught in his eyes. It is marvelous. So rewarding. I have captured his attention. He is in the palm of my hand. He nourishes me. He is mine. I have him. It's so wonderful. His uncertainty. How precious it is, it fulfills me. I am feeling utter delight. No need to hurry. I will tease him a little more before allowing him to hear my reveal and then acknowledge pure dominance, my absolute greatness, to him completely.

"Mr. Green, I know who left the bank last," he said.

"You do." Edward spoke but not in a question.

"Yes! And it is in my opinion that whoever left the bank last, before the murder was detected, is the one who committed the cowardly act."

Surely, he is mocking me, thought Edward. *Perhaps I should shoot him right now, regardless of consequences. I might as well hang for two murders if he is about to accuse me and hang me for one. The punishment is meted out exactly the same.*

Maybe I can hit him with something instead. No, the struggle would draw even more attention, and I'm no match for him in size or physicality. It would not end well for me.

The Count had not ceased talking, and Edward turned from his own thoughts to the Count's words and also concentrated on his body language to see if the man intended any sudden movement. Edward's muscles, his tendons and bones, stressed and prepared for any possible action he could take . . . attack, depart, surrender.

"Constable Abbott has said as much, and it is my strong compulsion that he is right, and therefore my stronger assumption is that I am right. I know who did it."

"You do?" This time Edward's inflection was a question.

"I do."

Edward's fingers were desperate; they were mere inches from the handle of the drawer. *Just a little farther, a little farther,* he thought, stretching his arm as far back as he was able.

In a whirl, the Count stepped toward him briskly and clamped his hands down hard on both his shoulders. Edward frantically tried to reach for the drawer handle, willing his body to contort in that direction, but it was too far away, out of his grasp. Plus, the larger man's grip was strong, pushing him downward, rooting him in place. There was nowhere to go now—the man had him in his clutches.

"I have told Abbott of my suspicions, my knowledge of the crime, and more importantly, who the very criminal is!" The Count was smirking.

"You have?" Edward's voice was feeble. His bad leg ached from the downward pressure. He was surprised his fear began to blend with some relief. The guilt of killing his friend had been overwhelming. The secrecy, the avoidance of talking about the murder when all the town could speak of nothing else, wore on his mind and spirit.

If the Count had informed the constable he was the murderer, and the detectives from Boston were aware as well, then the jig was up. There was no sense in killing this man who presented himself as some sort of royalty. Edward decided he would submit and take his just punishment. *I will be jailed or executed. Clara and Alice will lose a husband and a father. This has all been for naught. All is lost now,* thought Edward.

"The murderer should have known, there's no avoiding my clasps!" said the Count, and Edward prepared to surrender. His body grew flaccid, he had no more energy to flee from the man's grip. He was caught.

Chapter Twenty-Nine

"I<small>T WAS</small> B<small>AILEY</small>. It must be Bailey! I have brilliantly deduced it!"
Numbness. Confusion.

"I, the Count Joannes, shall be rewarded. It was George Bailey. He is the perpetrator. You are safe now. I have proven, since he was the last person to have a check cashed by Frank Converse, that he is the killer. With my guidance, the police have arrested him, and I shall be rewarded. I have told you, and I am telling all in town. I am a hero. I caught the murderer. It was me that laid the hands of the law upon him, when he least suspected it."

The Count released his grip and took a couple steps back. He was absolutely beaming. "He, no doubt, supposed he would get away with it, but I concluded by interviewing him and others that Bailey was the last one to have been noted clearly leaving the bank. It was Bailey! He is the villain! The combined reward is seventy-five hundred dollars, and I have earned it."

Dumbfounded, Edward paused to think for a moment. He had killed his friend to gain $5,000. This fool had accused the wrong man, an innocent one, and was to earn $7,500 for his efforts. If this was to be, the Almighty was perhaps sparing him from the gallows but had determined a way to slight him, nonetheless.

"I have stopped by to visit all the happy townsfolk and businessmen such as yourself who no longer have to fear or doubt in their hearts about who the murderer could be. I wanted to alert you yesterday that you would be safe but you were not in. I have valiantly protected all of you. With my intelligence and efforts, the culprit has been ferreted out. And so, I would like to allow you and all others an opportunity to thank me graciously, directly to my royal face."

The Count had pointed his finger at the wrong man, and his reward, even if it was greater than Edward had gained from the vile act, was of no matter. If another was condemned for the murder, Edward would, with this man's assistance, be able to pay off all his debts except the most dear, which was his very life for the crime he had committed. He was free! This man's act of foolishness had, if successful, disguised his own act of greed and violence. Edward started to smile. He could not help himself. He would perhaps attempt a jig if he thought his legs would consent, but instead he convulsed with uncontrollable giggles.

"Thank you! Thank you! Thank you so very much!" Edward clasped the Count by his arms. Though he could not reach the larger man's shoulders, the two men laughed and hugged. The Count noticed the tears running down the poor fellow's cheeks. He was quite impressed by this Green. No other person whom he apprised of his heroics this day had acted so spontaneously, so graciously and respectfully to his clever efforts to expose the cruel murderer.

The answer, he told himself, was so plain to a man of his intellect, where the less educated and unworldly were unfortunately oblivious. Perhaps, he thought, this tiny, somewhat malformed fellow was the most grateful since he was clearly not able-bodied and also worked so close to the crime committed. And so, the postmaster held the utmost esteem for the Count as his true hero which, of course, the Count deemed himself to be. "No need to worry, my dear man, my brave actions have kept you safe!"

"Indeed they have," exclaimed Edward, and he hugged the tall man even tighter. *Now, thanks to this vain idiot, Bailey can be my patsy,* thought Edward. The two men released their embrace but continued to gaze affectionately at one another.

"It has been my pleasure to meet you! My name is Count Joannes."

"We've met two times before," said Edward, who had been unaware of the Count's investigations up to this point as he had left Amos in charge of the post office the week after Alice was born and was one of the only local merchants not interviewed by him. Edward had purposely avoided being interviewed by the detectives, but it was only by chance that he had done so with the Count.

The Count scoffed. "Oh, sometimes, when one's as famous as I am, the general public feel they know me when indeed they do not. Anyways, as I said, it is pleasant to have made your acquaintance."

"I'm very glad you've come to tell me this wonderful news directly." Edward cared not if the man remembered him; it was serendipity, perhaps, that the fool had not. "You've assured my safety, and perhaps, as you implied, very much saved my life, and I will always remember you for that!" Restraining a snicker, Edward continued, "What an absolute delight to meet a royal and honorable man such as yourself!" Edward hugged him tightly once more. This charlatan was his salvation.

Edward reveled in the protective embrace of the Count's own greed. Edward clasped to the man as if for dear life, the tears continuing to stream down his face.

Such appreciation, thought the Count. *A true fan. If I have overlooked you, not interviewed you about this crime before today, I won't forget you now or ever again, Mr. Postmaster.*

Earlier that day, the Count, with a warrant in hand issued by Judge George W. Warren, of Charlestown Police Court, entered the stove and tinware business of George Bailey. Deputy Sheriff John Dearborn of Charlestown, assisted by Detective Whittier and Officers Goss and Stone, all of Charlestown, accompanied him.

Bailey, in his work clothes, put down a tea kettle he was polishing and then used his shirtsleeve to wipe his brow. He stared with surprise at the large group of stern-looking men before him, two of which were dressed in the blue pants and jackets that policemen had started to wear across the country in the last couple of years—surplus uniforms from the Union Army. Two other more serious fellows were in stiff suits and bowler hats but still had badges pinned to their lapels.

The deputy sheriff looked uncomfortable standing in the open door. Bailey had known him for many years. The others were strangers to him except the last one who was clearly not an officer of the law. This man dressed to the nines and being well-groomed by the barber next door, had recently become overly familiar to him.

The Count stepped forward and spoke first. "We are here to arrest you for the murder of Frank Converse."

"You are what?" said Bailey.

Dearborn stepped forward, taking the warrant from the Count and handing it to Bailey. He explained the purpose of their visit. "George, this was not my idea whatsoever but we have a court order to search your business. Please comply."

"I have nothing to hide, John. You can search away." The men all stepped past Bailey with just Detective Whittier remaining by his side. Bailey turned to the detective. "I ask your permission, please, to go to the bank next door to pay a note and also to speak to my wife and make her aware of this situation."

Whittier called to Dearborn, repeating Bailey's requests.

"Sure, Whittier, stay with him for a while. I will conduct a search and then allow the others to do a second pass as you and I go with him on these tasks."

Several minutes later, the three men left.

The remaining men investigated the premises and two nearby storehouses belonging to Bailey without, however, discovering any of the stolen money or any other evidence of his guilt. The Count had gone into every nook and cranny of the place several times and implored the others to do so, but after being thorough the second time through, they refused, knowing, if necessary, the order of the court would allow further search.

Bailey was transported to the jail in East Cambridge. Several citizens of Malden visited Bailey and conversed with him on the day following his arrest, including his good friend Thomas Dowling.

"How are you holding up, George?"

"No worse for wear, Tom."

"So, this is all the doing of that prissy fellow, this so-called Count."

"Yes. In some ways, honestly, this circumstance is not a great shock to me. In the days since Frank's murder, the fellow was always poking endlessly about the square. So, when he soon started questioning me about the murder, I supposed him at first to be a reporter for the public press, and so I answered his queries freely."

"And all the while the scoundrel's agenda, apparently, was to pin the foul deed squarely upon you."

"It appears so, but have no strong concerns, my friend—I am an innocent man and have faith in God that this will be cleared up and I can soon return home."

"You will be cleared," said another friend earnestly.

"You better be," said Dowling as he pounded his fist against the bars separating himself from his bosom buddy. "This Count better watch out if I see him!"

Mr. John Griffin, Bailey's attorney, spoke to reporters outside the jail and read the following statement:

"It is but just to my client, George Bailey, to state his arrest was not at the insistence of the detectives, or any of the parties most especially interested in the matter. George denies all knowledge of the murder and robbery. His reputation has always been good, and at the worst, the evidence, so far as we can learn, is only of a circumstantial character, which he believes he can overturn by the most positive proof. George, his dear friends, and I are all confident he will be discharged by Judge Warren without the necessity for a trial before the superior court."

After a weekend in jail, George was brought before the police court in Charlestown Monday morning, to answer the complaint charged against him by Count Joannes for the murder of Frank E. Converse.

To the question of "Guilty or not guilty?" he answered, "Not guilty." During the proceedings, George looked cheerful and confident, and he appeared to consider the whole affair, so far as it implicated him, as absurd and incredible. A number of his friends were there to support him, and they expressed to all present that they doubted the idea of his guilt. In the absence of the district attorney and the want of adequate preparation, he was remanded back to the East Cambridge jail to reappear before the court in two days' time for examination.

The Count held an impromptu press conference outside the courthouse. The reporters, having dealt with him directly or being wary of his reputation with the press, still clamored toward him, for the Count, if nothing else, always delivered good copy regardless of his perceived lack of morals or character. The public ate it up and hungered for more. Several of the press openly wondered if the Count held any outlandish aspirations of entering politics, even though he had never held any public office before. His last press conference was when he presented the newspapermen a letter he had written to Abraham Lincoln in 1861, soon after his inauguration. He was quoted as saying, *It is not wise for Lincoln to start a war with the Southern states. My personal fear is that this action will lead to an uprising by the slaves and the toppling of the plantation economy.*

"Why have you lodged the complaint of murder against Mr. Bailey, Mr. Jones?" asked one reporter.

"Please refer to me as Count Joannes. I have completed a very thorough investigation. There are twenty-one witnesses I will call, and I possess with me a number of documents I will present to sustain this charge. I will not rest until the vile evildoer pays for his crimes. I am dedicated in this as is my calling in all things I do. In fact, I will return this very evening to Malden to secure even more proof."

At the back of the crowd, Thomas Dowling stood and smirked at this last piece of information.

As the Count walked past Bailey's building later that day, Dowling crossed the street from his tailor shop to confront him.

"What sort of man are you?" asked Dowling, standing within inches of the Count's face.

The Count took a step back. "My dear man, I could ask the same of you, but I will answer your query nonetheless. I am a man of the arts, perhaps the greatest talent that has ever graced the stage, a prestigious author of fascinating literature, and now a great detective in the most terrible of crimes!"

Dowling bent over and laughed for several seconds. "You are merely a blathering charlatan!" he said and then, changing demeanors, charged forward and shook his fist in the Count's face. "You've accused the wrong man, and you'll get yours!" At this threat of implied violence, the Count turned and ran as fast as he could, his long cape flapping behind him, as Dowling stood there both amused and satisfied at the reaction he had elicited. Soon, the Count arrived at the Evelyn Hotel to collect his valise and then minutes later was at the depot to take the train back to Boston.

The way the Count responded to any injury, real or implied, was rarely face-to-face; he preferred to act through the courts instead. The next day, a peace warrant was granted to the Count, at his request, against Dowling, alleging the tailor threatened or attempted to assault and kill him. Dowling was subsequently arrested on the complaint.

In addition to lodging this charge against Dowling, the Count had also written a letter to a Boston paper to reveal the causes which led him to fasten the guilt for the murder on Bailey:

> *I hasten to request the inserting of the subjoined letter by me to the selectmen of Malden, that you may, if possible, extract the poison of the libelous publication this day in your columns concerning me and my motives, by some correspondent who signs himself "a citizen of Malden." The charge against me is almost as atrocious as the murder itself —that the "arrest is only a business of speculation"! You state, "The Count Johannes has already notified the selectmen of Malden that he shall claim the reward offered by them for the arrest and conviction of the murderer." Where in my subjoined letter have I mentioned "reward"? "I claim all rights," indeed—right to have free action in the case; and through "all dangers also," I did not think my life would be so threatened and jeopardized as it was in Malden by a friend of Bailey's, to prevent my receiving additional evidence and witnesses in the case, from intelligence I received Saturday evening. My noblest answer to libel is the very letter alluded to by the libeler, wherein my public spirit, motives, and humanity rise superior to all thoughts but public justice. The charge is only equaled in its falsehood by the distinct statement as fact (by your reporter) that the prisoner "had a protracted conversation with District Attorney Morse!" Had that been true, that talented gentleman would be unworthy of his high responsible office; and he justly said this morning that it was a published falsehood.*

> *Respectfully yours, George, THE COUNT JOHANNES BOSTON, MASS., JAN. 4, 1864 6 Tremont Street*

January 5, 1864
Boston Daily Advertiser
Our reporter visited the prisoner, yesterday, with a party of
Malden gentlemen, and found that Bailey's cell was spacious
and he was well cared for. He is cheerful and confident of
being discharged at the coming examination. He offered no
objection, saying, "I suppose, under the circumstances, it is
better to let the prosecution take the ordinary course, until
my innocence can be established." The evidence so far is only
confirmatory of what was given at the coroner's inquest and
does not in the least implicate Mr. Bailey. The public waits
impatiently to hear what facts the "Count"—who, by the way,
has not a very enviable reputation where he is best known
—may attempt to fasten this cold blooded murder upon a man
who has always held a good name as a neighbor and citizen.

Chapter Thirty

"M R. BAILEY'S A good man," said Emily. "It doesn't seem possible that he could have committed these horrible crimes."

"I'm very sure he did not," said William.

The husband and wife strolled along the Spot Pond Brook. They stopped and stood by the water's edge, perhaps a few hundred feet from their boardinghouse and a ten-minute walk for William to his workplace.

"Wait"—Emily paused and stared at him—"You are? Did you see him anywhere near the bank the day of the murder?"

"Yes, he went in perhaps twenty to twenty-five minutes before I saw Frank after he had been shot. But it couldn't have been him," he said and then thought, *for I know who the murderer is.*

"If that is so, you must testify."

"It's never a good idea to bring attention to ourselves, my dear."

"William, you ought to do the right thing." When Emily's face straightened and the tone of her voice deepened, William knew she was adamant about something, and he focused on her as his compass. William depended on her perspective and clearheadedness. He always had, and he clung to the notion that he always would. He wished he could share with her his strong suspicions about the postmaster, but anxiety prevented him from doing so. "You're right, darling," said William, "it is not just that Mr. Bailey should be punished for someone else's crimes. I will speak to his attorney. I have heard told that the man was seeking witnesses."

She stopped, reached out both her palms, and grasped his. "Thank you. I married a good man."

"I have my charms," he said as he kissed her, and she held him tight. It was a pleasant and rare event for them to spend these moments alone, away from the children, even if it was just for a few minutes.

"I have to get back home," she said. "Esther could only stay with the kids for a short time."

"And I have to head down to my shop and then see a man about testifying," he said with a glint in his eye. "I love you."

"I love you," Emily replied and turned to go. As she strolled farther away along the creek, William watched her, and then her reflection, grow smaller and gradually disappear; one and then the other faded from his vision. He didn't want to lose her or put his family at risk. It was his utmost imperative to keep them all safe. William would assist George Bailey, who was an innocent man, but he wondered if the only way to guarantee the welfare of himself and his family was to entirely safeguard the knowledge he held about the postmaster being the murderer. William prayed for guidance and courage to prove that he truly was as good a man as Emily viewed him to be.

George Bailey's examination was continued on Wednesday, January 6. The courtroom and all the passages leading into it were densely crowded. William stood amid the throng, positioned as to have one foot planted firmly in the hallway and the other one just barely inside the courtroom. Glancing around at so many familiar faces, William was not surprised that the postmaster was nowhere to be seen.

The case was opened briefly by District Attorney Isaac Morse of Lowell:

"There has been speculation, but I wish to quell those false rumors. I've neither seen nor conversed with the defendant. I appear simply as the law office of the government, and will allow all witnesses called by the complainant, the Count Joannes, to be summoned."

Charles Shepard was called first. He repeated his earlier testimony from the inquest, of finding Frank bleeding on the floor in the bank after being summoned by young Robert Merrill and how he had lifted him toward the door and attempted to soothe the boy.

Foster Lichfield testified next, recounting how he had first helped Mr. Shepard carry Frank to the door and then compressed the wound with a pillow slip until the doctor arrived and soon declared that the boy would not survive. "I saw half a pint of blood near where we found him. He bled some three pints afterward."

At this mention of blood, a young woman, weeping, fled from the court-room. William thought, *Poor* young *Miss Sprague!* The crowd scattered to clear a path for her. William clasped the doorjamb for balance as the hectic motion of the mass of bodies in such a tight space, heaving in all directions, almost pushed him completely forward into the chamber. Gripping tighter, he held his ground.

After the commotion, the prosecutor asked Foster if he had observed any smudges left upon the victim that could have come from being touched by the assailant or someone else, such as a tradesman who worked with polish on metals such as tin. Foster responded, "No person, as I know, put his hand directly upon the wound. There were no finger marks. The body was lying on its back, with the feet pointed toward the entrance."

Attorney Griffin asked, "What happened next?"

"I applied water with my hand, rubbing his neck and wrist to restore con-sciousness. I did it rather hastily for ten minutes, until the doctor came in."

Both attorneys now satisfied with Foster's answers, the judge called Dr. Burpee to the stand. Dr. Burpee relayed to the jury his actions and observa-tions at the scene, emphasizing that he "did not probe the wound, nor did any physician in my presence." He stated his belief that two pistol balls were still in Frank's head, and corroborated Foster's assessment that there were no smudges made by fingers. The use of fingerprints to reveal a suspect was still several decades from being implemented as a crime-solving tool. "The black-and-blue marks were evidently traces of powder from the gunshot and not from another source, such as from a tradesman's hands."

In response to Griffin's cross-examination asking about his relationship to George Bailey, Dr. Burpee replied, "I have lived ten years near George; his reputation has always been good."

William noticed George nod and smile at the doctor. The barber was growing tired standing and wished to sit. However, the only available chair was the one at the witness stand. He knew his turn would come soon enough, and was in no hurry to sit in it.

Dr. Sullivan testified next, and when asked by Griffin if there was the possibility that a second shot injured Converse, he replied, "I should think no other ball went in; there is no evidence of it, although it is in the bounds of possibility. The undertaker was unwilling to have me examine much on account of hemorrhage."

His mind preoccupied with his own thoughts during most of the first doctor's testimony, William was shocked when he heard the second's more clearly. *The postmaster shot Frank twice?* thought William as he gasped. *And now Mr. Bailey sits on trial in place of that greedy coward!* The barber's face grew hot, his heart rate increased and his fists clenched. He leaned forward.

Charles Merrill testified as he had in the inquest, that he left Frank with $5,000 and found him dead upon his return from Boston. "My first impression was that Frank shot himself. After a little while, it occurred to me that it might have been done some other way. I went to search for the money and found it gone but saw some notes that I had left with him. I went with my son to the small room behind the counter and examined the bank pistols there. The first was in the table drawer, rusty and unfit for use; the second was one which the directors had given to Mr. Murray, the young man who had the privilege of sleeping in the bank, acting sort of like a night watchman but more so out of charity since he had nowhere else to sleep, after the fire at his rooming house on Clement Street. The pistol was kept under his pillow; it was not a reliable weapon. I saw no pistol in the outer room."

Charles waited while the pistols he was referring to were produced, and the jurors confirmed that none were in working order. Charles continued, "My impression, on a sight examination, is that the shot entered under the right ear."

He was then asked about the check that George had cashed. "The check presented by Mr. Bailey was dated thirtieth of November last, drawn by the Rubber Shoe Company, of which Mr. Converse is treasurer. By agreement, I punch the checks I receive with five holes, and Frank made ten holes.

Yesterday, I handed this check to Thomas Lang, clerk of the company. It had been punctured ten times, so it was by Frank's hand. It is my opinion from this fact alone that Mr. Bailey conducted his business at the bank, left, and is clearly not the murderer. The books show there had been two deposits made and three payments during my absence. Mr. Bailey's was the last check presented before the murder so it seems foolish to me that a guilty man would leave so obvious a piece of evidence behind."

William nodded and thought, *There is no bigger fool than the Count, and now, besides perhaps the charade of his phony royalty, this attempt to besmirch Mr. Bailey is his life's biggest deception.*

Charles continued, "The place had been thoroughly searched, but no trace of the pistol ball could be found. There was a slight egg-shaped indentation on the strip which runs along the room to protect the walls from the chairs; it appeared as if a ball had hit the floor and glanced up. I deemed it best to go to Boston at once to take action on the matter. I checked and locked all the money up in the vault. I asked Bailey to remain an hour and a half while I went to Boston, because he sympathized in the affair. He is well acquainted with the Converse family. I think there were others there in the bank when I left."

"Please describe what you know of Mr. Bailey's reputation in the town," asked Griffin.

"I have known George about fifteen years, knew him as the son of the past president of the bank. His reputation has been very good, as far as I know. He is known as a gregarious, kind man. The directors always discounted his notes when presented. He always appeared to be easy in money matters. We were notified by him that he still had that one-hundred-dollar bill which he drew at the bank, and he returned it to us."

William's left leg was rooted so firmly in the hallway as to grow numb. He wanted to soothe it, but could not reach his arm down in the cramped passageway. He looked at George Bailey sitting there stoically, being accused of a crime he did not commit. As a gap opened directly ahead of him, William stepped forward so he was now completely in the chamber. He rubbed his leg for relief and breathed deep.

At this point, Morse submitted Bailey's earlier testimony from the coroner's inquest into the record.

Mrs. Caroline Vinton then testified. "I remember the time of the murder. I reside in the first house behind the bank. Thought I heard a pistol discharged at half past eleven on that day. I was sewing at the time. My girl Bridget was with me. The time may have varied five minutes past half past eleven o'clock. I think I said to my girl that I heard a shot fired; heard but one report. I couldn't tell whence the sound proceeded. The wind blew violently at the time. Peering from my window, I saw a man come down the street walking toward Pleasant a few minutes before the report. He looked like a foreigner; had on a fur cap, and sad, rather faded or tan-colored coat. That wasn't Bailey, and I didn't see Bailey until this excitement."

As William stood in the back of the court, he knew he would soon be called to testify. He glanced down at his palms. There was some sweat there, and he rubbed them together and then against his pants leg to dry them. He scratched along the side of his face. Seeing one of the detectives he had spotted in the square sitting in the gallery, he sized up the man, considering him, but averted his glance when Heath turned to look back at him. William was called to the stand and swore on the Bible to tell the truth. He pleaded with God to grant him the fortitude to be brave as he did so. *I have to be subtle about Green. I can't accuse a white man, while the Count can accuse anyone willy-nilly and have them arrested. He is truly a dangerous man, but so is Green. All of these men can place me and my family at a terrible risk so I must be quite tactful now.*

William gasped a deep breath when he was seated. He longed to scratch his scar but used one hand to restrain the other from doing so. "Sir, I am a hairdresser in Malden; my shop is located within twenty feet of the bank. On the morning of the murder, I was busy until half past ten. After that, I was unemployed and sat staring out the windows from ten thirty until three minutes past eleven when Mr. Rich came in to be shaved. Got him done by eleven twenty. When he left, I prepared to go and shave a man by appointment but soon had to deal with a stray dog behind my shop and didn't hear all the commotion at the bank at first."

"Sir, I left the shop at twenty minutes to twelve, and when I crossed the street, I saw a young lady run out of the bank with nothing on her head on such a cold day. The bank door was open, and I saw a man lying there. Young Converse was on the ground and bleeding. Mr. Lichfield was on his right, and Mr. Dowling's journeyman was on his left. 'For God's sake, help,' said one of them."

William hesitated for a moment, looked directly at the detective, then gathered his courage and continued, "I saw the postmaster clearly go into the bank twice. I think between ten thirty and around eleven." William paused and glanced at the gallery again, then looked back to the attorney and continued, "I saw Mr. Perkins stop a horse car and Mr. Lichfield throw a pair of ice skates into the bank. I saw Mr. Bailey, perhaps twenty minutes past eleven or so go into the bank. On the next morning, I was with Mr. Bennett when he said he spotted by one of the entrance posts before the bank, a piece of copper. He picked it up and handed it to me. Not knowing how to properly proceed, I walked into the bank and handed it to Mr. Merrill. I have heard since that it is part of a patent of an exploded pistol cartridge, however, I heard no pistol discharge, sir."

At this point, the Count motioned to Morse, who rose and produced the piece of copper from a purse, and James A. Leighton was called to the witness stand. "I am employed at Palmers & Bachelders in the military department. Have been there about a year." He took the copper in his hand and said, "I should judge this caliber to be a thirty-two one-hundredth of an inch. I should say it was adapted to a number two Smith & Wesson pistol. The indentation shows it to have been fired."

Dr. Charles Jackson, the Count's personal doctor and dear friend, was called to testify next and was asked if it was possible that the assailant had left evidence of his trade, such as stove polish, upon the victim. "I have not done an examination of the deceased yet I am a medical man. A man could not survive long with such a wound that has been described; not more than ten or fifteen minutes, depending upon the course taken by the bullet. Blood is very adhesive, and if a hand on which there was loose dirt, or lead, or stove polish, were placed on the wound, particles would be there."

William, now standing in back of the room once again, heard the Count chuckle and then saw the man raise his fist as if in triumph before staring down at his notes as he shuffled through the many pages before him.

At this point, District Attorney Morse, after a short, hushed conversation, with the Count's hand cupped repeatedly to his ear, requested to postpone the examination until the next day, so as to allow certain witnesses to be called.

Mr. Griffin objected, saying, "I would have admitted all that had been proved this morning, facts which were notoriously public, had I known no other evidence tending to incriminate my client would be added. I object that the examination should be unnecessarily protracted simply for gratifying the purpose of private speculation for a man of some perceived royalty." Luckily for the court, the Count was not present for this last remark, since after speaking to Morse he had whirled around, his cape flying high above and behind him as he sped toward the door in his quest to procure his witnesses.

Disregarding Griffin's objection, Judge Warren granted the motion for postponement, and at a quarter of two in the afternoon, the court adjourned.

William returned to his shop and remained busy with clients the rest of the day. When he arrived home, long after the sun had set, Emily was waiting for him outside their boardinghouse.

"I did it. It may have been one of the hardest things I have ever done, but I told what I was capable of saying, Emily."

William detailed to her the specifics of his testimony as well as the statements of others called to the stand.

Emily hugged him. "I am proud of you. You did what is right. William, I wish someone could point a finger at the stranger Mrs. Vinton witnessed, but it is good that you contributed to help Mr. Bailey, who is innocent."

She noticed William's face appeared uncertain, and so she said, "You did well, my love, as best as you could." She hugged him and William considered what he had done and what he could have done. He was ill at ease at not confiding completely in his wife.

I wish I had the bravery to tell you everything, to admit to you that I believe Mrs. Vinton's strange man and the one I saw last near the bank are one and the same. And that man is Edward Green.

Emily released her hug and kissed him on the cheek and reached for his hand. "You look weary; come upstairs."

When they entered the apartment, William knelt and kissed each one of his children on the cheek and then fell onto his bed and was fast asleep.

Chapter Thirty-One

THE NEXT MORNING at ten o'clock, George's trial resumed. His own testimony out of the way, William returned to witness the remainder of the proceedings. First on the stand was one of the defendant's childhood friends, Henry Jones. He testified that George had told him the following: "Went into the Malden Bank about eleven twenty on the day of the murder and deposited money. No one came into the bank while I was there. Frank Converse was alone as I left."

After Henry's unenlightening testimony, it was time for the complainant himself to testify. William had to restrain a snicker at the sight of the Count Joannes as he took the stand with an exaggerated strut. The barber knew the Count was thrilled for this chance to perform before a packed room.

Before the attorney's first question, the Count began to address the audience, his arms stretched wide as if it were possible for him to capture the whole room in his clutches at once. "Out, out brief candle! Life's but a walking shadow, a poor player that struts and frets his hour upon the stage and then is heard no more." The Count paused and decided it was best not to recite the next lines.

"Please sit down," said Mr. Griffin.

The Count complied, but before the attorney could utter another word, the witness, who had not been sworn in as yet, continued, "Blessed people of Malden, it is for your privilege that I have traveled here today. I know Mr. Bailey by sight since his abolitionist rant weeks ago at a local tavern."

At this point, the Count paused, his eyes narrowing. Distracted and staying silent, he then stood once more when directed and repeated the oath recited to him, his left hand on the Bible and his right extended as if he was inches away from touching the ceiling.

Moments later, he was again speaking as he scanned the room, seeking for any trace of admiration aimed toward him. "I heard of the murder the evening after it occurred. Days later, I went to Malden and first visited the bank once told of its location. I inquired who was the last to cash a check. I was told it was George Bailey. I asked where to find him and afterwards called at Mr. Bailey's store. He was at his desk writing. I said I know who you are but please verify for the record that you are Mr. George Bailey. He replied in the affirmative. Inquired if he kept at any time pocket pistols or powder and ball, he replied no. I asked him if he ever kept such articles for sale. He replied no. I then asked him at what time he went to the bank on the day of the murder, and he replied, 'About twenty past eleven, or it might have been a little later.' At my request, Mr. Bailey stated the particulars of his visit at the bank that day."

"Please sit down, sir!"

The Count, interrupted in the midst of his perceived marvelous performance, slumped surprisedly into his seat, but paused only an instant before continuing his rehearsed soliloquy.

The Count flailed his arms to appear as a larger man than he was and said, "Mr. Bailey stated to me he had known Frank since he was a child, and he knew Mr. Merrill, the cashier, quite well. He further stated Merrill had left him in charge of the bank when he returned from Boston after the murder. I informed Bailey that Mr. Merrill remarked that Mr. Bailey possessed a small pocket pistol which would carry a ball through a three-inch plank. He didn't respond to my query on this matter. Such a gun, even a tiny one, I am convinced could be fatal, my belief that it is the murder weapon in this hellacious crime is unequivocal. Bailey had mentioned at the earlier inquest that after he had left the bank, it being very cold, he ran down to the storehouse and stayed some ten to fifteen minutes and that when he heard about the murder he was near the Baptist church, and it was about twelve o'clock.

"I told Bailey I had a distinct recollection of circumstances attending the murder of Captain Joseph White in Salem—that the murderer was discovered by means of a vigilance committee and that my father was the discoverer. I proposed to Mr. Bailey a vigilance committee of the like should be formed in Malden. Mr. Bailey gave no word or look in encouragement of this proposition.

"I stared at the clock and it was almost a quarter past twelve. I remarked that at this time on the day of the murder, poor Frank was alive. But Bailey said, without hesitation, 'He was killed before this time.' My next interview with the defendant was on the day after Christmas."

Count Joannes continued his evidence by detailing at considerable length his conversation with Bailey at this interview, saying that Bailey's statements as to the time of occurrences on the day of the murder showed some discrepancies from the time stated in his first interview.

The Count here referred to a memorandum, of which he had several, and then continued with details of the conversation at the interview. The Count said he asked Bailey that if he was an innocent man, why had he not offered himself up to examination to prove it. "Bailey said it looked very bad for him as he was the last man in the bank, and many suspected him of the murder; I remarked to him that Constable Abbott had said that a gentleman had bet him two hundred dollars that the man who presented the last check certainly was the murderer.

"Bailey said there was no need of running his neck into a noose; let them take him up if they chose. He stated the fact that Converse entered the transaction in the ledger proved his innocence. Charles Sprague came into the store, and I repeated to him the conversation I had with Bailey. In speaking of the danger of his being accused, Bailey again said that Frank Converse had entered his check in the book and on that he would base his innocence."

When the Count was finally finished with his long-winded testimony, Mr. Griffin produced a copy of a letter which appeared in the *Boston Journal* on the fifth of January and asked his first question. "Mr. Jones—"

"Count Joannes, please."

Griffin shrugged. "Count Joannes, did you publish this letter?"

The Count looked askance at the letter, then turned his head to scan the room to see if others agreed the question was indeed a foolish one. "I did not."

"I will ask a second time, since your name appears on it. Did you publish this letter?"

Rolling his eyes, the Count said, "I did not publish the communication in yesterday's *Journal*—the editor did." Laughter erupted in the courtroom. Even William let out a chuckle, knowing no one in the court room directed any attention toward him.

The Count, not acknowledging the sound, continued, "I wrote it and sent it to him. The rights I speak of in that communication are not the rights to the reward, but the rights to collect evidence, and to seek witnesses. I would not ask for monetary reward; I seek justice. I despise money and those who seek it."

"Did you request of the selectmen permission to lecture on the murder of young Converse?"

"I never requested of the selectmen permission to lecture on the murder. I did request permission to lecture them on the Salem murder, of which I am well acquainted as my father helped solve it. This was Christmas Day. I offered a free lecture, to give suggestions for conducting the search for the murderer. Mr. Hubbard Russell, chairman of the selectmen, consented. I then had an interview with Mr. J. P. Converse of Woburn, the victim's uncle. He had no objection. I asked Mr. Converse to serve as chairman of a vigilance committee; he said his feelings toward the loss of his nephew would not permit him. I asked the clergyman who officiated at the funeral to serve on the committee as well. He also declined."

"In your interactions with Mr. Bailey, was there any other person present?"

"There was," said the Count, "a man sitting quietly at the stove. I believe it was that brute Dowling in Mr. Bailey's shop during the first interview. At the second, there was a very tall man in the store who asked Bailey if he could produce an alibi to the time of the murder, and Bailey replied to him that it was his misfortune that he could not."

"Were your actions of complaint taken in conjunction with others, or have you endeavored in this alone?"

"No part of my labor was undertaken at the request of the directors of the bank or the selectmen of the town." The Count strained to make eye contact with all those assembled at once. *The reward will be mine alone,* he thought, smiling. He continued speaking, now with his voice rising in a well-practiced flourish: "This has been my solitary quest, to right the terrible wrong done by this crime by deducing whom the perpetrator was."

Pointing at Bailey, he said, "This man's trade and polish-smudged hands upon the victim betray his crime, his mark as Cain! I seek justice for the victim, his family, and the security and peace of mind for all the concerned townsfolk. They can once more enjoy the safety they deserve, now that the said criminal has been apprehended by my very brave actions." The Count paused, "In fact, one of your merchants was quite moved by my heroics when I informed him that Bailey had been arrested. Tears lined his cheeks, and he embraced me in joy for the very security I had provided for him."

Griffin, taken aback by the performance and wishing to give this fool no further stage to wrongly persecute his client, decided against any additional questions. The Count stood and strutted away from the stand, preparing to bow triumphantly, but no applause came. Disappointed, he returned to his seat in the gallery. With the distraction of the Count's performance over, William stepped back, attempting to hide in the crowd. He could not camouflage himself, yet he could go unseen.

The next witness was one he knew well. John Rich, who had been in for a haircut the morning of the murder, stated, "I was in the barber's shop about eleven o'clock. I went from the Palmleaf works, of which I am a superintendent of the production of hats, and went directly to the shop. It was a very windy day and the snow started to accumulate. After leaving the barber, I met Mr. Bailey on the opposite side of the street talking to a gentleman whom I do not know. I merely nodded and had no conversation with him. I can give no description of the gentleman with whom he was conversing, as I did not notice him particularly. I am but little acquainted in Malden as I have been there but a short time, since October last, but Bailey I knew, as he had done work for me."

Deputy Sheriff John Dearborn testified next and described how he had arrested George and searched his premises thoroughly, finding nothing. "Bailey remarked after I had completed my initial search of his building that if any bank notes were discovered on his premises, some person had put them there to place blame on him. He said it was getting too hot for the murderer and he might have placed money there to divert suspicion from himself."

"We found no money but what he had on him, and no pistols except miniature ones with the barrel, lock, and stock cast all together. They were not real, mere toys, and I found nothing to feed any morbid suspicion. Again, they are truly harmless." A mild laughter filled the court and William put his hand over mouth to avoid joining its chorus. "Mr. Bailey did not express any concern when I arrested him. He behaved no differently than from what he has for the last ten years that I've known him. After the arrest, we left to go to the bank, Mr. Bailey desiring to pay a check. As we exited his establishment, Bailey remarked to George Jones that he hoped he was now satisfied, as all the rest of Malden was."

The Count was then recalled to the stand. "A child's gun, even a toy, can be dangerous." There was more laughter than before. Bowing his head, the Count realized he could not win over this audience. He continued, changing tack: "At the arrest of Bailey, I assured him I would not prosecute the good but only seek out the wicked. I would do all in my power to prove his innocence if the evidence led to him being a moral soul." A roar of disapproval was the response from those crowded into the courtroom and then more laughter as well.

The prosecution's evidence was then closed.

Mr. Griffin arose and said that if all the people in Massachusetts knew both the accuser and the accused as well as the people of Malden did, he would say nothing and offer no proof, for there would be no need to prove Bailey's innocence. "You can all plainly see by the reaction to the complainant's testimony, in Malden, no man, woman, or child can be found, after twenty or thirty days' talk and discussion, who entertains the slightest or feeblest suspicion of the defendant. The testimony of Mrs. Vinton that a stranger had been seen to go past the bank and not return proves Mr. Bailey was not the last man in the bank."

Mr. Griffin next brought forth more proof on this point, that a stranger may have been the murderer, with his next witness: Marshall Shedd. William listened intently to hear what the postmaster's close friend had to say.

"I am a baker. On the day of the murder, I was driving my cart from Cambridge through Medford to Malden. I arrived at the depot in town at eleven o'clock, and from thence went directly to Hill's Tavern. As I passed the depot, I saw two strangers there. I drove by the post office and the bank on my way to my bakery. I then ran up the yard and went to the bakehouse, and then directly toward the post office. Looking into the office and seeing no one present, I did not enter as was my custom. Instead I went to Dowling's next door"—*I saw you*, thought William, as the baker continued—"and there I saw a man go through the stone posts before the bank and go up to the door and look into the glass panes. He had on a brown coat and fur on his hat or around the neck. His attire was somewhat similar to the strangers I had seen. He paused there for a minute before he went in. The time was about twenty-five to thirty minutes past eleven."

I saw you as you were watching him . . . not knowing who he was, but when I did see, I knew. I wish someone else had witnessed the postmaster as well. He can easily gain refuge with a strange coat. Clothes offer me no similar disguise, thought William.

Next, E. B. Putnam, a grocer in Boston, testified that he saw Mr. Bailey on the day of the murder at his new home on Middlesex Street and that there was nothing unusual in his talk or appearance when he conversed with him about twenty minutes after eleven. He heard of the murder about twenty-five minutes past twelve.

Next, Griffin called an employee of George Bailey to the stand. Joseph Freeman testified that he was at work in the storehouse on the day of the murder, and at twenty-five minutes past eleven, George had entered and assigned his colleague, Mr. Rhodes, a job to do.

When asked during the cross-examination how he was certain of the time, Joseph stated, "The reason I know it was twenty-five minutes past eleven was because Mr. Rhodes looked out of the window at the clock on the church and stated that it was the time."

Griffin then presented the bank's account book, which was soiled and much disfigured with blots, and called Ezra Lamson to the stand. "I am the director of the bank and examined the book. When the book was handed to the Count, at his request, these marks were not there. After it was returned, they were."

The Count arose and indignantly denied the insinuation, saying the charge was false; he had traced the figures with a lead pencil on trace paper.

Griffin ignored the interruption and called Hubbard Russell, chairman of the selectmen of Malden. "I was at the bank the day of the murder. Between twelve and two o'clock we made a thorough but unsuccessful search for the bullet. Mr. Bailey was keeping watch at the door at the time. None of the selectmen had anything to do with this prosecution. Mr. Bailey's reputation is above reproach, as far as I know."

Charles Sanderson, one of the town's selectmen, and Charles Sprague, one of the bank's directors testified similarly.

Another bank director, Gershom L. Fall, testified as well. "I have resided in Malden for twenty-five years. I went to the bank shortly after twelve and searched for the bullet, assisted by Dr. Burpee and others. Mr. Bailey came into the bank about fifteen minutes after I got there." Fall stated that he was in the bank when Frank died, and when asked about Mr. Bailey's character, he answered the same as all the previous witnesses, stating that it was excellent.

Everyone loves George Bailey! thought the barber.

On the commencement of the examination, the Count had proclaimed that he had twenty-one witnesses, but he failed to show evidence of having one-third of that number. The judge said, "The evidence as far as I am concerned, is now closed. There has been, frankly, more wild assumptions and conjecture than I hold the stomach for. I will deliberate briefly, but the judgment to anyone who was listening is clear-cut. Regrettably, this has been a waste of everyone's time." He threw up his hands.

District Attorney Morse arose immediately, even though he had sat through most of the proceedings. "I came here without knowing the facts of the case. But after a fair investigation of the evidence, I do not feel, even were Bailey a stranger instead of a respectable citizen, that the evidence is such as would bring a conviction before a grand jury or warrant the court in holding him, therefore I humbly advise Your Honor to discharge the accused. I regret that any party should be charged with the crime and that the prisoner had been brought into such close proximity that suspicion should point to him. I believe the complainant has acted in good faith and honorable motives in the prosecution, but the case should be dismissed due to the lack of evidence."

Mr. Griffin stood to reply. "It would be an injustice to my client to leave the matter without uttering a word. Mr. Bailey had behind him, in support of his character, an unsullied life of more than thirty years in the town of Malden. This the prosecutor knew as well before the arrest as now; the fact the deceased was shot through the head was known then as now; the circumstances under which Mr. Bailey drew his check were equally well known, and many other circumstances the prosecutor brought forward were well known before the examination and were irrelevant.

The district attorney says the accuser, the Count, as he calls himself, was, in his judgment, driven by a pure motive. I do not believe the accuser spent any time in this case without singularly just a pure desire for the reward! His testimony in relation to his letters to the selectmen and the bank cannot be relied on as honest. 'Rights under the arrest' means 'the reward' and nothing else in his letters. Jones, Joannes, Johannes: the man has more names than he has scruples. Reading of the murder, its deep atrocity suggested rewards. He scented this at once. This vulture is a true carrion kite of the courts, flying high above and then swooping down upon the excited people of our town to take advantage when they have been so injured, merely to pick their bones clean. His main goal of all this chicanery is to gain himself prestige or wealth from the atrocious murder of one of Malden's sons. It is truly despicable, his actions pointing his false finger toward Mr. Bailey and also, by extension, his sin toward all of us by distracting us from ascertaining the true felon of this most horrid of deeds. Within the cramped confines of this court room, it was impossible for my ear not to hear, before the question reached the witnesses, whether the stove polish from a freeman's hands, if mingled with human blood, would be soluble and discolor the surface of the victim's skin! As if Bailey, going from his daily labor, committed this murder on the body of the youth, then dabbled or paddled with his sooty fingers in the blood he had shed to leave evidence of the crime! I expected to have proofs, after this, how my client had bestowed those 'hangman's hands,' where he had gone to wash away the filthy witness therefrom, and even that those missing bank bills were found under Bailey's pillow streaked with the bloody and sooty evidence of his guilt, for surely I thought so infamous a suggestion must have foundation in fact or it never would have been uttered in the first place. But in vain I waited. George Bailey may have soot on his hands, on occasion, from his noble profession, but they are not stained in blood. This accusation of murder is much more dangerous than someone doubting the royal pedigree of someone who calls himself 'the Count' when the man is surely just a vain actor that has inserted himself into our tragedy far from any of the pious reasons he claims. Why should anyone believe a suspected fraud? He can sue for libel if he wishes, but I am saying the following in open court: the man is certainly more likely a jester than a count."

William detected an emotion he had never seen before upon the face of his frequent customer: the Count sat there stewing, his lips pursed, his eyes squinting, as a chorus of laughter swelled around him. Griffin smirked directly at him and took joy in the success of silencing his client's accuser for a moment before continuing.

"In respect to the pistol shell the barber brought to Mr. Merrill's attention, an expert from Boston comes to tell us it might have been fired . . . *some time*, by *somebody* from *some pistol*. This opinion tends to convict any other inhabitant of the earth's surface just as strongly as Mr. Bailey. And these are the only facts not earlier testified at the coroner's inquest upon which the prosecutor seems to rely. No two facts the Count produces cohere. He approaches the 'door of truth,' as he quotes in his letter to the *Journal*, by such leaps and so spirally, that no man can follow him, the prosecutor, a learned attorney, getting befuddled even in an attempt to do so. Every material circumstance presented here, and the fact the people of Malden, and indeed the population of the whole world over which the story of this murder has gone, has already been discussed and debated thoroughly long before Mr. Bailey's arrest. There is nothing novel in these proceedings. A deep wrong has been done. Mr. Bailey has no redress. An execution for damages against the complainant would be no more fruitful than if issued against Lazarus at the rich man's gate. Truly, the Count cannot be counted on. Four nights in jail for my client, four days separated from his family and his native town, with more than three decades upright and an unspotted life therein, and an accusation of deliberate and willful murder on the records of the courts across the country, to remain there forever and sent abroad by the press to all the corners of the earth where the story of this strange homicide gets told—a murder that shall be memorable long years to come—these are the outliers of what the speculator in throats, blood, and reputation, this Count, has, without any honor of his own, besmirched Mr. Bailey's good name."

All those in the court sat silently still, staring intently at the defense lawyer. The Count alone fidgeted restraining himself from offering a vigorous response, his face an open scowl. "I am sorry," Mr. Griffin continued, "that the public prosecutor has seen fit to endorse this assassin of better reputation than his own after the scurrilous accusations of Count Joannes. It is a good time to utter a healthful word in the public ear against Mr.

Jones, the stirrer-up of unfounded and scandalous prosecutions and suits, which embroil communities and corrupt the morals and degrade the names of the towns in which they occur. The annals of such mischievous men furnish no noble comparison. The hand which executed this deed to blemish an innocent man and the brain that decided it must be considered a nuisance among men, and it is quite a good time that some prosecuting officer should so strengthen his spinal column as to say so. And as the district attorney said, while he concurred fully in the opinion that no evidence had been produced against my client, he has strongly dissented from the notion that any unworthy motive animated the complainant. It most certainly did."

At this, the Count began to rise from his chair, but Morse tugged on his jacket sleeve. Reluctantly and defeatedly, the Count remained seated.

Judge Warren reviewed the principal points of the testimony and expressed his belief that the counsel on both sides had performed their duties faithfully. He stated he did not see that any witnesses had been called on unreasonably and hoped perhaps their evidence might lead to future discoveries. The judge stated the district attorney, the counsel of the defense, and the accused had all acted with decorum. He also agreed with the motion of the district attorney in the belief that the evidence did not point to any known party but instead more certainly to some strange party. He concurred in the opinion of the district attorney that after a fair and impartial examination, there was not sufficient evidence to hold the defendant, and therefore George Bailey was discharged.

This announcement was received with tremendous applause and cheering. William unsure of how to respond, decided to join in and felt the rare feeling of being part of this community. George was immediately surrounded and was almost overwhelmed with the congratulations poured upon him from all sides by numerous friends. During the commotion, the Count quietly sulked away from the courtroom, shocked somewhat that Bailey was hoisted up in admiration and joy instead of him as he had visualized.

Thomas Dowling, who had been charged by the Count with assault and battery for shaking his fist at him, was also discharged. A dinner was provided for George, and he was carried home to Malden in triumph, riding in a large eight-horse sleigh. As the party passed through Cambridge, George happily bid a farewell to his old quarters in the large stone house and prayed to never lay eyes upon it again.

As Mr. Deloraine Corey, a close friend of the Converse family (and who would one day write a history of the town), was on his way home that evening, he passed by the post office and called to Edward, "George Bailey's been released and is coming home tonight! We're going to throw him a big reception in town hall, and we want to be sure that you and everyone else attends."

Edward shrugged and walked away. Corey thought this strange, but then Edward turned back to him and said, "His release is no surprise to me. It couldn't have been him. I knew all along that George Bailey was an innocent man!" Edward quickly turned his back on Corey and walked away, leaving the man dumbfounded.

Upon his return to Malden, George was greeted by a large throng of his fellow citizens and escorted to the town hall, where two thousand townsfolk were gathered to celebrate his release, proving that the townspeople thought the charges were trumped up by an adventurer solely for the purpose of obtaining the reward offered.

The throng was so immense that Constable Abbott had to fight with considerable effort to reach George, who was standing atop a buggy. Abbott pushed two men aside to allow himself to climb up next to him.

"George, I want you to know that I deny the statement made by the so-called Count that the last person who drew a check was certainly guilty of murder, as had been claimed. I never suspected you, and by this turnout, you can see plainly that only this vain interloper did so."

"I'm aware that this is all his doing. Don't worry, John, I hold no grudge against you."

"Thank you. It's been weighing on my mind that you might. I am so relieved that you don't." The constable waded back into the masses, awaiting the moment George would start to address them. Before he could utter a word, the Count Joannes stood upon his own buggy and addressed the crowd in a practiced baritone that could be heard in the far reaches of any amphitheater.

"Honorable citizens of Malden, I am elated that George Bailey is back amongst his many friends." The Count glanced all around, shocked to discern that this was the largest audience he had ever addressed, and the greater realization that they had not been drawn there to see him perform but to rejoice in Bailey's release caused him tremendous dismay.

He continued but perceived his voice was, at least to him, tremulous. "As you are all aware, great men such as myself and the prosecutor were seeking the truth and, more importantly, justice for Frank Converse. At the time, it appeared to us that George Bailey was the horrible murderer of the boy."

A clamoring hiss greeted this remark, and the Count had to steady himself at the shock of it and struggled to feign that it did not bother him, even though he was increasingly terrified he might tumble into the crowd and be devoured like a Christian in a Roman colosseum.

"We had the best intentions in our prosecution, yet we are thoroughly and without a doubt pleased that George Bailey was not charged."

At this, angry projectiles rained on him and a rock hit him square in the chest. Unknown to him, it was thrown by Thomas Dowling, who was exuberant that he had struck his target.

The Count loved the stage but was also well practiced regarding when it was time to depart the spotlight. The Count threw himself down next to the driver and ordered the man to flee. The horses were lashed, and the carriage scurried away as more projectiles were unleashed.

George Bailey stood tall and spoke in a voice as loud as he could muster. "Stop, please, let them depart in safety. I have no animosity toward this fool for falsely pointing his finger at me or for the days I spent in jail. I am free now; it was unpleasant but just a meager moment in life, a few days of being accused by an outside interloper, but my thoughts dwell with the sorrow and uncertainty visited upon the Converse family and all our town, for the pain of Frank's murder is indelible and no solace will be brought to us until the true criminal has been identified and captured." The masses cheered.

"I implore you to be vigilant, to be aware, to inform the detectives of any oddity or suspicion, no matter how trivial. Murder will out; the evil behind this will surface. There is no escape from the eyes of the citizens of Malden and certainly no escape from God."

At these words, the postmaster, who stood as far away as he could in the throng while still being able to hear, shivered and took a step backward with his good leg, but his bad leg remained rooted in place for a moment. Edward had held such great hope that the vain charlatan would protect him from justice, as if wrapping his fancy cape around him to shroud his sins, but now he was unnerved and unsure. The Count had fled in one direction as some of the townspeople chased his carriage; Edward limped off in another direction, blending in mostly undetected as he had for majority of his life. The barber, embedded in the crowd, was once again the only one to notice the postmaster's exit.

Chapter Thirty-Two

January 8, 1864
Boston Daily Advertiser
From the sublime to the ridiculous, there is but a single step. The Malden tragedy has been a farce not unusual in the courts of the Commonwealth. While the whole community has been shocked by the appalling crime in the neighboring town, while the whole machinery of the police stimulated by large rewards has been put in active operation to detect the criminal, causing some false reports, and while every good citizen stands ready to do his utmost in aid of the officers of the law, a highly respectable citizen is arrested, imprisoned and brought before a criminal court on the grave charge of deliberate murder. A large number of witnesses are examined: not a particle of evidence is produced against the prisoner, and he is discharged amid the plaudits of his neighbors.

Why was a warrant issued at all? Why was a man who appears to stand as well among his neighbors as any person in the Commonwealth, suddenly seized, imprisoned, held up to public odium and disgrace, and then coolly told there is not a particle of proof against him? Justices of the peace may issue warrants "against persons charged with criminal offenses." But against persons charged by whom? Upon what evidence? Under what circumstances? Clearly, the magistrate is to use his own discretion in some degree, and should not take the unsupported word of any vain or interested intermeddler who chooses to come before him, as a sufficient warrant for the gravest of criminal proceedings—or extremely mischievous consequences may ensue.

The arrest of George Bailey, of Malden, at the insistence of the notorious George Jones, who styles himself "The Count Johannes" on the charge of having committed the murder of young Converse, the Malden bank clerk, is pronounced by the Boston Journal as, "one of the greatest outrages which has been committed upon a citizen of Massachusetts, through the instrumentality of judicial proceedings." The Journal says "there was not the scintilla of evidence connecting Mr. Bailey with the murder, and Justice Warren, who issued the warrant for his arrest, deserves, as we think, impeachment and removal for his agency in this outrage. If there is any redress for Mr. Bailey against Mr. George Jones, under the laws in relation to false imprisonment, we hope he will seek it. But whether there is or not, the community should be protected in some way against the litigating mania of an individual who has obtained as much notoriety as this complainant."

January 13, 1864
To the Editors of the Boston Daily Advertiser:
While the admission into your columns of all the suggestions and opinions which the public might offer would overwhelm your paper, yet a reasonable amount of discussion might lead to such facts as would fix the foul murder done at Malden upon the fiend who perpetrated it. For this reason, I beg to offer a few hints, that appear to me strong, and tending to circumscribe the watchfulness of the public eye to the real spot where the murderer must be searched for.

It would seem that the business of the Malden bank is quite limited—else more than five thousand dollars would have been required by the teller, during the absence of the cashier, on the day of the murder, and a less youthful officer would have been left in sole charge of the bank. It is probable, also, that the business of the bank follows some pretty uniform rule; that the larger portion is transacted in the forenoon, and after dinner, and that there is a common interregnum about the hour of twelve. I assume that this is a fact, from the almost incredible audacity and confidence with which the bloody work was done. It is inconceivable, and almost impossible; that the murderer had not weighed his risks well, and decided upon the probable safety from discovery, at the hour the deed was committed. The murder could not have been done upon impulse—from sudden temptation, and regardless of the chances of detection. It was well and long, and carefully studied. The time, the hour, the safety and certainty of success were weighed, and the weapon for the deed prepared and ready at hand. Professional thieves are always wary, calculating and systematic, never rash, however daring. Banks, from the greater precautions taken to protect them, are studied carefully and the weakest point of attack determined before an assault is made; and all reason points to the moral certainty that this was especially true of the robbery and murder in the Malden bank—although it does not merely follow that a professional did the act. To suppose that an entire stranger, only knowing that there was a bank in Malden, entered the town suddenly, at midday, went to the bank, murdered the teller at once, robbed the drawer, and then left the town as quickly as he entered it, is absurdity run mad—and yet this seems to be the popular idea.

Assuming that the murderer had taken the time to study the facts—that he placed himself, or was, in position to learn well, and beyond a doubt, the daily routine of events that passed in the bank—that he must have been informed of the fact that the cashier, not only was, but would be, absent on that day—demonstrated that the murderer had been long enough a resident, or visitor in Malden, to have been well known to many citizens of that place. It was a long considered and thoroughly matured plan, and it could only have been matured in Malden; not elsewhere. It is possible that a Confederate may have done the deed; but it is altogether improbable—and the man is probably in Malden, or in this region, still. Not only robbery, but murder was intended from the first, and the weapon decided upon and ready at hand; and no stranger to the place is the guilty man.

Now, if the murder was the act of a stranger, who had taken the time to determine his course without exciting suspicion, he must have had some boarding place and been known as a stranger. Such a person, of the coolness, daring, desperation and cunning required for the awful deed of blood, would not have left the town, perhaps has not, even yet—certainly not until all risk was at end. If it was a resident, the same is true—for in the intensely excited attention of the people of Malden, when the murder was known, the sudden departure of a resident, even, would have caused remark—and more, if a stranger were to leave. I assume, therefore, as almost demonstrable, that the murderer of young Converse had been a resident of Malden, as a citizen or stranger, long enough to learn the customs of the bank and the course of its business without exciting attention, to deliberate and determine upon his plans; that he was well known, and that he is either now in Malden, or did not leave until some recent day.

It seems, to my judgment, that there is no escaping from this view and conclusion, from the facts of the case; and it is highly probable, that the intelligent citizens of the pleasant town of Malden, by thus regarding the probabilities of the manner in which the horrible deed was done, will yet ferret out and convict the worse than hell-hound, whose black soul conceived and bloody hand executed it—not by hasty and rash suspicions and flimsy imaginings; but rather by the calm, judicious and studious comparing and connecting of suggestive facts, however slight or seemingly insignificant.

S.L.R.

Chapter Thirty-Three

DURING THE EXAMINATION against George Bailey, Detective Heath had been sitting in the gallery of the Charlestown courtroom, carefully watching the proceedings. Of all the witnesses, William Shiloh, the barber, intrigued him the most. In fact, at one point, Heath perceived the barber was looking right at him as he paused during his testimony. From his windows, William had stated, he could observe anyone going in or out of the bank. He had testified to seeing Bailey going into the bank on the morning of the murder. When asked if he had sighted anyone else, he named two or three men whose presence there had been known, and whom the detectives had already questioned and eliminated as suspects. But this was the first time anyone mentioned that Edward Green had gone to the bank that day. William stated he had seen Edward enter the bank not once but twice that morning, and the second time was around eleven o'clock.

When he returned to the police station, Chief Savage said to Detective Heath, "Who is this Ed Green?" Heath stated he was the postmaster and a close companion of the deceased. Heath then made inquiries at the Boston post office as to what they could tell him about the Malden postmaster. They had an overall good report of Edward, but the detective still retained the gut feeling he should follow up on this lead. Heath soon realized suspicion of Edward in general was a natural thing because everyone else who had been to the bank that morning had come forward to tell what they knew, with the hope of throwing some light on the mystery. For whatever reason, Edward Green had refrained from doing so.

The detectives decided to follow this new evidence and hoped it would lead to the identity of the strange man in a fur hat and tan coat that Shedd, the baker, had spotted in front of the bank and a similar one Mrs. Vinton had also seen near the bank minutes before she heard a shot fired.

Caleb Shiloh swept the hair near the barber's chair deep into the corner by the door. He yearned to speak to his father but was reluctant to do so. He continued the back-and-forth motion of the broom as his mind also traveled back and forth. For a week he had been thinking of one thing over and over. He was curious about his father's statement during the hearing to determine if George Bailey was the murderer of young Frank Converse. William Shiloh had stated under oath that he had witnessed the postmaster going to and from the bank twice on the day of the murder. Caleb, as well as a large number of the town, had been sitting in the courtroom.

"Father, you didn't mention before to me what you said during your testimony at Mr. Bailey's examination. That you saw Mr. Green on the day of the murder exit the bank."

"Son, I saw him twice that morning clearly, as I testified. This was before you arrived at the shop. But those times I thought nothing of it, since it was a familiar sight to see him at the bank."

Caleb stopped sweeping and stared intently at his father. "Those times? Was there a third time you spotted the postmaster? Father, did you see Mr. Green leave the bank directly before Frank's body was discovered? Is that what you're not telling me?"

William's eyes widened and his shoulders tensed. Caleb noticed his father's hand massage the scar on his cheek, as he was apt to do in moments of contemplation. William, realizing where his hand was, dropped it back down to his side. "Son, I don't want to discuss this any further."

On the fateful morning that Frank Converse lost his life so violently, William watched as the postmaster exited the bank a second time. Sometime later, William planned to sweep the mounds of hair off the floor but Caleb, who had just arrived, volunteered to do so.

While Caleb was in the back room, fetching the broom and dustpan, William spied in his mirror a foreign person leaving the bank. The barber turned around attempting to see him more clearly, after the man had moved farther away into the stormy day. Even with the accumulating snow, William discerned the strut and gait of the postmaster. William had long ago mentally stored away his particular movements as he ambled through the square on his errands. No one else in town walked with such a prominent limp. Edward at first stood out but soon blended deeper into the fabric of the town with his impairment. To most, Edward became quite hidden by being so common a sight. After a while, one did not take notice of him for the mere fact that he was so noticeable. But as an outlier himself in Malden, William was cognizant of others who were also different in one way or another.

On the day of the murder, it appeared to William that Edward made a great attempt to mitigate his limp but was only mildly successful at doing so. The limp seemed even more exaggerated, as though the postmaster was not sure of his destination and appeared like he was pulling himself in two directions at once.

William stared at the tracks embedded in the snowy ground. They were uneven and clearly marked the awkward gait of the postmaster. After a few moments, they were covered over as if Edward had never walked by at all. The ground was pure white, the impressions hidden by a fresh canopy of snow. If William had been in the back of the shop instead of Caleb in that moment, it would have been as if no one had passed by his establishment at all.

Three, thought Shiloh. *Peter denied the Lord three times.*

The barber had only testified about seeing the postmaster twice during the Bailey hearing, but the third time was in a reflection and the man's outfit was different, even if his walk was not. William wanted justice for Frank, but he knew his very pigment complicated his condemnation of Edward immensely. William was also more than aware that the man who would kill Converse in broad daylight would not think twice about shooting a Negro who claimed to be a witness to his crimes—or even the barber's son, who was posing too many questions.

"Caleb, you must be quiet and obey your father for all our sakes!" said William sternly, wanting to scream this rational thinking at his son. God may desire him to tell someone, but perhaps it was best to tell no one, for all the someones that could affect his life were of a lighter complexion.

William looked Caleb in the eye and said, "Let white men settle white men's business." His son stared at him for a few moments and then, realizing his father's tenuous position in the town and so also his own, Caleb nodded. William was content with Caleb's silent understanding of this delicate issue. They had to tread lightly; there was great danger in this town always for the family, but the present situation was quite precarious. The barber trusted in his Maker. Whatever God deemed to happen would, and William prepared himself to be called upon to respond as God wished. Yet, he prayed he could somehow not offer his opinion outright that the postmaster was the murderer. For doing so would quite likely only further imperil himself and his loved ones. William prayed that his Savior understood his first imperative was always to protect his family.

I can parade around, curtsy as I ply my trade as a barber, be their waiting man if it pleases them, but I am no great detective, as the Count falsely claimed himself to be. These white men must solve their own crimes. I can only contribute from the perimeter, for that is the only place they allow me to dwell. I wish to be helpful but also must remain cautious. The punishment for Edward's crimes could easily be pinned on me or my family, regardless of our proximity to the offense.

All William concluded he could do was pray that he supplied the proper bait during his testimony at Bailey's indictment—his statement that he had seen the postmaster twice before the murder—which would hopefully lead the detectives right to his barber pole. If the detectives came fishing, asking the right questions, the barber would then guide them to the right answers. And maybe all of this could be over. They could arrest Edward, and the Converses could perhaps obtain some tiny solace that their son's murderer had been captured. The barber as well could gain relief and the peace of mind that he had acted in a virtuous manner toward God and the Converses while also securing the safety of his family and himself.

Detectives Heath and Jones wished to question William Shiloh. Constable Abbott, who was the only law enforcement presence in town, relayed to them what he had learned from the barber in the days after the murder. Now, the detectives wanted to speak to William directly, just in case there was anything else he had initially forgotten to share with Abbott. They were compelled to jog his memory. This was not the first murder case the pair had investigated; there had been a handful of others in the five years they had worked together. Jones was in awe of Heath for his role in the arrest of Professor Webster in 1850 and was devoted in following the lead detective in hopes of solving this crime.

This was a similar case, with a prominent victim and a crime splashed across the front pages of newspapers around the country and the very world. Heath and Jones were under tremendous pressure to solve the murder, and the stress wore on them as time went by without any definitive answers.

The two detectives were neighbors on South Bennett Street in the city and were starting to feel like they were spending far more time with each other than with their wives and families since the murder. Heath was fond of his friend but loathed the fact that when Jones met him each morning, the younger man reeked of burnt eggs and tobacco.

There had been so many leads that went nowhere and more to follow up on. Hours and hours together. Both were anxious to return to their normal police work and quiet domestic lives. But mostly, Heath and Jones, who had spoken with Mr. and Mrs. Converse on many occasions since the horrible day deeply considered it their duty, their very obligation, to solve the mystery and bring the villain to justice. The detectives were impelled to supply whatever solace they could provide to the Converses and also to the citizens of the town. Were there any clues that William had omitted to the constable which another conversation could bring back to the surface of his mind? They were compelled to see if he would bring up Edward once again to them, as he had offhandedly mentioned him during his testimony. It was certainly worth their effort if it could allay the concerns and utter grief of the most prominent family in town, or any family, for that matter.

The barber set his scissors down on the counter as Heath and Jones entered his shop. *The white men have come to seek their justice,* thought Shiloh. *They can have it, for it is just, but I still must parse my words for them. The Count, up until recently, had been my best customer, but I would desire to tell him, if I could, what an utter and cruel fool he is for accusing Bailey and that Green has been the villain all along. All those moments sitting in my chair after the crime, and the amateur detective never inquired of me if I saw anything the morning of the murder. It is of little surprise to me that two of the only people the Count never interviewed about the crime are the criminal and the witness with the best view of the bank. He underestimated us both. Shamed as he is, I feel his noble cheeks will never grace my well-shined chair again and while it will affect my earthly ledger, it will put my heavenly one further into the black.*

"Hello, Mr. Shiloh, after your testimony at the Bailey hearing, we have some questions for you if you don't mind," said Jones.

"Yes, sir. I wish to do all I can to help."

"That is great to hear. We have a list the constable has given us of men you mentioned seeing enter or exit the bank on the day of the murder. Was there possibly anyone you omitted?" said Heath.

"Yes," William said, scratching his head. "There was another man who visited the bank the morning of the murder, but I thought nothing strange about it since he was always going in and out of there. So, I didn't think to mention it previous to Bailey's inquest. He is the postmaster and he was Frank's dear friend. Nothing about his travels seemed out of the ordinary."

Most of the townsfolk including the constable had mentioned to the detectives the close friendship of Frank and Edward. This bond had put Edward out of bounds in the minds of many, including the detectives, as a possible suspect.

Convinced the barber had nothing of substance to offer and believing this was a waste of their time, Jones stood up and prepared to leave, but Heath grabbed him by his suit jacket to stop him and continued speaking to the barber. "Mrs. Vinton and Mr. Shedd, the baker, stated they saw a strange man in a fur cap and tan coat around the time of the murder. Did you perhaps see this man as well from your window?"

There you have it, thought William enthusiastically. *That was the right question.*

"Yes," he said.

"Yes!" repeated both Heath and Jones at the same time. Jones sat down and fumbled in his pockets for his pad and pencil, then said urgently to William, "Tell us about that, please."

"Well, I was looking in my mirror at the time and saw the figure of the man exiting the bank. The clothes seemed different, no question about that"—William paused and gasped a deep breath before continuing—"but the limp looked familiar."

"Could it have been the postmaster?" said Jones.

"It could have been so," said William after another pause, not wanting to appear either too eager or too certain to these men, yet he immediately noticed by their changed facial expressions that the detectives were very pleased by his answer.

"Thank you so much, Mr. Shiloh!" said Heath, placing a gentle hand on the barber's shoulder.

"You have been quite helpful," exclaimed Jones.

The demeanor of the detectives, which had gradually become sluggish as the days dragged on without any promising lead, now lightened considerably after hearing the barber's words. Hours before, at first light, the two had begrudgingly set eyes upon each other outside their adjoining houses for what seemed like the umpteenth time in this endless investigation, but each now hoped they held a strong possibility to bring it to its conclusion.

They had a solid clue, perhaps a real suspect, instead of following all the false leads and false accusations manufactured by the Count and others merely seeking reward. The detectives nodded at William and began walking back to the depot.

"Shiloh has no need to lie; he has no real chance of claiming any of the reward," said Jones.

Heath shrugged his shoulders and said, "We both know that. Regardless, he's stated clearly what he observed," and then, placing his hat on his head, Heath continued, "that the man whom he saw leave the bank soon before the murder was discovered might have been the postmaster. This, finally, is a true lead for us to follow."

Jones agreed. "It is not the strongest lead, but it gives us a focus, and we can begin to investigate Green in earnest instead of spinning about in circles as we have been doing for the past month." *And finally end this investigation once and for all,* thought Jones, a smile starting to develop on his face.

Heath was thinking a similar thought as they arrived at the depot to head back to Boston: *Mr. Green, we're coming for you, and if we find definitive proof that you are the culprit of this vile deed, rest assured, you will be in our custody forthwith.*

William watched the detectives walk away, just as he observed everything that happened on Pleasant Street. A faint hope blossomed within the barber that he had not allowed to muster since the murder. *It is done. All I am capable of doing, in fact, willing to do. Wisely, I am not accusing Green directly, but now the detectives are on the right track with my assistance. Speaking this truth is the relief I've been seeking. Hopefully, they will arrest the postmaster soon, and I pray Green has no reason to suspect I've played any part in his capture.*

The barber was attempting in his mind to provide an alibi for a crime he didn't commit to protect himself from the possible wrath of the criminal. *If only I was white; my life would hold some difficulties, sure—Green has had his share—but I'm certain it would be a far easier journey, nonetheless, for me. Mine is not an easy road to wander, for I must tread softly as I do so, but with the intention that each one of my steps lends itself to a greater purpose.*

If I am to leave my just mark on this world and continue to walk with some respect and safety, my *actions must be fastidious and sound in every manner. I pray I have decided well in this Green matter, for I wish this situation to come to its just conclusion for the well-being of myself and my family.*

That evening as he walked home, William felt lighter, free. Edward had not been arrested or even accused, but the guilt William felt at staying silent had eased, the shackles had loosened. Yet one burden on his conscience remained. He had kept all of this internal struggle secret from Emily, the woman he loved, the lighthouse that, throughout the years together, had guided him through the worst of storms.

As they lay in bed that night, William stared upward in the blackness. Emily was curled up against him, and he could sense her breath along the scar on his cheek.

"There is something I have to tell you, that I haven't told you."

William felt the caress of warm air against his face cease. "What is it?" Emily asked.

"The detectives came to visit me today."

Her breathing became more rapid as she asked, "What did they want from you?"

"Information, and I sort of told them, at least pointed them in the right direction."

Emily, in a calmer voice, said, "How so?"

"I am almost certain the postmaster is Frank's killer."

"You are?" Her body jerked in the bed as she sat upright.

"Yes, I testified, with your support and guidance, that I saw him twice that day. What I haven't told you until now, and only implied to the detectives, is that I saw him a third time exit the bank, minutes before the boy was found slain."

"Oh, my gosh!" Emily had to will herself not to jump out of the bed in surprise.

William sensed her fear and unease. "I'm sorry to have kept this from you. I worried Green was a dangerous man, and my firm belief is that he remains so until he is arrested, which I hope will happen soon."

"You should have told me!" William could sense Emily frowning in the darkness. He heard a rustling and then a match strike as she lit a candle at their bedside. The light flickered on the face he loved, and she kissed him directly on the wound he carried from his past.

"William, free yourself of torment. I am not mad. You did as you felt just, but it is not right that you should have endured such a heavy weight alone. I am always at your side to assist in our struggle."

"You are so sweet, my love. I will never hold back such a thing from you again. I promise." He pulled her body close to his own, her hair brushed against his face.

"Good, now get some rest, both of your body and your mind. They will arrest him if he is guilty, and we will retain only our normal concerns, which are numerous enough." Emily laughed.

"Yes, the struggle continues," said William, giving a light chuckle back, "but we will survive, as we always do. Good night, my love."

She blew out the candle, and William allowed one eye and then the other, with a small bit of reluctance, to close.

William, although he didn't know it for a fact at this point, had shown Edward Green his fate this day, yet it would be someone much closer to Edward who would soon seal it.

Chapter Thirty-Four

A DAY OR TWO later, Charles Merrill wrote Ezra Lamson a letter and, instead of mailing it, dropped it off at the bank director's door. Imploring secrecy, he detailed his strong suspicions against Edward for the crimes. His reasoning was the knowledge among many in the town of Edward's numerous debts and his lack of being a witness at any hearings or interacting in any conversation about the robbery and murder. But he summed up his skepticism of Edward with "Green is the only individual who visited the bank on the day of the murder who has not sought out the detectives to talk about his interactions that day with Frank. The only one."

By this time, the Boston detectives had already started tracing the postmaster's movements. The money Edward spent in the previous month was being scrutinized. It was discovered that he had paid off some of his most pressing obligations and, in doing so, had used notes of the Malden Bank. Heath and Jones began searching in earnest for further clues of the postmaster's guilt.

The directors of the bank, immediately after the commission of the murder, devoted themselves unceasingly to the labor of detecting the criminal. Along with Detectives Heath and Jones, they investigated many circumstances and reports which were brought to their ears, and many persons eventually known to be innocent were for some time closely watched by police.

Two men from Portsmouth, New Hampshire, were induced to come to Malden, ostensibly to make arrangements for engaging in the substitute business (able-bodied men who, for money, assumed the place of a rich man on the battlefields of the war), but really to see if either of them answered the description of the stranger said to have been seen on the day of the murder.

They were walked across Malden Square, little knowing that half a dozen people, including Caroline Vinton and Marshall Shedd, were scrutinizing their motions to see if they could be recognized.

Fortunately, they did not answer the description and returned home without knowing the real purpose for which they were called to Malden. Other parties were also suspected, and a warrant was actually issued for the arrest of a Charlestown man whom Boston police conceived to be the murderer before it was dismissed.

Heath and Jones started interviewing townspeople discreetly about Edward, and there was no better place to do so than at Hill's Tavern. The detectives had not visited here prior to this and thought they could still pass as two of the many ubiquitous mustachioed, suit-wearing men who had journeyed through the town since the railroad had arrived. Many visitors traveling farther north or south stopped and stayed overnight at the hotel near the depot.

The barkeep had encountered more strangers in the past couple of years than he had during his whole life living in the town, and so he didn't pay these two particular men any special heed.

There were very few customers as they set foot in the tavern. The detectives, having placed their badges in their pockets before they entered, sat at the bar and ordered a couple of ales.

"Where are you gentlemen from?" asked the barkeep.

"We're from out of town," stated Heath.

"We're traveling about seeking answers to life-and-death questions," stated Jones, and Heath shot him a look.

Yet this casual conversation led the barkeep to talk about Frank's murder.

"You two are aware of the murder that happened here?"

"We are," said Heath.

"Frank was a fine boy," said the barkeep.

"Yes," said Jones, never having met him.

"The whole town is torn up with fear the murderer could strike again, but mostly with anger," said the barkeep as he wiped down the counter.

"Yes, it is all most people can talk about, it seems," said Heath, hoping to encourage him to keep speaking on the subject.

"Most people, true, but not all," said the barkeep.

"You see a lot of people here, drinking and having long discussions in general and about the murder in particular now, I assume," said Jones.

"Yes, but one fellow is here all the time and has not uttered a word about the murder."

Heath and Jones both put down their glasses.

"Which fellow?" said Heath.

"The postmaster. Usually, his voice fills the joint, but he has seemed cool and indifferent since the crime, truly out of his character. Some say it is because he was so close to the boy, but others are starting to say this should make him even more vocal about the crime. In fact, he was in here last week, drinking ale after ale, as he is known to do, and some shots of whiskey, which was a bit out of the normal for him. Well, as I was saying, he was here when Dowling, the man who threatened that fool, the Count, as you may have heard"—the detectives nodded and the barkeep continued—"Dowling said that if the murderer became known and he heard that a mob cut the bastard up to pieces, he would be very glad. A lot of the men cheered, but Green looked straight ahead and kept drinking. I returned soon after to fill him another mug of ale, and his stool was empty."

With this new information in hand, Heath and Jones thought it imperative to immediately update Ezra Lamson, the director of the bank. Ezra acted as the chief advisor to Mr. Converse on any new evidence gathered in solving the crime.

The detectives met with Ezra at his home to discuss their investigation. Charles Merrill was also present.

"Have you started to look into Green?" asked Charles.

"We have," said Jones.

"After interviewing the barber, we have made further inquiries, and I believe at this point, the postmaster should be the focus of our investigation," said Heath.

"Agreed," said their host. "The deacon and I have discussed the details about the growing suspicions against the postmaster"—he nodded at Merrill—"and so, he has requested that we collectively keep an eye on

Green and see what evidence we can gather and then ferret him out if, truly, he is the guilty party."

"That is a good idea, sir," said Heath. "Jones and I will wear out our shoe leather to interview the townsfolk and follow Green and report to you."

"Gentleman, if you wear out your shoes, Mr. Converse will certainly supply you with new pairs until his son's murderer is captured, whether it is Green or someone else," said Ezra.

And so with the approval of Mr. Converse, who was consulted at every step, Ezra formed a secret circle, a kind of vigilance committee, for the purpose of watching the suspected man. Its members, all influential men and friends of the bank and the Converse family, included two other directors of the bank, George Blanchard and Caleb Wait; town selectmen Hubbard Russell, Charles Sanderson, and Charles Sprague, who was also a director at the bank; and Constable John Abbott.

The secret circle was now working on the hypothesis that Edward Green was the murderer. They had first met on the evening of January 9, a week after Bailey's arrest, and since then had met several times.

On private investigation, it was ascertained Edward stood well with the good people of Malden, excepting that, like many other persons of irreproachable character, he had the misfortune of being involved in debt.

A couple of days after its formation, Ezra visited the post office, knowing that Edward was not present.

"Hello, Amos. How are you today?"

"Fine, sir. How can I be of service?"

"I would like to ask you a question, and could you promise me not to tell the postmaster I have inquired?"

The boy shrugged. "Sure, I suppose so, sir. What is it?"

"Does Edward have a gun in the office?"

"He did."

"And no more? When did you last see it?"

Amos pondered for a moment, his face grew taut, and his eyes stared at Ezra. "Mr. Green had a pistol. It was in this drawer." Amos pointed to the desk before him. "I noticed it an evening or perhaps two before Frank's murder but not since. In fact . . ." The boy hesitated. "As I recall, Mr. Green frequently practiced shooting in the lot behind this office in the days before the murder but never afterward."

Both were silent for almost a full minute.

"Where did he get this gun and how long did he have it?"

"He mentioned it was a pistol which his brother used in the army and said he just received it from the South. That was in early December. But I knew that could not be true."

"Why is that?"

"Well, it appeared to be brand new, certainly had none of the wear and tear one would expect from battle."

"A fine observation, son. Brand new, you say?"

"Yes."

"And you have not seen him with it since?"

"Not in the normal drawer he liked to keep it in. He may be carrying it upon his person. I know not."

"Okay, Amos. I again ask your discretion."

"Is Mr. Green a suspect?"

"There are many suspects," lied Ezra. "We just have to be sure to check everyone out. You understand."

"I do. And I miss Frank. And I know Mr. Green misses Frank terribly. I have heard him crying when he thinks I am out of earshot. Please, catch Frank's killer, sir."

"I intend to, son. Good day."

Chapter Thirty-Five

ABOUT A WEEK after the secret circle formed, Marshall came to Ezra in some distress of mind and confidentially informed him that he suspected Edward to be guilty of the crimes. He stated his concerns about Edward's increased spending habits and his indifference to the murder of his dear friend. A topic that was central to every conversation of all the townsfolk, with the exception of the postmaster. But the paramount reason that induced Marshall to visit one of the directors of the bank, and the close friend of Elisha Converse, was his discovery in Edward's stove at the post office.

"I was in the post office the day after the murder. It was late morning, and Edward was sitting by the stove. I sat down beside him, and he seemed uncomfortable about my arrival. I spied in the stove what remained of a fur-trimmed hat and a few metal buttons with foreign markings on them. Seeing the scorched buttons was very disconcerting to me. They appeared like pairs of fiery eyes staring out from the embers. I inquired as to what he was burning. He made no response to my question. Instead, Edward stood, sealed the stove door, and said, 'Marshall, you'll have to excuse me. I must close the office and spend some time at home with Clara. The baby's due within days.'

"I hadn't known Edward to burn clothing before in the stove, just wood and trash. The clothes seemed very different than the style I knew him to own. I wondered if they were the items I saw the stranger at the bank wear. That's why I'm here, Mr. Lamson. Edward has had lots of financial concerns.

It's hard to believe he would murder Frank, yet his behavior recently has been very odd. On my next visit to his office on the following day, Edward was sitting at the stove and was quite jovial to see me. He invited me to sit down. The strange items I had noticed in the stove the day before had been removed. I asked no further questions of him but decided I must come and talk to you, sir, about my concerns. I apologize for waiting this long. It has been a great weight on my conscience, but Edward has been a dear friend to me and it has been quite difficult for me to think of him being capable of such a deed." Marshall rubbed his forehead with a rag to dry the sweat. "But I believe now that he is guilty."

"I am grateful to you, Mr. Shedd. This information can be quite helpful in our investigation of Edward Green."

Marshall took a step back and said, "You've been investigating Eddie?"

"Indeed, we have." At this, Ezra then informed Marshall of the existence and objects of the secret circle and made him a member of it. Soon, Detective Heath, excited to have someone so close to Edward reporting to them about his activities, engaged Marshall at a salary of three dollars a day to do nothing but travel about with Edward and report to him what his closest friend was doing. Detective William Calder was assigned to monitor Edward from a distance as Marshall watched him from a close proximity.

On the next Saturday, the two friends went to several places in Boston, and Edward purchased a mirror worth thirty dollars at a store on Hanover Street. They visited the furniture establishment of A. J. Carter of Charlestown, on the corner of Union, and selected $271 of carpets and also furniture for Clara. The carpeting was cut, but the articles were not delivered, as Edward proposed to call and pay for them in a day or two.

"You say your address is in Malden? Oh my. What an evil act by an atrocious fiend! Tell me, has there been any news of the arrest of the vile murderer?" asked the shopkeeper.

"As I said, I will return with the funds and then you can have them delivered, please," said Edward.

"We are unaware what the authorities know and who they suspect," said Marshall.

As they returned home through Somerville, they met a man who was heading in the opposite direction and stopped his carriage next to theirs.

"Hey, you're the Malden postmaster."

Edward wearily said, "I am."

"What news of the Malden Murderer? Have they captured the bastard? Does the law have any clues?" The man glanced at Edward and then at Marshall as each returned silence. Marshall was driving the carriage and paused there, waiting to see how Edward would respond before driving off. Edward glared at Marshall.

After a brief, uncomfortable pause, Edward turned to the man and said, "I believe they are after somebody," and then added, "The next thing you will hear is that Green, the postmaster, will be shot through the grates of his office."

"Let's hope not, for your sake, sir," said the man and drove off. Marshall pulled the reins and their carriage trotted forward.

Marshall thought his friend's response very strange and almost a deflection of his guilt as it bubbled to the surface, and he reported as much to the secret circle the next day.

"Marshall, his guilt seems obvious to you from his behavior," said Ezra in his parlor as the rest of the circle listened intently.

"Unfortunately, it does, sir."

"We have to find a way to make him confess," said Jones.

Heath considered this and then said, "Marshall, I have an idea. Go with Edward to the Boston Museum tomorrow. You have said he is a great fan of John Wilkes Booth, correct?"

"He idolizes the man. Thinks he is a terrific actor."

"As he is. The play just premiered the other night to tremendous accolades. The deacon is attending tomorrow's performance."

"What do you have in mind, Benjamin?" said Ezra.

"The thing is to surprise Green and put his guilt front and center so he confesses to his dear friend."

"How will I elicit that?" asked Marshall.

"Sometime during the evening, leave Green for a bit and then when you are driving home after the play, inform him that you heard Deacon Converse state he held no personal grudge against his son's murderer and did not believe in capital punishment; moreover, if he could have the mystery cleared up, the deacon would do what he could for the person who would own up to it and relieve him and his family of the terrible suspense."

Marshall promised to follow these instructions, but the next day, neither he nor Edward attended the play.

Heath went directly to the bakery the following morning.

"Marshall, we are so close."

"What if we are all wrong and Edward is innocent?"

"This is no time for second thoughts. You came to us, joined our circle, and do I have to remind you that we have paid you to report on your interactions with Green?"

"No, sir."

"If he is innocent, he will not confess. We have to place him in this situation to know for sure if he is the murderer. I know he is your friend. But think of Frank, think of the Converses, please. Booth's play is scheduled for at least the next week, but the sooner we do this the better. The deacon greatly enjoyed the performance last night, but you cannot expect him to see the play over and over again, can you?"

"You are right on all counts, sir. I will talk to Edward today and convince him to attend tonight with me."

Marshall guided the carriage, Edward sitting beside him. Traveling through Scollay Square, they tied the horses near King's Chapel Cemetery, where John Winthrop, the first governor of the commonwealth, famous for his sermon about Boston being a "city on the hill," was buried among others of renown. The friends then walked to the magnificent building known as the Boston Museum.

The museum contained mummies from both Egypt and Peru; galleries of stuffed animals, encompassing an elephant, an orangutan, and a platypus; and a mermaid, depicted as a "curious half fish, half human," but was really just a head of a young monkey sewn onto the body of a fish. There were over three thousand different specimens of birds, and many other animals were preserved in alcohol, comprising hundreds of reptiles and fishes. The museum also displayed paintings, engravings, and statues. The charge for admission was twenty-five cents and included entrance to the grand exhibition hall, where comedians, an orchestra of musicians, and actors performed. Special upgraded seating for such entertainment was available for fifty cents.

Dabbling in opium before the murder, Edward had increased his use since killing Frank. Millions of opium pills were being distributed daily among the Union Army for a variety of ailments serious or minor, whether gunshot wounds or mere stomach discomfort. The hypodermic syringe had become more available as a delivery method in the past decade, but Dr. Burpee had prescribed a tincture to relieve Edward's pain. His hallucinations, which the physician was unaware of, started with scary clouds and had only expanded since. Reality and remorse had blurred for Edward Green more and more into a maze of everyday uncertainty.

Edward and Marshall strolled through the high-ceilinged hall that contained a wax museum. Edward stared anxiously at the figures, perceiving that all of them were real, especially the tribes of Natives standing next to teepees. He worried as he passed them that they would suddenly spring to life and attack him, but he forced himself to take a deep breath, then removed his flask from his coat pocket and took another pull, trying to distract himself from the fears that always resided so close to him. After Edward purchased their tickets, he and Marshall walked down to the front few rows.

Marshall, conditioned to climbing the stairs to the balcony, was befuddled. "Eddie, are you sure these are our seats?"

"Yes, Marshall, it's my treat. Don't concern yourself with the price."

They sat in the third row, a little right of center, and Marshall gazed intently at the stage, having never been this close to it. Edward sat massaging one of his legs and took another long pull from his flask. Marshall turned his head back toward the left several rows behind and nodded at Detective Calder, who returned the gesture. Edward also glanced around the theater, left and right and then up. He frowned, imagining vivid images of clouds painted on the ceiling. Since the murder and his increased use of opium, the clouds sometimes now appeared to follow him indoors as well. Edward wished to ignore them so instead darted his eyes quickly around the room.

He heard a familiar voice close by and realized, to his shock, that Deacon Converse was seated in the middle of the front row with some of the directors of the bank. Edward became quite anxious and thought about getting up and exiting the venue. Just then the curtain fell, and the performance began.

The lights went down, and the clouds disappeared from his vision, with the only illumination being the spotlights upon the stage. Edward breathed a little easier and allowed himself to enjoy the show, amazed by Booth as he always was.

During intermission, Marshall excused himself while Edward traveled down to Beacon Street in front of Boston Common, the oldest city park in the United States, and stared up at the light-yellow dome of the State House in the moonlight (the dome would not be gilded with its familiar gold leaf until 1874). The Bell In Hand Tavern being closed, Edward wandered over toward Faneuil Hall to the Green Dragon and consumed one ale and then quickly another.

Edward did not wish to look upon Mr. Converse or gaze upon the clouds he imagined on the ceiling once again, so he walked back to his seat after the house lamps were dimmed and the show had resumed.

On the way home, Marshall related in a casual manner what he overheard Deacon Converse, surrounded by a group of men, say during intermission when asked of his son's murder: "'I forgive Frank's murderer, for forgiveness of others is a gift unto oneself.'"

Edward exclaimed, "Did he really say that?"

When Marshall confirmed that the deacon indeed had, Edward was silent the rest of the way home. From the moment this was relayed to the secret circle, there was little doubt within its membership that Edward would make a full confession when confronted by their evidence and his money trail.

On Tuesday, February 2, while out riding with Marshall, Edward spoke about the murder and asked Marshall if he thought a man who had been suspected was guilty. Marshall replied, "No, I don't believe that he is any more guilty than you are."

Marshall stated to the secret circle that the manner of Edward at this suggestion was very embarrassed, and the two did not speak as they returned to town.

Many in the circle, having become morally certain of Edward's guilt after these two conversations, called for his immediate arrest. Heath held out against it, on the grounds that if Edward did not confess, it might be much more difficult to secure evidence against him than it would be if he were allowed to remain at liberty under the long and short shadows of Detective Calder and Marshall as evidence continued to build. Growing impatient, a number of the members disagreed with the detective, convinced that if Edward was apprehended at this point, he would unquestionably admit his guilt. So, when Heath was away in Portland hunting whitetail deer with his brother, they made up their minds to arrest him. Detective Jones learned of this plan and telegraphed Heath to return at once, which Heath did.

Heath rushed from the depot to Ezra Lamson's home; Jones was waiting outside for him. The detectives entered the drawing room and stood in the middle of a half circle of gentlemen seated in maroon armchairs, some smoking pipes and others sipping whiskey. Marshall sat farthest from the center, his tumbler recently refilled after consuming at least two other whiskeys while waiting to see if the group would proceed with the arrest of his friend. He took a long swig at the sight of Jones and, especially, Heath, who was still dressed in a long red coat, the tails of which covered a large section of his white trousers tucked neatly into his Boston Rubber Shoe Company boots. A bloodhound lay by his feet. Taking off his rounded black cap and holding it to his chest, Heath spoke in the vernacular of a hunter, matching his attire. "With all due respect, my friends, we cannot act in haste. We must be absolutely sure of capturing our quarry before we spook him off. We are tracking Green. We are close. Perhaps days away. Let's be patient, please. We will follow his trail and we will snag him."

Some discussion followed, but the sight and authoritative words of Heath were enough for the detectives to convince the circle to stay patient for the time being. The secret circle investigated Edward's personal affairs carefully and soon were aware of what bills he was paying and how he was doing it. It was ascertained that Edward was suddenly settling debts as small as twenty dollars as well as some very much larger in the short period which ensued since the murder. He had paid $500 to Mr. Gray in Boston as an agent for the schoolbooks. The payment due by the first of the year was paid in full, all in bills on the Malden Bank, three days early. Edward also settled a debt of about $200, which had been due for almost two years, nearly all in bills on the Malden Bank. The detectives concluded this was unquestionable proof against him. The sudden possession of so much money for Edward to pay his debts, and the fact that the money was entirely or mostly on the bills of the Malden Bank, were additional links in the chain of evidence against him. It was known Edward was not in a position to pay such an amount of money from his own property, having no income except about a $600 yearly salary from the post office.

The secret circle was informed, and these facts also were brought to the attention of some personal and intimate friends of Edward, including his brother-in-law, John Chapman, who with great reluctance yielded to the unavoidable impression that circumstances were strongly against Edward, even satisfactorily demonstrative of his guilt.

In this way, a considerable amount of evidence was gradually accumulating. It was not thought advisable to make an arrest too soon, yet the detectives were prepared to do so on short notice if necessary. The danger of losing Edward through his discovery of their half-matured plans, and his chances of flight, were considered by police from the first, and a large number of his photographs were obtained, unknown to him, from a Boston photographer for the purpose of sending them all over the country in case he made his escape. Among the other means taken by Ezra to watch Edward was that of boring a hole through the partition from an apartment adjoining the post office, and at various times the movements of the suspect had been observed through this aperture.

On the morning of Sunday, February 7, Ezra placed himself at that lookout, expecting Edward would visit the office as he normally did. But he did not arrive, and it was learned quite late in the day that the suspected man had been seen to leave town in a carriage. It was feared Edward might have gotten intelligence of the storm that was gathering over his head and attempted by flight to escape the coming danger. A man was dispatched in haste to Boston to inform the police.

Chapter Thirty-Six

Earlier that morning, Marshall had encountered Edward on a buggy at Jackson's livery.

"Shall I join you?"

"No, Marshall. I prefer to ride alone today, if you take no objection." The baker shook his head as Edward rode off, not looking at him or waiting to see his reaction. Marshall noted that Edward turned right on Main Street heading south.

The two horses, Virgil and Homer, brayed. Jackson had informed the postmaster they were two of his finest horses, and that had pleased Edward.

Edward required the best team since his destination was one he had never ventured to before, one he thought he was thoroughly unable to travel to on his own two feet. However, Edward was also uncertain whether a team of horses could carry him to his desired location, but he had gathered his nerves as best he could and even sipped on a bit of whiskey, followed by a dose of an opium tincture, before Marshall arrived and asked to join him.

There was no company allowed on this journey; this was one Edward knew he would have to undertake on his own. Edward kept the horses at a short gallop as he collected his thoughts. He knew if Marshall accompanied him, he would only desire to talk about the murder of Frank as he increasingly had for the past few weeks, and there was only one soul in town to which Edward was capable of speaking about the matter. The time had come to confess and ask forgiveness. He would never dare speak to Clara about it, due to her fragility and his shame. Marshall was a loyal friend, but Edward could not reveal his thoughts on the murder to him either.

The team followed the route they knew well; it was one they traveled almost daily. True beasts of burden. The side streets were blocked from view by their blinders; all they could behold was the road ahead. But the rider they transported was well aware of the streets that intersected his path as he was being carried away from the center of the only town he had ever known. When his own body was the only means of his travel, Edward looked hither and fro as his limbs carried him. Even now, forced to sit straight on the carriage as it moved, he still retained the tendency to not focus solely on the destination before him. Edward eyed each side street clearly as he headed farther south—there was Madison, Newhall, and Wigglesworth, in honor of the preacher and author of "Day of Doom." Everyone in town knew the lines of the famous book and certainly walked over the poet's grave at one point or another. The last line of Cotton Mather's eulogy for the Malden reverend stuck in Edward's head as the horses marched forward and away: "And waits with joy to see his Day of Doom."

Next, Edward passed a street that was the same as his last name. He thought it peculiar that Green Street lay beside the next street, named after the father of his dear friend Frank Converse. Edward knew the only thing named directly after his own father was the gravestone under which Reuben lay, one barely paid for by his family with the help of Elisha Converse. Frank and Edward had wandered on nearby paths, their lives were close and intersected, much like these two roads, but also like these roads, they differed in their topography—Green Street was a bit crooked while Converse Avenue was ramrod straight. His family, with a common name of Green, had a common history.

However, Edward thought he would not be surprised if one day, the town of Malden would be renamed as Converse, a much more renowned surname, due mainly to one man, Elisha, who owned more of the town than anyone else. In fact, the street, named after Converse only in the last few years, was not one in which the deacon lived, but he owned several plots on it as well as several more throughout the town. It lay somewhat between his opulent home and his factory. If he was only pretending to be a pious man, Edward Green thought, Elisha Converse could easily rule over the whole town, eventually, as his fiefdom.

The next block contained the largest mansion in Malden and any nearby vicinity. Virgil and Homer seemed to slow their pace without any discernible change in how Edward held their reins.

Should he go inside, speak to the deacon or even his wife, Mary, if she was home alone and equal in grieving and longing for an answer to their shared pain? Edward hesitated and took a deep breath. *No. What good would it do? How could it ease their suffering?* Edward had just one he intended to talk to directly, and that conversation was long overdue. He tightened the reins and sped up.

Edward regarded the deacon's ornate and decorative buggy outside as he passed. Elisha's driver nodded at him as he did so. Edward recognized him but did not know his name. He nodded back and continued to ride, the team feeling the initial tug of the reins but never breaking stride. Elisha must be inside. Edward allowed a small glance backward as he was pulled forward and away. He drew tighter on the reins, and the velocity of the buggy increased. He was going farther south and downhill; he took one left turn and soon after, another. The day was chilly but Edward was nervous and sweating. He pulled out a handkerchief, loosened his scarf, and wiped his brow.

As he drew closer to his destination, Edward realized he and the team were driving in circles without ever arriving at it. Unable to find the proper entrance, he counted a total of nine circles altogether. Were these rotations an attempt of his scared subconscious to not enter into this desired destination? He brought the horses to a trot. Edward wondered what Clara and Alice were doing. He should have stayed with them, soaked up the love the three of them shared as a family. Alice had been so beautiful on this morning in the small floral dress paid for by the blood money her father had struck down a young man to attain. Clara smiled so lovingly at him, and then his daughter had as well.

Edward possessed all he wanted in life, and yet he felt he possessed nothing at all. He told himself he should have faced the consequences of his debt and devoted himself to the solemn responsibilities of being both a husband and a father. He should have never killed the boy, who was his friend, someone's child as Alice was his now.

I never truly understood the gift and the fear of fatherhood until I held my baby, my firstborn, thought Edward, *and at this moment, I realize Elisha had once done the same and now holds nothing but complete grief and confusion. I, Edward Green, have brought about both of these latter feelings, I know, and worse still, I've betrayed my friend. I know not the expressions of the Converse parents, their raw emotions when they looked upon the corpse of their offspring on that December day, but I know all too well the final look in the boy's pleading, confused eyes as he saw the face of his killer—a man who, in many ways, was his dearest friend, the closest thing he had to an older brother—ending his life. What I committed was fratricide, pure and simple.*

Dizzy, a bit shaken and unsure, Edward endeavored to continue on the journey he had set out upon. He was sad yet determined. There was no more avoiding it. It was time to visit his friend. He attempted to lead the horses through the gate. They were reluctant to enter. They looked forward but their muscles were rigid in place.

So, he secured them to a post, wrapping the rope tight. He wanted to make sure that they didn't flee, so he retained a way back home. He followed the animals' gaze and detected a shimmer in the air, barely visible like a gossamer curtain between two places. Edward approached the gate with trepidation. As he did so, he thought, *Should I abandon all hope?* He recalled a book Frank had once lent him which described someone crossing over a river named Styx.

His bad leg strained with pain, as usual, as it steadied on the ground, preparing to propel the other, good one forward. Edward exhaled deeply but had trouble inhaling until he crossed the threshold from the land of the living to that of the planted dead. Many of them were recently slain in the war, which seemed without end. Some of the fresh grave markers held familiar names. They had fought and died, but he was not called upon to do so, for he was not able-bodied. Edward could easily be among them if not for his bad leg. Frank had avoided joining their ranks likely due to his father's wealth and position but, nonetheless, now lay beside the dead soldiers through an act of equal violence, not of war but from a more cowardly, singular cause.

Wandering to find Frank's final resting place, Edward discovered the grave-stone was exactly how he had envisioned it. The ground beneath Edward's feet was unstable, each one of his steps tenuous. The headstone contained the protruding, lifelike image of Frank Converse. Two angels curved above his carved face and partial torso and "Frank Eugene" was written in rounded letters below. Frank's earthly countenance sculpted with intricate, skillful detail upon the stone marked his final resting place, the cost of his memorial of no consequence to his affluent, grieving parents. Frank had been so young and promised all the wealth and happiness his earthly father could provide; now his body withered beneath the feet of the man who, just two months prior, had stolen his last breath and, in fact, had glanced into his eyes as he did so. The friends were never closer or further apart but in that very moment. Edward now imagined they had been both somewhat surprised at the circumstances, one changing his destiny by ruining the path of the other, who retained no malice in his heart but only shock at the violence perpetrated against him, the one he held as his dearest friend bringing about his very demise. There were fresh flowers on the ground and a weathered piece of paper with a Bible verse written in the hand of Elisha.

> *And I will bless those that bless you. And the one that*
> *curses you I will curse. And in you all the families of the*
> *earth will be blessed.*

Reading it, Edward wept as he thought of his Alice and thought of Elisha's heartfelt desolation at losing his son. Edward was unsure of this journey today and had been unprepared. He wanted to honor his friend, to mourn him. Edward walked to a nearby grave and took a fresh bouquet and placed it before Frank's grave, adding his purloined flowers to the memorial of those left by his victim's father and others. The sculpted resemblance of his friend's face on the alabaster headstone was so accurate, it appeared to him that young Converse was actually an apparition before him and so Edward, tormented by his sin, fell penitent to his knees.

"Frank, I am so sorry. Truly, I am. I have put you in this place. I robbed far more than the bank on that snowy day. I loved you more than words can say, and I violently sent you to the spirit who resides in the sky. I took you from this world. I'm truly sorry, and I know not what will happen to me. I deserve far worse than I've bestowed upon you, but now I'm not just a husband, but I'm also a father."

Edward bowed deeper; he wanted to divert his eyes from Frank's realistic image but could not. "Alice was born on Christmas. It's such a strange conundrum—I took your life to be able to provide for hers. It's neither of your faults; I've been unwise with money. I remember how elated you were when I told you that Clara was with child. I'm now a murderer and a parent, both the taker and giver of life. I feel for your parents. I would weep if my little girl was snatched as cruelly from Clara and me as I've stolen you from Mr. and Mrs. Converse."

Edward straightened himself up as much as he could and stared directly at the face before him. "It's not right, it's not fair. But it's never been fair. I've no proper excuse for my sins other than you were always who you were, and I was and am always who I am. God made us this way. It's not your fault; I believe it's only partly mine. I was given free will, but you and I were also given far different circumstances in our lives. You were blessed, at least until the moment I walked into the bank on that snowy day, and I was cursed, an outcast in plain sight. You were able-bodied, I was crippled by form and fate. The very hand of our Maker chose how we would live. I'll walk the earth for the remainder of my days asking him why He made you one way and made me another. It was not your choice to be favored by Him and envied by me. We both loved you. He was your Creator, as He is mine. I became your destroyer. Did I have a choice? I did. I'm a sinner, and I repent to you and to Him. I'll continue to pray to each of you and hope earnestly one or both of you hear my pleas for forgiveness."

The carved likeness of the friend he murdered lay so very clear, so vibrant before him, almost glowing in the late morning light as the sun rose behind him, that Edward expected an answer. He paused for several moments. He imagined what Frank would say to him now if he was able to communicate or if he had been able to do so as their eyes met before the firing of the second chamber. But the stone's image of his slain friend just stared past him and deliberately into eternity.

Not being able to gaze any longer at the very face he had smote, Edward looked around for any distraction. Of all the myriad flowers, those left by Elisha were the finest, most likely from his private greenhouse. Edward glanced at the note from Elisha once more and then picked up the roses that the father had left for his beloved son. He took two of them, one in each hand, and held them with arms stretched out at his sides, gazing toward the sky.

"He was given so much by you, and I, so little. Whhhhy?"

The sun hid behind a cloud. Was God ignoring him? He squeezed on the flower stems as an offering. The thorns pierced just below his wrists and Edward bled. "I am your son too," he said, and there was only silence in response.

If God would not speak to him, he would wrack his brain for scripture. But only one line came to him as he stood above the boy he had slain: "What have you done? Listen! Your brother's blood cries out to me from this soil."

There had been a flurry of snow the day before, but now it was sunny and clear; yet the snow remained on the frigid ground.

Edward left irregular footprints as he staggered away from the grave. A few drops of blood from his wrists fell to the ground among his crooked steps. They mingled with the snow and stained its purity. This evidence would remain throughout the rest of the day, until it would begin to warm and melt it, but for the moment, these marks seemed permanent.

Edward rejoined his team outside the gates. As Edward ventured from one cemetery to another, he saw the dead as his traveling companions throughout the journey. Both his parents, who had given him life, and Frank, whose life he had taken, were embedded deep within his thoughts. He drove home along the marshes in Chelsea and past Black Ann's Corner as he entered back into East Malden and then Maplewood Square on Salem Street. The buggy galloped west, and Edward watched a train south of him head east on the Saugus Branch. The line that was connected to the Boston and Maine Railroad originated in Edgeworth, close to the Boston Rubber Shoe Company, and winded north through Saugus and into Lynn.

Edward pulled on the reins as he passed Waite's tavern, opposite Webster Street, where his father had once toiled before becoming postmaster. It was the only tavern nearby that Edward would not visit; it reminded him too much of the past and raised troubling questions about what he suspected may have brought about his mother's demise.

Edward conveyed the purloined roses to the cemetery where his parents lay. Their stones were meager. Edward had not brought any flowers there since his father had passed. He placed the roses, with their blood-soaked stems, on each of his parents' graves and lay down on the spot between them. He outstretched his arms, palms facing upward, and then clutched them by his sides. The family was together again. Edward was exhausted, his eyes beginning to shut. He took a deep breath, exasperated by this sojourn to call on spirits once so dear to him. Feeling as if he were a castaway in between two realms, Edward fell asleep.

When he awoke, little of the day's light remained, and Edward knew he must get home, back to the stables, back to Clara and Alice. He had no one to guide him in or out of this realm except his team. The horses appeared to gather new verve as they transported Edward away from his day of visiting the dead. It had been his first trip to see the memorial of his friend, and it would be his last.

Chapter Thirty-Seven

WHEN IT WAS ascertained Edward had left town that morning, fears were revived that he was aware he was suspected and had fled. The train leaving for New York on that evening was kept under careful observation and a man was sent to render it certain that Edward did not enter at any of the way stations. Detectives Heath and Jones went to the residence of Ezra Lamson to consult, as they had previously done, with the secret circle. While there, Marshall relayed the conversation he shared with Edward at the stables—that he had offered to go riding with his friend that morning, but how Edward had insisted that he intended to go riding alone, which struck Marshall as odd. Fearing that Edward had taken the alarm, felt the noose closing on him and wished to escape, it was determined by the committee that he should be arrested at once, upon his arrival, before he could return to his boardinghouse on Pleasant Street.

So suddenly was this agreed upon, however, that no warrant was obtained, as Justice Hill could not be found. So, it was determined that Edward would be apprehended by the constable without that authority, and the charge against Edward would be lodged by Detective Heath on the following day.

Before nightfall, the moon starting to reveal its fullness in the sky, Edward returned to the livery. He took each horse and, with a double knot, tied one to the post and then the other.

Constable Abbott had been waiting for Edward for many hours. Abbott breathed heavily, deciding what to do. He allowed Edward to enter the post office and exit again before approaching him.

"Mr. Green."

"Yes?"

"Mr. Lamson has requested your presence, please, at his home."

"For what purpose, Constable?"

"It would be best if he told you personally, please." Abbott was trying to choose his words carefully, having rehearsed what to say to the postmaster. He had to lure Edward in somehow, and there was one tactic he knew would be guaranteed to be successful.

"He would like to have a talk, perhaps a quick drink with you. He has assured me it would not take much of your time."

"A quick drink, you say?" Edward said and looked at the town clock. "My wife expects me home, but I suppose I have a bit of time to spare for a quick drink."

Edward, looking first at the post office and trying not to gaze at the bank but then forcing himself to do so, shed a tear. Edward hoped he had wiped it away before Abbott could glimpse it. Edward readily accompanied the constable and another man who had joined them to Ezra's house on Summer Street, a few houses north of the train depot. They entered a room in which several gentlemen were seated including, to his profound surprise, his dear friend Marshall, who sank into his chair at Edward's recognition.

"Edward, you are under arrest for the murder of Frank Converse," said Constable Abbott.

Edward remained as if struck dumb yet exhibited no marked emotion and made no reply. He continued to stand silently while his person was searched. In his pockets two bills were found—one five-dollar and one two-dollar, both on the Malden Bank; and while the search of his pockets was being presented, he held in his hand a roll of more bills, which he placed on a table near where he was standing.

After the search of his person was concluded, Edward, in the company of Lamson, Abbott, and Blanchard, retired to an adjoining room, where Ezra said, "Your movements have been closely watched, and everything you've done is known. It's in your best interest to tell at once where the money is."

To this, Edward offered no reply. Then Ezra told him some of the circumstances which had come to their knowledge including the payments of money which they knew he had made beyond his means. "Now," said he, "how much of this money did you use?"

After a moment's silence, there came the practical confession, "Not more than four hundred dollars."

"More than that," said Ezra, and gradually Edward told the whole story, yet still without perceptible emotion.

"I went into the bank three times the morning of the murder. The first time, at about half past ten, I was in the act of drawing my pistol to shoot Frank when I saw a pair of skates. The conductor of the horse car had just thrown them in before I entered the bank. At the time, I thought they were Lichfield's and he would return for them at any moment, so I went back to my office. The second time was eleven o'clock, when I got into the bank and was again preparing to execute this purpose, when I was interrupted by the entrance of Mr. Gray and then Mr. Stone."

"On entering a third time, I walked into the directors' room, and seeing that no one was there, drew my pistol—a six-chamber Smith & Wesson revolver—placed the muzzle within a foot of young Converse's head, and fired, the ball striking under or back of his ear, the shot felling the boy to the floor. I soon after discharged a second shot, toward Frank's temple, while he lay on the floor. The murderous deed having been consummated, I seized the bills on the counter and those in the drawer and eventually, after initially being uncertain what to do, returned to my office."

After detailing these facts, Edward informed the persons present that a portion of the money was concealed in a piece of newspaper in an old boot in the post office, and the balance of the stolen money was secured under the flooring of the Volunteer Engine House.

Constable Abbott and Ezra Lamson immediately escorted Edward to both places to search for the money. They found $615 at the post office and $3,454 at the firehouse, all in Malden Bank bills, in the same condition in which they were stolen from the bank, for a total of $4,069. Upon the wrapper were the figures and the ten punch holes made by Frank, which could be identified as his mark. Besides the Malden money in the package, there was a one-hundred-dollar bill on the Exchange Bank of Boston, which Charles Merrill had known about. The detectives had been expecting that Edward would spend this bill first, but it appeared he had no knowledge of the contents of the package.

When the discovered money was added to the several sums paid by Edward, all the stolen bank money was accounted for.

Edward said that in the weeks before the murder, he had purchased the pistol with which he committed the deed from the store of Mr. Reed, in Boston, and that he also bought a quantity of ammunition; that he loaded the pistol and kept it in a drawer in the post office until the thirteenth of December, two days before the murder, when he often took it from the drawer and carried it about on his person. The officers, of course, already knew that Edward possessed the revolver, since the boy in his office, Amos Tenney had informed the circle.

Soon after returning to his office, after perpetrating the double crime of murder and robbery, he had reloaded the two discharged chambers of his pistol and the additional chamber he forgot to load before the murder, and threw the remaining ammunition into a creek near his office.

Edward informed Jones and Blanchard that the pistol was in a bureau drawer by the chamber pot in his apartment. Heath and Jones walked over there and knocked on the apartment door. Clara opened the door.

"Mrs. Green, your husband, Edward, is in custody for the murder of Frank Converse," said Jones. "We're here to—"

Before he could finish, Clara was on her way to the floor, fainting at the news of her husband's arrest.

The two detectives carried her to the bed and laid her down gently. Jones fetched the landlady to keep an eye on her and her baby while he went to retrieve Dr. Burpee. Heath stayed and first checked on the baby, Alice, who appeared undisturbed and slept soundly, and then he searched the bureau where Edward said he stored his gun.

Opening a drawer, he found the weapon, with all the chambers loaded and capped as Edward had described them.

After the confession was made and the money and weapon were recovered, Edward was placed on a carriage to be transported to Boston by Heath and Jones that night. Edward held a lantern for Heath so he could see to guide his horses through the muddy road in the dark. Edward revealed no emotion except when passing the residence of Deacon Converse.

At this point, he laid his head upon Jones's shoulder, as if fearing to look upon the home he had rendered so desolate. He sobbed and, after the carriage passed a distance and left Malden altogether, once again lifted his head. He remained quiet for the rest of the ride, but his thoughts tormented him. *Mr. Converse, you treated me so well. Been a benefactor to myself as you were to my father and the whole town, and how have I repaid you? By tearing your world asunder with the slaying of your son. I am—*

Heath yanked on the reins suddenly, his green gloved hands clenching tightly and straining them back toward his stomach. The pounding of the horses' hoofbeats echoed in Edward's heart. The cacophony was interrupted by a stutter. He felt dizzy, bewildered. The metal of the animals' harnesses clanged every split second, then after a full second, and then two. The horses gasped hard as Heath continued to tug on the reins so the team would not descend the slope in the road too quickly, inhaling each breath as if it were their last. Doing so, they carried Edward Green away to his fate.

"Sorry," said Edward, feeling he was responsible for the horses' distress. As the road leveled, the team and Edward searched for a deep exhale of relief, and they found it, at least for a moment.

At the Boston police house, Edward admitted his guilt once again, and his confession was recorded:

> *It was my intention to pay up the loss of funds by installments at different times. My troubles began by the mismanagement of the schoolbook accounts. I had sold schoolbooks for the town, and in not keeping any separate account of their money from my own, I had spent the money not thinking whose money I was spending until I found myself greatly in debt. Then there was trouble and I did not know how to get out of it. I had a wife and a baby on the way. My debt and my expenses seemed without end. Then I attempted to burn down the post office in order to burn up all its contents, including my bills, and I thought I might get excused from paying my*

debts. Having access to the Volunteer Fire Department, I fed several small coals along the hose to block or tear it and thus slow aid to smother the fire. The reason I didn't burn the office directly was, I thought of the people that lived in the building. I thought they would not have any proper chance to escape; and so, I gave that up and burnt the next apartment, adjoining the office, thinking that it would burn enough of the office to destroy its contents. But I failed in accomplishing that, and then my trouble grew worse and worse, until I hurried into this awful deed. The fire was several weeks before the murder was committed.

The way I came induced to carry a pistol on my person for the first time was a couple of years ago, I had been out of town to spend an evening, and I was returning home very late one night—I think it was in the autumn of sixty or spring of sixty-one. When I got into Malden, opposite Washington Street, a man, who was sort of dressed like a Union soldier, stepped into the street and stopped my horse. I struck my horse with the whip, then the horse gave a sudden spring from the man, and I drove on until I reached the stable.

I told Jackson, the hostler, of it and I also told some of my friends about it, and they asked me how I knew that it was someone intending to rob me. I didn't know what his intention was. He may have been attempting to steal my soul from my very body. My friends thought if I was in the habit of carrying money with me, I ought to have something to defend myself in such a case, as it was very easy for anyone who felt so disposed to watch me wherever I was when I closed my office and follow me wherever I went and whenever there was an opportunity to rob me; and so I bought me a pistol. I sold that pistol to a friend who was going down to a Nova Scotia gold mine. I owned it several months when I sold it to him. When he got back home, he had a new one, and wanted to sell it to me. I took it and kept it sometime with the intention of buying it; but as I didn't make him any offer for it, he took it back.

I did not have a firearm for over a year. Then as I was in Boston one day last December, I passed Reed's gun store. I stopped and looked in the window and saw a pistol I took a great fancy to, and went in and inquired the price of it; and as it was very much less than I supposed, I bought it. When I went in, I didn't have any intention of buying it. I swear to you and I would not lie. I am not known as a liar or someone who would exaggerate. This was two or three weeks before the murder. Again, I didn't buy it with the intention of using it for any wrong purpose whatsoever. It was just a fine weapon. I made no schemes at all to use it. The thought would never cross my mind to injure my friend for any reason. It was impulsive. Earlier this evening, I went to the post office to fix my stove for Monday morning and when I came out, I was met by the constable.

Then Edward described his arrest.

At Mr. Lamson's house, Constable Abbott said I was arrested for the murder of young Converse, then I was searched by Detectives Heath and Jones. Then, Mr. Lamson called me into his private room. He said he wanted the money and in the name of the Malden Bank, he demanded it. He wanted me to tell them where it was so they could go and get it, or for me to go with him. He said I should lead them, Abbott and Lamson, to the hidden cash. Then we all went to the post office and I gave them what money was there and got the rest from the engine house. On our way downtown, Mr. Lamson asked me if I shot Frank for the money, and I answered yes. When we got back to the house, Lamson, Heath, and Jones counted the money. Then they questioned me to know where I had spent the rest; I told

*as near as I could remember. Constable Abbott asked me
if this was the first crime I had ever committed. I said yes.
Mr. Lamson uttered something about being on my track. I
don't remember for certain what he did say. He also asked
me if I bought my pistol at Reed's and took one from his
pocket and asked me if mine was like that one. Then I was
asked where mine was. I told them it was at home; and
as Heath and Jones were leaving the room, I asked Mr.
Lamson a question in regard to a picture that was hanging
on the wall. He noted it was a painting of Icarus, and I had
no further questions.*

*As I was going through Mr. Lamson's kitchen, I asked
for a glass of milk; they only had water. One was fetched
for me and I drank it as quickly as I could since they were
all silently staring at me. I could feel them trying to probe
my mind with theirs to see what I was thinking. Soon
I was taken to Boston. This is all I remember that took
place on this evening. I do not remember having been
asked any other questions, whatever, of any kind. The
arrest was very unexpected, and so sudden that I am still
completely stunned. My motive in writing this statement
is to show the facts as to what caused my trouble, and also
to show that it was not a premeditated, forethought act.*

I am yours,

Edward W. Green

Edward Green was jailed in the Tombs in Cambridge, taken there about midnight. The jailers noted Edward's demeanor retained an element of calmness, even after the extreme brutality he had described committing upon a young man he perceived as his own brother.

Before being locked in his cell, Edward inquired of his keepers the time and carefully set his watch. He suddenly remembered the stove at the post office.

He had failed at intentionally burning down the building and the evidence of his money troubles; now as he sat in his jail cell, he worried he would burn down the post office by mistake, having lit the stove before he was arrested. They would check it, he thought, and knew either way, they couldn't blame him for arson from where he presently resided.

Edward thought of Frank, he thought of Clara and Alice. He really wanted a glass of milk. He thought of himself as a young boy without a mother, then with a mother he didn't want. Edward remembered the years he had spent bedridden, which fueled his unquenchable desire to live and enjoy his life to the fullest once he was somewhat able to do so. Now all that appeared to have come to an end. He had killed his best friend, his brother, Frank. The boy was gone.

Now, all the money he had stolen, and his very freedom as well, had vanished. Edward's sore leg remained . . . as did the spite of his good one. Everything had changed, and also, nothing had changed, whatsoever.

About the Author

MICHAEL CLOHERTY is an Emmy award–winning video editor who has worked in Boston television news for more than twenty-five years. Over the past decade, he has expanded his storytelling with short videos about the local craft beer scene and a documentary about the Dropkick Murphys. He has also bungee jumped and performed open mic stand-up, twice each; both were equally terrifying and thrilling. He lives in Malden, Massachusetts, with his wife, Jen, and their miniature pinscher, Guinness. For more information, visit MichaelCloherty.com.

Made in the USA
Middletown, DE
17 June 2021